Community Languages: A Handbook

Multilingual Matters

Aspects of Bilingualism in Wales
  COLIN BAKER
Australian Multiculturalism
  LOIS FOSTER and DAVID STOCKLEY
Citizens of This Country: The Asian–British
  MARY STOPES-ROE and RAYMOND COCHRANE
Communication and Cross-cultural Adaptation
  YOUNG YUN KIM
English in Wales: Diversity, Conflict and Change
  N. COUPLAND in association with A. THOMAS (eds)
The Interdisciplinary Study of Urban Bilingualism in Brussels
  E. WHITE and H. BAETENS BEARDSMORE (eds)
Key Issues in Bilingualism and Bilingual Education
  COLIN BAKER
Language and Ethnicity in Minority Sociolinguistic Perspective
  JOSHUA FISHMAN
Language in Geographic Context
  COLIN WILLIAMS (ed.)
Language Planning and Education in Australasia and the South Pacific
  R. B. BALDAUF and A. LUKE (eds)
Marriage Across Frontiers
  A. BARBARA
Mediating Languages and Cultures
  D. BUTTJES and M. BYRAM (eds)
Migration and Intercultural Education in Europe
  U. PÖRNBACHER
Multiculturalism: The Changing Australian Paradigm
  LOIS FOSTER and DAVID STOCKLEY
Multiculturalism in India
  D. P. PATTANAYAK (ed.)
New Zealand Ways of Speaking English
  A. BELL and J. HOLMES (eds)
Our Own Language
  GABRIELLE MAGUIRE
Story as Vehicle
  EDIE GARVIE
Teaching and Learning English Worldwide
  J. BRITTON, R. E. SHAFER and K. WATSON
The Use of Welsh: A Contribution to Sociolinguistics
  MARTIN J. BALL (ed.)

Please contact us for the latest book information:
Multilingual Matters,
Bank House, 8a Hill Road,
Clevedon, Avon BS21 7HH,
England

MULTILINGUAL MATTERS 67
Series Editor: Derrick Sharp

Community Languages: A Handbook

Barbara M. Horvath and
Paul Vaughan

MULTILINGUAL MATTERS LTD
Clevedon • Philadelphia • Adelaide

Library of Congress Cataloging in Publication Data

Horvath, Barbara M.
Community Languages: A Handbook: Studies of Languages Used in Predominantly
English-Speaking Countries/Barbara M. Horvath and Paul Vaughan.
p. cm. (Multilingual Matters: 67)
Includes bibliographical references.
1. Sociolinguistics — Handbooks, manuals, etc. 2. Linguistic minorities —
Handbooks, manuals, etc. I. Vaughan, Paul. II. Title. III. Series: Multilingual Matters
(Series): 67.
P40.H69   1991
306.4'4   dc20

British Library Cataloguing in Publication Data

Horvath, Barbara M.
Community Languages: Studies of Languages Used in Predominantly English-Speaking
Countries (Multilingual Matters: 67).
1. English-speaking countries. Languages.
I. Title. II. Vaughan, Paul.
409

ISBN 1-85359-091-6

Multilingual Matters Ltd

UK: Bank House, 8a Hill Road, Clevedon, Avon BS21 7HH, England.
USA: 1900 Frost Road, Suite 101, Bristol, PA 19007, USA.
Australia: P.O. Box 6025, 83 Gilles Street, Adelaide, SA 5000, Australia.

Typeset by Editorial Enterprises, Torquay.
Printed and bound in Great Britain by Billing and Sons Ltd.

Contents

Preface

Host countries in the past couple of decades have had a change of heart about the languages that migrants have brought to their countries. There is now much more acceptance of those languages and government policy often supports the maintenance of the languages of past and recent migrants. Sometimes the support is in the form of language teaching at school, or interpreter services for a wide range of government institutions, or radio and television programmes. In addition, there are often government agencies that have been put in place to ensure that multilingual people understand their rights and responsibilities as citizens of the new country. Along with this new government-supported willingness to accept the fact that migrants are reluctant to give up their languages and prefer to add another comes the problem of making and implementing policy concerning a large number of languages, many of them unfamiliar to the people responsible for instituting change.

There are many people nowadays who find that they need to become familiar with a large number of languages: employers, teachers and others working in education, people working in the media, and many who in the course of their daily lives interact with bilingual people. In addition, acquaintance with such a large number of languages awakens a curiosity in the predominantly monolingual English-speaking community about these languages and the general public becomes interested in finding out more about the history and sociolinguistic structure of the languages. The school curriculum often includes some discussion of the languages and cultures of migrants.

This book attempts to respond to the need for information about languages which migrants have brought to countries that are primarily English-speaking: this is reflected in the choice of languages included in the book. Not all languages are represented because that would probably include most of the world's languages. Nevertheless, we believe that we have included the languages that represent the majority of those involved in migration movements to English-speaking countries this century.

The information included in the chapters on individual languages is constrained by a number of factors. Primarily we have included information that we think will be useful in multicultural settings: Chapter 1 discusses what we mean by 'useful' in some detail. Two other factors, however, need to be clarified. First of all, our search for material on the languages is limited to that produced in

English and further to those materials that were available to us locally. We are grateful that the Fisher Library at the University of Sydney has a substantial collection of such material. The bibliography for each language is placed at the end of the chapter on that language for the sake of convenient reference; it represents a valuable resource for anyone wanting more detailed information on any of the languages.

The sources for some languages (Armenian, for instance) were not extensive and on some occasions we called upon experts for advice. We are grateful for discussions with the following people: Dr Gasinski of Macquarie University (Byelorussian); Mr P. Hoffman of the University of Sydney (French); Mr R. Coll formerly of the University of Sydney (Irish Gaelic); Dr Vickery of the University of Adelaide (Khmer); Dr A. Diller of the Australian National University (Lao); Drs A. Koscharskij and M. Harasowska-Luelsdorff of Macquarie University (Ukrainian). These people are in no way responsible for the selection or interpretation of information that we included in the reports; that responsibility remains ours.

The second factor limiting our work was time. These reports were written to fulfil a contract with the Special Broadcasting Service, Australia, a radio and television system which provides programmes in all of the languages in this book. They needed the reports fairly quickly in order to use them as part of the procedure for selecting radio programme staff. Even so, we took far longer than anyone had anticipated. We allowed approximately two to three weeks for each language. We are grateful to SBS for their support of this project and especially to Meryl Gowing of SBS and Stepan Kerkyasharian, formerly Head of Radio at SBS and now head of the Ethnic Affairs Commission of New South Wales for their personal support and encouragement.

The division of labour on this project was: Horvath after a good deal of negotiation was given a contract by SBS to produce sociolinguistic background papers; Vaughan researched and wrote all of the reports; and Horvath wrote Chapter 1.

We are grateful to the word processor operators who helped through various phases of production: Lucy Rogers, Sonia Robinson and Arlene Harvey.

Sociolinguistic Profiles: A Guide for Multicultural Policymakers

In recent years countries on the receiving end of the world's migration routes have become somewhat more enlightened about the languages and cultures of the people who come to live and work among them. The melting pot philosophy of earlier migration periods, most often identified with the United States but not unfamiliar elsewhere, called for the newcomers to shed their foreign ways, preferably on the boat on the way over, and to take on as quickly as possible the lifestyles and ways of speaking of the host country. Henry Ford literally required the migrant workers in his automobile factory in Detroit to change their clothes so that they would look and feel like American workers.

It is well-known, however, that many migrants were not in the least anxious to shed their language and culture and that this implied no necessary rejection of the host, only a strong attachment to their own ways. In fact, many people were motivated to migrate because, oppressed in their home countries, they hoped to be able to practice their religion and speak their language in a new and freer society. Many of the migrants worked long and hard at setting up institutional support in the form of clubs, schools (even universities), churches, newspapers and radio programmes to maintain their heritage, usually without government assistance.

A move away from the melting pot philosophy does seem to have taken place. No longer is assimilation the unquestioned policy. Sweden, for instance, ranks high among the host countries which regard it as a government responsibility to support a multicultural policy; that is, a policy that eschews absolute assimilation and favours the maintenance of the language and culture of the migrants, albeit in the context of learning the language and ways of the host country. It is a context where migrants are asked to add to their cultural baggage, not to replace one set of cultural values with another. When a country adopts a multicultural policy, it usually means teaching a variety of languages in schools, collecting information about language knowledge and use for the government census, providing interpreter services, issuing government notices in a number of languages, and perhaps supporting radio and television programmes on

1

government-owned or publicly-owned stations. As a reflection of this policy change, from assimilationist to multiculturalist, labels such as 'foreign' language or 'migrant' language are replaced by 'heritage' language (Canada) or 'community' language (Australia).

The adoption of a multicultural policy requires a deeper understanding of community languages than has been necessary in the past. If we take the case of English-speaking countries, for instance, it takes quite a while before people in policy-making and administrative positions begin to appreciate how unlike English the community languages can be, not in the obvious ways in which the structures of language differ but in what we, in writing this book, have called the sociolinguistic profile. English has an international standard variety that is used for schooling and formal speech and writing; the dialects of English are quite close to that standard in terms of grammatical structure and the lexicon. The major differences among the dialects of English are to be found in the phonology: a wide variety of accents can be found within a country and between countries; some of the accents are held in high regard and others are not so highly regarded.

Clearly not all languages have a sociolinguistic profile like English. In many cases the written language is so different from the spoken that linguists would not hesitate to call them separate languages, even if the speakers insist that they are the same. In fact, there are many cases in which linguists find themselves disagreeing with speakers. Sometimes speakers claim that their language is different from a neighbouring language, but linguists would insist they are the same. Sometimes the differences between the dialects are as unimportant as they are in English, but more often they are so different that speakers of dialects of what is purported to be the same language cannot understand each other.

Unless the people who make policy and those who implement it understand these possible ways in which languages can vary sociolinguistically, misunderstandings result which could lead to programme failures. A few examples from the Australian experience will illustrate how good intentions can go astray. In 1981 the New South Wales Minister for Education announced that thirty specialist community language teachers would be added to the primary school system (Di Biase & Dyson, 1988: 57). Very quickly thereafter the teachers were hired and educators had to decide on a whole range of issues: what languages would be taught; would any student be allowed to study any language or would these teachers concentrate only on native speakers of the community language; what basic approach to community language teaching was to be adopted. The first step, however, was to interview and hire the teachers. Above all, they had to know the languages they were to teach. Initially this was done in a very great hurry; if you were a member of the community and claimed to speak the language fluently, you had a chance of being hired as a community language teacher if, of course, you had primary school teaching qualifications. The appropriate method was also quickly decided upon: you start with the language the children speak and then introduce literacy skills just as is done in English.

Despite the good intentions of the education department, many mistakes were made. An Egyptian teacher was hired to teach Lebanese children; although Egypt and Lebanon are both Arabic speaking countries, the spoken languages of these two speech communities are not mutually intelligible although the formal spoken and written language is. So much for starting with the language that the children speak. Administrators quickly learned that Serbo-Croatian was not a single language; Croatians are particularly adamant that their language is separate and distinct from Serbian no matter what the linguists might have to say about it. Suddenly the Anglo-Celtic population was shocked to learn that most of the Italian migrants did not speak Italian; they spoke 'dialect'. Again an apparent problem for the 'start with the language children speak' approach, although it was, we were told time and again by respected members of the Italian community, not something to worry about.

Another example of initial confusion in implementing a multicultural policy in Australia concerns the 1976 national census in which for the first time a question was asked about languages spoken. The third largest migrant group (after Italians and Greeks) comes from Yugoslavia and there are at least four languages involved: Serbian, Croatian, Slovenian, and Macedonian. The census questionnaire lists only Serbo-Croatian but the derived census tables also indicate how many speakers there are of 'Yugoslavian', a figure which is based on the false assumption that language is the same as birthplace. Not only does this provide data which is inadequate for educational planning purposes (speaking 'Yugoslav' is in some respects like speaking 'Swiss'), it fails to count the children born in Australia of Yugoslav parents who speak one of the four languages. In another case, people who reported their language as Lebanese or Egyptian were coded not as Arabic speakers, but aggregated as 'other' speakers or as speakers whose language was the same as their birthplace. Again the second generation of Arabic speakers is lost by using this method (Clyne, 1982: 2–4).

The area of public policy that has led most directly to the research on the sociolinguistic profiles in this book, however, concerns the media, particularly radio. Ethnic radio stations were supported by the Australian government in Melbourne and Sydney from about 1975 on. Initially, these were all run by volunteers from the various communities, representing forty languages in Sydney and forty-one in Melbourne (Clyne, 1982: 85–8). These stations were later incorporated into the Special Broadcasting Service (SBS) which produces both television and radio programmes in the community languages. Management at SBS decided to replace the volunteers with trained broadcasters as part of the professionalisation of the radio stations. By this stage in the development of multicultural policy, people, especially the English monolinguals among the managers, had become somewhat more aware of the complexities involved in making decisions about the community languages, although that awareness often came from an inefficient process of trial and error.

Although a set of simple principles often seems the best way to operate in a multicultural setting, the diversity of sociolinguistic situations must first of all be taken into account. For instance, it seems simple enough, and fair, to allocate radio time to languages not to nations. Even when we set aside the problem of sorting out what constitutes a language, some languages, such as Spanish, are associated with a number of nations and the media needs of the Chileans may well not be met if the broadcaster is European oriented. Some cultural groups, i.e. Australian Jews, have neither a nation nor a language in common but they still want time on the radio.

In 1985, as a result of a restructure, SBS needed to recruit broadcasters and journalists for the radio programmes in fifty-eight languages. The programme presenters naturally had to speak their languages properly, i.e. in a variety of the language that people from the speech community would find appropriate for radio. The managers were by now very sensitive to the difficulties involved in selecting people from such a diverse group of languages and they sought advice from linguists before beginning the interviews. They asked for a simple statement of what it meant to speak properly or appropriately on the radio; they wanted to adopt a simple principle on the standard of language required for radio announcing. We had no simple answer, at least not any that would be useful in the selection process. However, after a period of negotiation, we suggested that we could provide the selection committees with sociolinguistic background information on the fifty-eight languages and it is these which form the basis of the sociolinguistic profiles in this book.

Sociolinguistic Profiles

Just as it is impossible in a multicultural situation like the Australian one for a policy to exist that simply states that children will all be taught a community language according to a single principle, so it is not possible to have a simple principle for deciding what is the appropriate variety of a language for use on the radio. However, making decisions about individual languages can be made much easier if some background information is known about the language. In the area of public policy, it is not good enough to consult a formal grammarian to find out whether Serbo-Croatian, for instance, is one language or two before deciding to hire one or two broadcasters. Relying on the criteria formal grammarians use to determine the relationships among languages can lead to just as many difficulties as basing judgements on naive understandings of a language; it is critical to understand how the speakers regard their language and its relationship to other languages. Sufficient understanding is needed of the history of the speech community and the way in which language has been used to signal symbolically the political relationships between the Serbs and the Croats, before any policy decisions can be made.

The sociolinguistic profiles in this book are meant to give sufficient information about a language so that policy makers and implementers can go about their business with an intelligent understanding of any issues relevant to that language that ought to be taken into account before decisions are made. No formula or checklist was used to put the profiles together; nevertheless, there is a certain set of characteristics of a language that are likely to be important to know in order to make intelligent judgements concerning them. These characteristics are standardisation, functional distribution, historical development, the relationship to other languages and variants, and the social evaluation of the language by the speech community and others. (See Fasold, 1984, Chapters 1–3, for a thorough and sometimes divergent view from the one proposed here.)

Standardisation

If a language has been codified in some way, either it has a dictionary or grammar, then that codified variety is considered the standard. It is the language that is taught in school and people who write in the language are expected to follow the code. In some cases there may be more than one code (Norwegian) and there may be some controversy over which code is the acceptable one. Usually, when there is some question of which code represents the standard, there are political issues such as one code being used as a symbol of nationality, e.g. Urdu and Hindi. In such situations the issue of correctness is extremely important to speakers because of its symbolic association with the recognition of their rights as a separate nationality.

Functions

Perhaps the most important characteristic of a sociolinguistic profile is the determination of the functions associated with the varieties of the language that have been isolated. There are many sociolinguistic situations in the world where there is a strict separation of the functions of varieties of the language. When a language has (at least) two varieties that are functionally separate, one reserved for written and formal spoken occasions and one for informal spoken occasions, we refer to the situation as diglossia (Ferguson, 1959). Arabic is probably the best known among the diglossic situations, but there are many such in the world. Perhaps the most interesting aspect of diglossia for multicultural policy is the different perceptions of the relationship between the two varieties held by linguists and those held by the speakers. Linguists tend to see a very great difference between the two, related but very distant in terms of the grammatical and other systems. The formal variety has to be learned at school and is often not completely understood even by adults and is never used in casual conversation; the informal one is learned at home and is used conversationally. In some sociolinguistic situations, of course, the functions of language are split between two languages resulting in a bilingual speech community.

The functions that are usually discussed concern whether the language/variety has official status and is therefore used for governmental functions; whether it is used as a medium of education in primary, secondary, and/or tertiary levels; whether or not it has a body of literature written in it (in this regard, having a 'holy' book written in the language takes on particular significance); and whether it is used in church services. (Fasold (1984) discusses these points in detail.)

Historical development

Languages differ with respect to their histories. Some languages have remained in one location for thousands of years and have had a written variety for a thousand years or more (Slavic languages). Other languages have long histories but have introduced a written variety only recently (Fijian). Yet other languages have been 'purified', a language-planning process in which borrowings from other languages are expunged and the new codified variety is brought back to an earlier state, often with new words based on an earlier or 'purer' stage of the language. Perhaps the speech community has been politically dominated for a long period by another language community and upon gaining freedom they resurrect an earlier form of the language, change the writing system (e.g. to a different alphabet) or the spelling system; they may even attempt to have people speak the new language purified of all its borrowings from the former oppressors (Latvian). There are also new languages (creoles) or languages newly standardised (Indonesian). Languages differ with respect to how consciously planned they are; English, for instance, is regarded as having developed without much conscious planning whereas a language like Turkish was and still is quite consciously planned by a government-appointed language standardisation committee.

Relationships to other languages or varieties

The most difficult aspect of the sociolinguistic situation to sort out is the relationships between the varieties within the language as well as the relationship of the language to neighbouring languages. Once again the linguists often come into conflict with the speakers. The first relationship to consider is that between variants, e.g. the written and spoken mode: are these two modes close or distant? Next, what are the relationships between the dialects: are they all more or less mutually understandable or is there a dialect continuum in which dialects close to each other geographically are mutually intelligible but those more distant geographically are not? If there is a standard dialect, how close is it to the other dialects? Is it closer to some dialects but distant from others? As we have seen with the Serbo-Croatian case, it is quite common for speakers to judge as different two varieties of a language regarded by linguists as the same. Often, as is the case with Serbian and Croatian, a different alphabet is used in the written language which, along with some lexical variation, emphasises the differences between the varieties.

The fact that the speakers of a language use a different set of criteria to determine closeness or distance among its varieties than that used by linguists has an important impact on the literature available on languages. It is often very difficult in consulting the literature to determine clearly what the relationships are among the varieties and what criteria are being used to determine the relationship. Descriptive linguists may only describe the standard variety and not discuss the question of dialectal variation; they may ignore what the speakers' perceptions are altogether. On the other hand, works written by speakers of the language may fail to point out the distance between the dialects or exaggerate the difference between the language and a neighbouring language.

Questions like what is a dialect or what is a language and what is a close or distant relationship between dialects or languages are difficult for linguists. The Chinese language consists of dialects that in Europe would be regarded as separate languages; Macedonian and Bulgarian are separate languages that are so close as to be dialects. Since the linguistic community is not able to define these fundamental terms without equivocation, there is added reason for policy makers to take account of the speech community's perceptions on these matters. Especially for any kind of multicultural policy planning and implementation, it would be a grave error in judgement to ignore the speech community's understanding of its own language.

Social evaluation

Despite the fact that linguists regard all languages and their variants as equally systematic and capable of fulfilling the needs of a speech community, varieties of a language rarely exist without being evaluated by members of a speech community. Some varieties are claimed to be good, beautiful, educated, proper, appropriate to particular functions while others are thought to be bad, ugly, uneducated, improper or inappropriate. Sometimes an ex-colonial power regards its variety of the language as proper while the variety spoken by the former colonies as not real or proper. (Spain and the Latin American countries might provide an example here.) Needless to say, the former colonies do not necessarily accept or share this evaluation. Again, failure to take account of the evaluation of a variety can be disastrous for a multicultural policy designed to foster language or cultural maintenance.

Types of Sociolinguistic Situations

Classifying the sociolinguistic profiles in this book according to language seems to be the natural place to discuss the characteristics we have just examined, i.e. standardisation, functional distribution, etc. However, as we will see, it is possibly not the best place to start. In fact, there are three possible ways to arrive at a sociolinguistic profile: we can characterise the language or we can consider the linguistic repertoire of the speech community or that of the nation. Sometimes, as we have seen, the functions of language within a given speech community are distributed between two languages. If we start with a language, e.g. Welsh, and describe only its history or dialectal variants, we might fail to notice that most if not all speakers of Welsh also speak English and it is likely that English would be the dominant language for most. We can also get into trouble if we take the nation as the place to draw up a sociolinguistic profile. Although one could correctly identify Canada, for instance, as a bilingual nation based on its two official languages, English and French, we would be mistaken in believing that there were many bilingual speech communities in Canada. By and large, Canada has communities of monolingual English speakers and monolingual French speakers. Further, looking only at the 'official' languages we would fail to note the many bilingual communities that do exist in Canada, that is the so-called heritage language communities where either English or French is the second language. Another problem with starting with the nation is of course that language boundaries and national boundaries quite often do not coincide (Macedonian). Furthermore, some languages have no nations (Assyrian/Syriac or Kurdish).

The unit of social organisation that is probably most useful from a language planning perspective is the speech community. If we start with the speech community, we can still profile the specific characteristics of a given language but we will not fail to note other languages which function in the community. To take a specific language-planning situation, a program directed to a Hebrew-speaking audience in Australia could conceivably consider having some programmes in Yiddish and some in English because one can reasonably expect at least these three languages to function within the Hebrew-speaking community.

Therefore, although the sociolinguistic profiles in this book are classified according to language, the speech community is usually taken as the starting point for a description, especially in cases of bilingualism. As well, it is sometimes necessary to refer to the nation for languages such as Macedonian or

Tamil in order to understand fully what is often a complex sociolinguistic situation.

Four basic types of sociolinguistic situation have been revealed in the process of putting together these profiles: sociolectal, standard plus regional dialects, diglossia, and bilingual. For ease of reference, we will include multilingual situations under bilingual. The primary characteristic that is used to arrive at this four-way classification is the relationship of the variants in the speech community to each other.

Sociolectal

In classifying languages according to sociolinguistic type, one must assume that they all will share certain kinds of sociolinguistic variation. That is to say, there will be variants that are associated with social class, gender, level of education, and the formality of the situation. However, in what we are calling the sociolectal type, the spoken and written variants are very close and the main differences in the spoken varieties are phonological, i.e. in the pronunciation or accent, not in the grammatical system. There is a continuum of dialects with a standard written language and all dialects are mutually intelligible once a speaker gets used to the accent. English is a good example of this sociolinguistic situation.

Standard plus regional dialects

In the standard plus regional dialect situation there is an unbroken chain or continuum of dialects but those dialects not close to each other geographically will not be mutually intelligible. Often this geographical continuum of dialects goes beyond national boundaries; however, each nation will have a standard language that all members of the speech communities can also use. The standard will usually be close to some of the regional dialects but will be more distant from others. The functional distribution of the standard and dialect will usually entail informal or local situations in which the dialect is used and formal or national situations in which the standard is used. German stands as a good example of this sociolinguistic situation.

Diglossia

The variants of the language here represent a broken chain; that is to say, the variants are related to one another historically but are so distant as to be mutually unintelligible. This characteristic plus the strict functional distribution, particularly that the formal variant is never used in conversation, distinguishes diglossia from the other three types. As noted earlier, Arabic is the classic diglossic situation. However, in the case of Arabic it is also important to take account of the national variety of Arabic; many of the spoken varieties of Arabic are not mutually intelligible.

Bilingual

A speech community is bilingual if at least two distinct languages are required to fulfill the linguistic functions of that community. While it does not necessarily imply that every individual in the speech community is fluent in both languages, it does indicate that most educated speakers would be. It is also the case in a stable bilingual speech community that there is a functional distribution associated with the two languages. Some situations or settings call for the use of one of the languages and the other language is appropriate in different situations or settings.

Table 1 attempts to classify all the languages in this book according to these basic types; it is very difficult to feel confident about labelling all of the languages because the information available is not comparable across all and in some cases we were not able to judge the quality of that information. The classifications, then, should be regarded as tentative pending more information.

TABLE 1. *Sociolinguistics types*

Language	Type	Comments
Albanian	Sociolectal	May have some dialects geographically distant that are not mutually intelligible
Arabic	Diglossia	Great variation in spoken dialects; Modern Standard Arabic (MSA) represents a new development which could eventually qualify as a standard and dialect type
Armenian	Sociolectal	Two written varieties; one used in the USSR and the other maintained by those living outside the USSR; nevertheless, the varieties are close

TABLE 1. (*Continued*)

Language	Type	Comments
Assyrian (Syriac)	Standard and dialect	Not a national language, likely the speech communities bilingual
Bengali	Diglossia	Probably in a transitional state; a new literary standard has developed and is taking on certain functions; may see development of standard and dialect
Bulgarian	Sociolectal	On the same dialect continuum as Macedonian; literary language differs
Byelorussian	Sociolectal	A bilingual speech community over an extended time historically, now dominated by Russian; in a dialect continuum including Ukrainian and Russian
Cantonese	Diglossia	Not a classical case of diglossia and speakers would certainly disagree; however, the written language is Mandarin in grammar and vocabulary, making the written and spoken language distant; spoken varieties are standard and dialect
Croatian	Standard and dialect	Same dialect continuum as Serbian, Slovenian, Macedonian and Bulgarian
Czech	Diglossia	Language purism movement to develop a literary language which is also used for formal speech
Danish	Sociolectal	Probably moving from a standard and dialect type
Dutch	Standard and dialect	On dialect continuum with Flemish

TABLE 1. (*Continued*)

Language	Type	Comments
Estonian	Bilingual: Russian Standard and dialect	Long history of bilingual; German, now Russian
Fijian	Bilingual: English Standard and dialect	Fiji is a multilingual country; Fijian is a *lingua franca*
Filipino	Bilingual: English Standard and dialect	The Phillipines is a multilingual country; Filipino is a national language; both languages used for many functions
Finnish	Sociolectal	Earlier bilingual with Swedish, which is still a national language in Finland
French	Standard and dialect	
German	Standard and dialect	
Greek	Sociolectal	Before 1976, diglossia
Gujarati	Sociolectal	Only if exclude certain very diverse dialects
Hebrew	Sociolectal	Major recent changes to support a range of new functions
Hindi	Standard and dialect	Bilingual (as with all Indian languages): English; same as Urdu except for a different script; India is a multilingual country
Hungarian	Sociolectal	Historically a bilingual speech community

TABLE 1. (*Continued*)

Language	Type	Comments
Indonesian	Sociolectal	Like Hebrew, a national language given new functions in a multilingual country
Irish Gaelic	Bilingual: English Sociolectal	A dying language; diglossia earlier but the archaic literary language no longer functions
Italian	Standard and dialect	Dialects are very important so have regional standards as well
Japanese	Standard and dialect	Written language expecially complex historically
Kannada	Diglossia	
Khmer	Sociolectal	Formerly bilingual: French
Korean	Sociolectal	Now a northern and a southern standard
Kurdish	Sociolectal	Not sufficient information available; probably bilingual since not a national language
Lao	Sociolectal	Formerly bilingual: French and Vietnamese
Latvian	Standard and dialect	Historically bilingual: German, Polish, now Russian; has gone through a language purism movement
Lithuanian	Sociolectal	Historically bilingual: Polish, now Russian
Macedonian	Bilingual: Greek Sociolectal	Only recognised as separate language in Yugoslavia; a purist movement is going on

TABLE 1. (*Continued*)

Language	Type	Comments
Maltese	Bilingual: English Sociolectal	
Mandarin	Sociolectal	
Norwegian	Sociolectal	A difficult language to classify; previously diglossia which developed out of bilingual: Danish; now two competing codes: an urban and a rural based standard
Persian	Standard and dialect	
Polish	Sociolectal	Often historically dominated by other languages; has gone through bilingual, to the standard and dialect type and now appears to be emerging sociolectal
Portuguese	Sociolectal	Major difference between European and Brazilian varieties; Brazil has a creole continuum
Punjabi	Bilingual: Urdu/Hindi Sociolectal	Could be a standard and dialect; not sufficient information
Romanian	Sociolectal	Called Moldavian in USSR; underwent an earlier purist movement; not all Romanian speakers affected by changes
Russian	Sociolectal	Earlier diglossia with Old Church Slavic; probably has gone through a standard and dialect type and now emerging sociolectal

TABLE 1. (*Continued*)

Language	Type	Comments
Scottish Gaelic	Bilingual: English Sociolectal	A dying language; a spoken language with few literates
Serbian	Sociolectal	Appears to have gone through standard and dialect and now emerging sociolectal
Sinhalese	Bilingual: English Diglossia	Went through a purist movement; a clear case of diglossia
Slovak	Sociolectal	Close to Czech but separate literary language; literary language seems to have no spoken functions so not diglossia
Slovenian	Diglossia	Appears to be developing new forms especially for formal speech; perhaps becoming standard and dialect; long periods of bilingual: German; Hungarian
Spanish	Standard and dialect	Regional standards as well; Latin American varieties also have Castillian standard
Swedish	Standard and dialect	Does not appear to be one accepted spoken standard but there is a literary language; some dialects are not mutually intelligible; emerging sociolectal
Tamil	Diglossia	Previously bilingual: English; spoken language sociolectal
Turkish	Standard and dialect	Purification movement very effective starting in late 1920s with Ataturk

TABLE 1. (*Continued*)

Language	Type	Comments
Ukrainian	Bilingual: Russian Standard and dialect	Long history of bilingual speech community; have a literary language which is used in formal speech; may be diglossia
Urdu	Standard and dialect	Previously bilingual: English; same as Hindi but different script and borrowing language is Arabic rather than Sanskrit; a national language in a multilingual country
Vietnamese	Sociolectal	Long history of bilingual: Chinese, French, English
Welsh	Bilingual: English	A dying language undergoing maintenance movement; tradition of diglossia but few use the literary language; emerging sociolectal
Yiddish	Bilingual: Hebrew and other European languages	A dying language being replaced by Hebrew

Sociolinguistic Types and Policy

In the earlier discussion we gave some examples of where simple operating principles have gone astray in the implementation of multicultural policy. Community language teaching in schools and the selection of radio programme presenters involve such a diverse set of sociolinguistic situations that it is next to impossible to work with a single operating principle. Nevertheless, any organisation which has to deal with a myriad of languages must act and be seen to be acting fairly to all ethnic groups, and that means being able to set out in clear terms what the basis for decision making is.

Classifying the languages according to sociolinguistic type offers some hope of being able to arrive at an explicit set of principles. For instance, in a diglossic situation it will be necessary to address the problem of the formal variety of the language. Since one can predict that there will be a strong feeling in the speech community about what is the correct form of this variety and about its appropriateness for particular occasions, it is imperative that teachers or radio announcers know the formal variety well. Bilingual communities might have programmes in either language or might regard only one to be appropriate for education, given the particular functional distribution of the languages. Since it can be fairly assumed that almost all speakers in the standard and dialect sociolinguistic type know the standard, then it is the standard that is appropriately chosen for teaching in schools and for radio programmes, especially in a migrant setting where the 'local' use of the dialect is no longer appropriate. The sociolectal type is important to characterise, especially for English speaking policy makers. Although the simple principles that they come up with may be soundly based for languages that are of the sociolectal type, they are often not appropriate for other types. Making explicit the characteristics of the sociolectal type should clarify for policy makers and implementers which operating principles need further consideration for particular types of languages.

Needless to say, knowing the sociolinguistic type alone is not sufficient. Each speech community has its own history, its own understanding of functional appropriateness, its own symbolic interpretation and evaluation of the relationships among the varieties. Perhaps the best advice for policy makers is to listen to the members of the speech community and to be prepared to have to deal with controversy over linguistic matters. It is hoped that the profiles in this book will contribute to an understanding of the complex issues involved in multicultural policy formation and implementation.

References

CLYNE, MICHAEL G. 1982, *Multilingual Australia*. Melbourne: River Seine Publications.
DI BIASE, BRUNO and BRONWEN, DYSON 1988, *Language Rights and the School*. Sydney: Inner City Education Centre/FILEF Italo-Australian Publications.
FASOLD, RALPH 1984, *The Sociolinguistics of Society*. Oxford: Basil Blackwell.
FERGUSON, CHARLES 1959, Diglossia. *Word* 15, 325–40.

Albanian

Albanian is an Indo-European language, the sole modern survivor of its own sub-group (Encyclopaedia Britannica, 1985: 701). According to Pollo and Puto, the Albanians may be the direct descendants of the ancient Illyrians who were possibly the first inhabitants of the region (1981: 2ff, 32). The name Albania traditionally referred to a small area in what is today central Albania, though the origins of this name and of the indigenous name *Shqip* or *Sqiperi* are still the subject of debate by scholars (Encyclopaedia Britannica, 1985: 700). Albanian is today spoken by about two million people in Albania, by nearly the same number in adjoining areas which are now part of Yugoslavia, and by smaller groups in Greece and other countries around the world (Byron, 1976: 32).

Albanians are divided into two groups: the Gegs, sometimes spelt Ghegs, in the north; and the Tosks in the south (Byron, 1976: 32). Both the Roman Catholic Church and the Eastern Orthodox Church were active in Albania, and by about the tenth century Albania was also divided into two religious areas. In the north the Gegs were predominantly Roman Catholic, and in the south the Tosks were mainly Orthodox (Byron, 1976: 32–33; Pollo & Puto, 1981: 57ff). As a result, Latin was used as the official language in northern Albania, whereas Greek was the official language of the south (Pollo & Puto, 1981: 61).

After the Ottoman Turks conquered Albania in the fifteenth century Turkish also became an important language in Albania, particularly for the many Albanians who converted to Islam (Byron, 1976: 33, 39). Latin and Greek, though, continued to be used. In the north, because of the mountainous and inhospitable terrain, the Gegs remained relatively free of Turkish influence, while in the south the Orthodox religion was viewed favourably by the Ottomans and allowed to continue (Byron, 1976: 33, 38).

Writing in Albanian began in the fourteenth or fifteenth century, and in the sixteenth and seventeenth centuries a small number of works were produced, mainly in the northern, Geg, part of Albania (Byron, 1976: 36; Encyclopaedia Britannica, 1985: 701). According to Byron, these works were produced by the Catholic clergy during the Counter-Reformation, and to counter the spread of Islam (1976: 37).

For these writings the Geg dialect was used. However, the form of the language used was not uniform throughout the Geg area. As Byron says

Geg had two sub-traditions of literary usage, a southern Geg one, which was more widespread and another more limited tradition based on north-western speech forms ... (Byron, 1976: 38)

In the southern, Tosk, regions of Albania, writing in Albanian began only in the eighteenth century when the Ottomans began to intensify their efforts to convert the population to Islam. As a consequence:

the Orthodox Church was compelled to counteract Islamic influence by accelerating and intensifying Orthodox religious education. They attempted to do this by printing books in the vernacular, as the Catholics had been constrained to do earlier. (Byron, 1976: 38fn3)

The form of Tosk developed for literary use was less diversified than the forms used for writing Geg (Byron, 1976: 38).

Nevertheless, writing in Albanian was carried out on only a small scale. In the nineteenth century when many new schools were opened, the Turkish authorities refused to allow Albanian schools, nor did they allow the reading and writing of Albanian, though it was permitted to be used as a spoken language (Byron, 1976: 38–9). Instead, the Ottoman Turks insisted that Albanian Muslims be taught in Turkish, Greek Orthodox Albanians in Greek, and Catholics in Latin or Italian (Pollo & Puto, 1981: 114). Byron notes, however, that 'Catholic schools in the north were more tolerant of the vernacular' (1976: 39).

With the beginning of an Albanian nationalist movement in the late nine-teenth century, societies were formed to cultivate the Albanian language and to campaign for Albanian schools. Albanian was taught secretly in foreign-lan-guage schools and Albanian books were published abroad and smuggled into the country (Byron, 1976: 39). A further aim of the Albanian societies was to pro-vide a single alphabet for Albanian which up till then had been written using let-ters based on the Latin, Greek or Turko-Arabic alphabets (Byron, 1976: 39; Encyclopaedia Britannica, 1985: 701). Thus, for example, one author wrote in the Geg dialect using Latin letters, and in the Tosk dialect using Greek letters (Byron, 1976: 53).

In 1908 the Young Turks, who had just come to power in Turkey, declared Turkish a compulsory language in all state organs and in all schools (Byron, 1976: 39). Despite strong pressure from the Young Turks to adopt the Turko-Arabic alphabet, the Albanians, in 1909, decided to use the Latin alphabet for all writing (Pollo & Puto, 1981: 139–40; Byron, 1976: 39–40). And when Albania gained independence in 1912, Albanian, written in the Latin alphabet, became the official language (Byron, 1976: 40).

From the beginning of the nationalist movement in the late nineteenth century there had been some debate about which form of Albanian should become the literary standard (Byron, 1976: 52ff). According to Byron, the main proposals were: (a) Geg and Tosk varieties should be combined; (b) a central form such as the south Geg variety spoken around Elbasan should be adopted; or (c) Tosk should be elevated to national literary status (Byron, 1976: 554).

After independence, the Elbasan variety of Geg was used for a time as the official language and the language of education (Encyclopaedia Britannica, 1985: 701; Byron, 1976: 57). However, although some grammars of this variety were produced, and a few attempts were made to codify the norm envisaged, its use as an official and written form ended after the socialists gained power in 1944 (Byron, 1976: 57–8).

Even though the Elbasan variety of Albanian was officially recognised prior to 1944, many Albanian scholars point out that in practice writing in Tosk and Geg continued (Byron, 1976: 59ff). One scholar, in fact, stated in 1949 that:

> ... even during these last thirty years or so that we have been independent, and up to the present day, the greatest amount of work in the field of writing and publication has been produced by Tosks. Tosks have, so to speak, held the keys of the press and of publication. Aside from a restricted locality (namely Shkoder, where the Catholic priests worked, and whose production remained confined to that locality), the whole of Albania, by and large, has read and written in Tosk. (Shuteriqi quoted in Byron, 1976: 60)

When the socialists took power in 1944 the Tosk variety was elevated to the position of standard literary variety. In the period after the Second World War, the predominance of the Tosk variety was considered to be due to the fact that most of the leaders of the Communist Revolution were from the Tosk regions, and that most of the party literature was written in Tosk. Thus, 'when this southern leadership came to power, its dialect was established as the basis of Standard Albanian' (Byron, 1978: 398). Byron, though, believes that this is only part of the reason why Tosk was elevated to the position of the official standard form (1978: 398).

Whatever the reason may be, it is now accepted that Standard Albanian is based on the pre-1944 literary Tosk (Encyclopaedia Britannica, 1985: 701). Standard Albanian, though, is not identical to pre-1944 literary Tosk. Rather, literary Tosk forms the original kernel of standard Albanian, but elements from literary and spoken Geg and from spoken Tosk are also incorporated, and the standard form has been considerably elaborated by language planners (Byron, 1976: 61ff).

In their spoken forms, Geg and Tosk are mutually intelligible, in fact, according to Pederen:

the difference between the two Albanian dialects is much smaller than the dialectal differences found within most other languages; from the practical point of view they are quite insignificant. (Quoted in Byron, 1976: 41)

However, there are sub-varieties within each dialect which form a continuum, with the central regions of Albania being a transitional area from one dialect to the other. In consequence, even though neighbouring sub-varieties may cause no problems of comprehension whatsoever, at the extremes, i.e. the far north and the far south, the sub-varieties may not be so easily intelligible (Byron, 1976: 41).

The major differences between Tosk and Geg are in the phonology, the sound system. There are differences in vocabulary, but these differences do not necessarily denote dialectal differences; that is, the same word may be used by a Geg and a Tosk sub-variety, and in grammar what differences there are are relatively minor (Byron, 1976: 41ff).

The adoption and codification of standard Albanian has led to a standard spoken Albanian. The orthography of standard Albanian has been regularised such that when learning to read and write, Albanians also learn a standardised pronunciation (Byron, 1976: 77). The use of standard spoken Albanian, especially through education, the press, radio and other forms of mass media, is tending to level out dialectal variation (Byron, 1976: 69). And, according to Byron, it appears that efforts are being made to eradicate local forms of speech in favour of the standard. As she says, 'there is strong evidence that the political leadership countenances disappearance of regional dialects' (1976: 68).

In Yugoslavia, the Albanians in the Kosovo region are predominantly speakers of eastern Geg varieties, as are the Albanians in Macedonia. Since 1974 these Albanian speakers have widely adopted a common orthography with Albania (Encyclopaedia Britannica, 1985: 701).

Albanian, therefore, has a standard literary form based on the southern Tosk variety but with elements of the northern Geg dialect incorporated into it. The literary form provides a guide to a standardised pronunciation through the orthography. The spoken Geg and Tosk dialects are mutually intelligible, though there are many sub-varieties the extremes of which may cause some problems in comprehension. The standard spoken form is, though, tending to level these dialects, and there appear to be official efforts to eradicate dialectal variation in favour of the standard form.

References

BYRON, J. L. 1976, *Selection Among Alternates in Language Standardization: The Case of Albanian*. The Hague: Mouton (*Contributions to the Sociology of Language*, 12).

BYRON, J. L. 1978, Linguistics and the study of language standardization. *Current Anthropology* 19 (2), 397–9.

ENCYCLOPAEDIA BRITANNICA 1985, Albanian language. In: *Macropaedia* Vol. 22, pp. 700–1.

POLLO, S. and PUTO, A. 1981, *The History of Albania: From its Origins to the Present Day*. London: Routledge and Kegan Paul (Translated by C. Wiseman and G. Hole).

Arabic

Arabic belongs to the Semitic group, part of the Afro-Asiatic family of languages. It was originally spoken in the north-western region of the Arabian Peninsula (Chejne, 1969: 6). Until the early part of the seventh century AD Arabic was, it appears, mainly an oral language in which tradition and poetry were handed down from generation to generation by professional reciters (Chejne, 1969: 54).

By this time it seems that several dialects of Arabic were spoken, but one of these, the Quraysh dialect from around Mecca, was the most prestigious. The Quraysh dialect, originally the dialect of the Quraysh tribe, was used throughout Arabia as a common dialect for recitation and was understood by most Arabs (Chejne, 1969: 54).

By this time too, the Arabic writing system had been developed, though few traces of it prior to the seventh century AD have so far been discovered (Bakalla, 1984: 106–107). It seems that writing was used on a very limited scale and only by a small majority (Chejne, 1969: 58). The Arabic alphabetic system is written from right to left and originally contained only consonants. At a later stage diacritic marks, i.e. small dots or other marks above or below a letter, were introduced to indicate short vowels (Bakalla, 1984: 109).

Between 634 and 656 AD the single most important document in and for the Arabic language, the Qur'an (Koran), was written down (Chejne, 1969: 58). According to Moslem faith the Koran represents the word of God as revealed to the Prophet Mohammad, a member of the Quraysh tribe. The words of Mohammad were originally memorised by his followers and were written down by scribes on durable material such as stones, bones and leather (Beeston, 1970: 13; Chejne, 1969: 58). After Mohammad's death in 632 the first Caliph, or successor to Mohammad, (632–634), collected the scattered material on which Mohammad's words were written, the second Caliph (634–644) put them into book form and the third (644–656) revised the work of the second. This became the final and standard version of the Koran and the basis of Islam. It is still in use today (Chejne, 1969: 58).

Within a hundred years of Mohammad's death the Arabs were in possession of an empire which stretched from India in the East to the Atlantic and Spain in the West. In all of the conquered territories Islam was introduced with the Koran as the basic sacred text and Arabic as the language of worship. However, as Beeston notes,

> the Moslem conquests resulted in the adoption of the use of Arabic by vast numbers of non-Arabs ... and this led to a very significant evolution in the common language itself. (Beeston, 1970: 14)

Consequently, in the eighth century, Arabic scholars, feeling that the rapid evolution of the language brought about by the conquests would erode the ability of Moslems to read and understand the Koran, began to develop

> the sciences of Arabic grammar and lexicography, of which a principle aim was to establish a standard of 'correct' Arabic. (Beeston, 1970: 14)

In order to establish a standard the scholars adopted as models primarily the Koran, considered to be a 'paragon of purity and eloquence' because of its divine origin, and the Quraysh dialect (Chejne, 1969: 40).

It is important to note that the Arabic of the Koran is considered to be sacred and consequently occupies a very important position in Moslem life. As Ibrahim puts it:

> The position accorded to Arabic by Islam is probably unique among languages of the world. Not only is it the language of Islam's holy book, the Qur'an, and of all religious rites and services among all Moslems, but it is also probably the only language which provided its speakers with a verbal miracle, the Qur'an, which is miraculous by virtue of its having been revealed by God to the Prophet Mohammad in a form of language never to be surpassed or even equalled by any human being. (Ibrahim, 1983: 513)

And as Hitti says:

> The religious influence [the Koran] exercises as the basis of Islam and the final authority in matters spiritual and ethical is only one side of the story. Theology, jurisprudence and science being considered by Moslems as different aspects of one and the same thing, the Koran becomes the scientific manual, the textbook, for acquiring a liberal education. (Hitti, 1970: 127)

The Arabic scholars were successful in their aim since, as Altoma says,

> Classical Arabic as written or spoken today is basically governed by the same grammatical rules [as described by the grammarians of the eighth century], and that the deviations detected in modern usages seem to be of little significance in comparison to the bulk of classical rules being observed. (Altoma, 1969: 7)

And, as Beeston puts it,

> The grammar taught in the schools of the Arab world today is virtually identical with the grammatical system devised by the eighth century

scholars; and throughout the period from then to now this grammar has been the ideal aimed at by the educated classes for literary expression. (Beeston, 1970: 14)

In maintaining the grammar of Classical Arabic virtually unchanged for over a thousand years the influence of the Koran cannot be over-estimated.

Although the grammar of Classical Arabic has remained virtually unchanged, the same is not true of the vocabulary. According to Bakalla, 'Arabic vocabulary is in the process of changing and developing rapidly in order to meet the needs of the modern age' (1984: 13).

The form of Arabic used nowadays, therefore,

can be seen as an extension of Classical Arabic plus the modern elements which have poured into the main stream of the Classical Arabic. (Bakalla, 1984: 81)

This form is usually referred to as Modern Standard Arabic (MSA), though it is still sometimes called 'Classical' and some refer to it as 'written Arabic'.

According to Bakalla,

Modern Standard Arabic is, in fact, a cover term for the variety of Arabic, both spoken and written, which is utilised in education, mass media (including the press, radio and television) and general lectures, announcements, and advertisements. (Bakalla, 1984: 81)

In its written form MSA is virtually identical in all Arab countries and can be read and understood by any literate Arab. It functions as the official standard language in all the Arabic speaking countries (Bakalla, 1984: 85). In its spoken form too there is little variation, but

it is influenced quite readily by the speaker's regional background and one can tell without difficulty from which region the speaker of Modern Standard Arabic comes. (Bakalla, 1984: 81)

However, while MSA functions as the official written language, and the spoken language of education, the media and so on, it is not the spoken language learnt as a first language in the home, nor is it the language used in informal situations. As Ibrahim puts it,

this variety does not have a single native speaker and is not anyone's exclusive language of communication, not even highly educated people's. (1983: 509)

As far as the vernacular, or spoken language, is concerned the situation is complex. In each country there are many different dialects spoken. Bakalla notes that 'in Saudi Arabia alone one can count over 200 dialects scattered all over the Kingdom' (1984: 79). As well as geographical or regional dialects, Hain points out that there are dialectal differences between social and religious groups as well (1964: 12–13). According to Altoma, there is usually a standard or semi-standard form of spoken Colloquial Arabic in each country based on the speech of the capital city (1969: 3).

Although speakers of one dialect may understand other dialects which are fairly close geographically, as distance increases so intelligibility decreases. As Beeston says, '[the vernaculars] form a continuous spectrum of variation, of which the extremities, Moroccan and Iraqi, differ to the point of mutual unintelligibility' (1970: 11).

A recent development in spoken Arabic, according to Mitchell (1978) and El-Hassan (1978), is the growth of what they call Educated Spoken Arabic (ESA). ESA is becoming a pan-Arabic variety of the spoken language. That is, it is understood by all educated Arabs irrespective of which country they are from. Even though there are regional variations, these are not significant enough to cause problems of comprehension (Mitchell 1978: 227-228). As Mitchell puts it:

> Its users are motivated, first, to proclaim themselves as educated men and to converse on topics beyond the scope of particular regional vernaculars; secondly, to 'share' with other Arabs of similar background, whether of their own or other Arab countries; thirdly, to promote the forms of pan- or inter-Arabic that the forces of modernisation ... require; fourthly, to maintain enough local and regional linguistic loyalty without prejudicing supra-regional intelligibility or provoking ridicule, at the same time retaining the means to fulfil the more private, homely and familial functions of speech. (Mitchell, 1978: 228)

El-Hassan notes that ESA:

> ... draws upon both MSA and Colloquial [or vernacular] Arabic. MSA, ESA and Colloquial Arabic constitute a continuum. These varieties of Arabic are neither discrete nor homogeneous; rather they are characterised by gradation and variation. (El-Hassan, 1978: 32)

Thus ESA fills the gap between MSA, which 'requires a degree of formality which is seldom present in carrying out everyday activities' (Herbolich, 1979: 302) and Colloquial Arabic which differs significantly from region to region and can cause problems of comprehension.

Of the varieties along the Arabic 'continuum', i.e. MSA, ESA and the multitude of different colloquial varieties, only one, MSA, is written. This is because of 'the almost mystical regard in which Arabs hold their written language to the detriment of spoken counterparts' (Mitchell, 1978: 227).

As a consequence, MSA is the only variety of Arabic which is taught in schools and literacy classes (Ibrahim, 1983: 509). MSA, therefore, enjoys considerable prestige and is used in all formal situations, including radio broadcasting, whereas the spoken varieties, with the possible exception of ESA, are considered stigmatised and sub-standard. Altoma sums this up when he says,

> the colloquial lacks the prestige enjoyed by the classical and is looked upon, often with a considerable degree of contempt, as a stigma of illiteracy and ignorance. (Altoma, 1969: 3)

And as Ibrahim puts it, 'all varieties of spoken Arabic are sub-standard and stigmatised when it comes to achieving literacy in the language' (1983: 509). It should be noted that ESA, by its very nature as the speech of educated Arabs, draws heavily on MSA forms even though it is not used for writing.

Learning the written variety of Arabic, MSA, means learning what is virtually a different language from the one acquired in childhood. The syntax, vocabulary and phonology (i.e. the sounds) of MSA are very different from any of the colloquial varieties (Ibrahim, 1983: 511). Consequently, there is often interference from colloquial Arabic into the standard form and it is usually easy for an Arab to identify where a speaker of MSA comes from (Ibrahim, 1983: 511).

To sum up the situation, therefore, classical Arabic, nowadays known as MSA, is the prestigious form used for writing, formal speaking and in the media, and is the official language of all Arabic speaking countries. It corresponds to no-one's native tongue and must be learnt virtually as a second language. In consequence, many items of vocabulary and phonology are often transferred from the spoken, colloquial variety to MSA and this usually enables Arabs to place where a speaker of MSA comes from. Educated Spoken Arabic draws heavily from MSA but is also influenced by the regional colloquial varieties. It is becoming a pan-Arabic spoken language. The colloquial varieties differ from each other to a greater or lesser extent depending on distance, i.e. at the maximum distance, Moroccan to Iraqi, they are mutually unintelligible whereas neighbouring dialects are virtually indistinguishable. The colloquial forms do not have much prestige. As Ibrahim puts it,

> Spoken Arabic, the native language of every Arab, is simply not worthy of any attention according to the overwhelming majority of Arabs who are willing to venture an opinion on this matter. (Ibrahim, 1983: 514)

It is perhaps worthy of note that even though MSA is the language of education and literature and enjoys great prestige, it is not always used in tertiary education. As Zughoul and Taminian point out,

> English in particular remains the medium of instruction in most of the universities of the Arab world, especially in the schools of science, engineering and medicine. (Zughoul & Taminian, 1984: 156)

They also note that English is extensively used in business, industry and trade in the Arab world, and consequently, English is seen as a 'vehicle for educational and occupational mobility' (1984: 169–170).

References

ALTOMA, S. J. 1969, *The Problem of Diglossia in Arabic: A Comparative Study of Classical and Iraqi Arabic*. Cambridge, MA: Harvard University Press (*Harvard Middle Eastern Monographs* XXI).

BAKALLA, M. H. 1984, *Arabic Culture Through its Language and Literature*. London: Kegan Paul International.

BEESTON, A. F. L. 1970, *The Arabic Language Today*. London: Hutchinson and Co.

BLANC, H. 1964, *Communal Dialects in Baghdad*. Cambridge, MA: Harvard University Press (*Harvard Middle Eastern Monographs* X).

CHEJNE, A. G. 1969, *The Arabic Language: Its Role in History*. Minneapolis: University of Minnesota Press.

EL-HASSAN, S. A 1978, Variation in the demonstrative system in Educated Spoken Arabic. *Archivum Linguisticum* 9 (1), 32–57.

HERBOLICH, J. B. 1979, Attitudes of Egyptians towards various Arabic vernaculars. *Lingua* 47 (4), 301–21.

HITTI, P. K. 1970, *History of the Arabs from the Earliest Times to the Present*. New York: St Martins Press (Tenth Ed.).

IBRAHIM, M. H. 1983, Linguistic distance and literacy in Arabic. *Journal of Pragmatics* 7, 507–15.

MITCHELL, T. F. 1978, Educated Spoken Arabic in Egypt and the Levant, with special reference to participle and tense. *Journal of Linguistics* 14 (2), 227–58.

ZUGHOUL, M. R. and TAMINIAN L. 1984, The linguistic attitudes of Arab university students: Factorial structure and intervening variables'. *International Journal of the Sociology of Language* 50, 155–79.

Armenian

Armenian is an independent branch of the Indo-European family of languages, known as *haj* to native speakers (Comrie, 1981: 179). Armenian is spoken in the Armenian SSR as well as other Republics of the Soviet Union such as Georgia and Azerbaydzhan. It is also spoken by a large emigré community in Europe, the Middle East, America and Australia (Comrie, 1981: 179; Encyclopaedia Britannica, 1985: 683).

Armenian was probably introduced into the Transcaucasian region in the latter part of the second millennium BC and by about the seventh century BC had displaced all other languages of the area (Encyclopaedia Britannica, 1985: 683–4).

At the beginning of the fourth century AD the King of Armenia adopted Christianity as the official religion of the country (Lang, 1978: 264). At first Greek and Syriac were used as the languages of the Church, but in about 400 AD an alphabet was, according to tradition, invented for Armenian by Mesrop, an Armenian churchman (Lang, 1978: 266; Comrie, 1981: 179).

This alphabet was used to translate religious texts into Armenian and was soon also used to produce original literature in Armenian (Lang, 1978: 266–7; Encyclopaedia Britannica, 1985: 567). The literary language is traditionally believed to be based on the dialect of Tarawn on Lake Van, though it is not known to what extent the spoken language was split into dialects at this time (Encyclopaedia Britannica, 1985: 684). This form of the language, known as Classical Armenian, or *Grabar*, remained extremely homogeneous till about the ninth century. From the ninth century on, the influence of the spoken language began to be evident and, consequently, slightly different varieties of the literary language grew up from region to region. *Grabar* continued to be used as the literary language, though in more or less corrupted versions, until about the middle of the nineteenth century (Encyclopaedia Britannica, 1985: 684).

During the nineteenth century a new literary language emerged which was closer to the spoken language, though it used the same alphabet as Classical Armenian (Encyclopaedia Britannica, 1985: 684). The new literary form of the language developed in two centres, and, consequently, there are today two varieties of literary Armenian. One centre of development was in the east, where the literary form was based on the spoken dialect of Erivan; the other centre was in the west and was based on the spoken dialect of Armenians living in Istanbul (Encyclopaedia Britannica, 1985: 567).

Comrie calls these two varieties Modern Eastern Armenian, and Modern Western Armenian and he notes that the former is the standard literary and spoken form of the language in Soviet Armenia today, whereas the latter is the spoken and written language form used by 'Armenians in Turkey and of emigré communities in many Middle Eastern countries and the West' (1981: 179). As far as the two varieties are concerned, 'the differences between these two written forms of Modern Armenian are slight, constituting no barrier to mutual intelligibility' (Encyclopaedia Britannica, 1985: 684). Nevertheless, it is possible that the fact that the Eastern variety is the standard form in a Soviet Republic may lead some emigrés to prefer the Western variety.

There are numerous spoken dialects of Armenian, some of which are so different that speakers cannot understand each other. However, the influence of the standard varieties perhaps particularly in the Armenian SSR itself, is leading to a levelling of the dialects (Comrie, 1981: 179; Encyclopaedia Britannica, 1985: 684).

References

COMRIE, B. 1981, *The Languages of the Soviet Union*. Cambridge: Cambridge University Press.
ENCYCLOPAEDIA BRITANNICA 1985, Armenian language. In: *Macropaedia* Vol. 22, pp. 683–4.
ENCYCLOPAEDIA BRITANNICA 1985, Armenian literature. In: *Micropaedia* Ready Reference Vol. 1, p. 567.
LANG, D. M. 1978, *Armenia: Cradle of Civilization*. London: George Allen and Unwin.

Assyrian (Syriac)

Assyrian, or Modern Syriac, is a Semitic language. Assyrians have no state of their own, but live in areas of south-eastern Turkey, north-western Iran, northern Iraq, and also in parts of the USSR and Syria (Beyer, 1986: 54; Comrie, 1981: 282). Earlier this century, though, persecutions in some regions led to mass migrations, and, consequently, speakers of Assyrian are now found in several countries around the world (Beyer, 1986: 54). Estimates of the number of speakers of Assyrian vary from 100,000 (Comrie, 1981: 272) to a million (Crystal, 1987: 316).

Modern Assyrian (which should not be confused with the language of the Assyrian Empire, also called Assyrian, which has been extinct for about 2,000 years) is descended from Aramaic, which, by the time of Jesus, was spoken throughout the Middle East (Beyer, 1986: 10). By about the third century AD, Aramaic had split into Eastern Aramaic and Western Aramaic (Comrie, 1981: 272; Beyer, 1986: 43).

One form of Eastern Aramaic, known to most scholars as Syriac, became the ecclesiastical language of the Eastern-Aramaic speaking Christians (Beyer, 1986: 43–4). The script used for writing Syriac evolved, according to Beyer, from the original alphabet invented by the Canaanites about 2000 BC, via the Cuneiform scripts of various Semitic languages (Beyer, 1986: 56ff).

When the Christians split, in the fifth century, into the Nestorians in the eastern regions and the Jacobites in the west, Syriac also split into an eastern and western form. Over time, differences in pronunciation and in the script of the eastern and western forms evolved (Beyer, 1986: 44; Paulissian, 1978: vi; Oddo, 1978: x).

The spread of Islam, from the seventh century AD, led to Arabic taking over from Aramaic as the main language of the Middle East (Beyer, 1986: 10; Hetzron, 1987: 656). Some of the Christian groups, and also some Jewish groups, though, maintained their religion and their Aramaic language (Beyer, 1986: 44–5).

The descendants of both the Eastern and Western branches of Aramaic have survived into modern times. The descendant of Western Aramaic, though, is spoken at present only in a few villages near Damascus in Syria (Comrie, 1981: 272; Beyer, 1986: 55). The descendants of Eastern Aramaic are, however, still fairly vigorous.

The name Assyrian for the modern descendants of Eastern Aramaic is not used consistently. The dialects descended from Eastern Aramaic which are spoken by Jews are called, by their speakers, 'Targumic'. Most of these speakers have now migrated to Israel (Encyclopaedia Judaica, 1971: 948–9). Scholars use other names. Beyer (1986: 54) says that "Modern Eastern Syriac...[is] spoken predominantly by Nestorian and Chaldean Christians (who call themselves 'Assyrians')". Comrie calls the language Aramaic and notes that 'the people who speak it are usually called Assyrians' (1981: 272). Hetzron says the language is Eastern Neo-Aramaic (Modern Syriac) and he adds, 'the speakers are sometimes inappropriately called Chaldean, (Neo-) Assyrian' (1987: 656). But Crystal says the language is 'Syriac (or Assyrian)' (1987: 316), and Paulissian (1978) and Oddo (1978), who produced the 'Assyrian Dictionary', mainly use the name Assyrian, but also use Syriac. As well, the language has sometimes been called Nestorian, Chaldean and Jacobite (Paulissian, 1978: vi). It is possible, therefore, that the name by which the language is known has overtones of politics, religion, and group identity.

It appears, however, that Assyrian mainly refers to the forms of Eastern Aramaic spoken by Christians and known to most scholars as Syriac. This is the form, as noted above, which was used as the ecclesiastical language of the Nestorian, sometimes called Chaldean, Christians and the Jacobite, or Maronite, Christians.

The division of Assyrian, or Syriac, into two forms after the fifth century has continued to the present. Beyer notes that Modern Western Syriac is spoken mainly by Jacobite Christians around Midyat in south-eastern Turkey, while Modern Eastern Syriac is spoken by the Nestorian, or Chaldean Christians (Beyer, 1986: 54). Oddo also states that Western Syriac is used by the Jacobites, or Maronite Christians and the Eastern form by the Nestorians (Oddo, 1978: x). According to Comrie the Nestorian, Eastern form 'still survives as the liturgical language of most Eastern Aramaic speakers' (Comrie, 981: 272–3).

A new written form of Assyrian was devised in the nineteenth century based on one of the dialects of Urmia in northern Iran. This written form used the same alphabet, known as Estrangelo, as 'Classical' Assyrian but was designed to bring the written form closer to the spoken language since 'Classical' Assyrian was restricted to 'scholars, the clergy and very educated Assyrians' (Paulissian, 1978: vi).

According to Comrie, a writing system based on the Latin alphabet was also devised and used in Aramaic-medium schools between 1926 and 1938 (1981: 273). This writing system does not appear to be in use nowadays.

The writing system based on the Urmia dialect is apparently extensively used for publishing, but there does not appear to be one standard dialect used for speech. As Beyer says, 'everyone reads the texts [in the new written language] in his own dialect' (1986: 53).

In the spoken language, Beyer notes that 'Modern Eastern Syriac [Assyrian] is divided into several considerably divergent dialects...' (1986: 54). And Sara, although he calls the language Chaldean, says that among the Christian speakers of modern Eastern Aramaic in Iraq, various dialects with differing degrees of mutual intelligibility are spoken (Sara, 1974: 12).

It would seem, therefore, that although there is a standard written form for Assyrian, there are several spoken dialects which may or may not be mutually intelligible. It is possible, though, that the written form may disseminate the Urmia dialect and this dialect may become a spoken standard as well.

Assyrian, then, would appear to be the name given by its speakers to the modern form of Eastern Aramaic spoken by Christians and known to most scholars as Syriac. The name seems to have overtones of politics, religion, and group identity. There is a standard written form based on the dialect of Urmia in Iran, but there does not appear, at present, to be a standard spoken form. Rather, there are several considerably divergent dialects.

References

BEYER, K. 1986, *The Aramaic Language: Its Distribution and Subdivisions*. Gottingen: Vandenhoeck and Ruprecht (Translated by J. F. Healey).
CRYSTAL, D. 1987, *The Cambridge Encyclopaedia of Language*. Cambridge: Cambridge University Press.
COMRIE, B. 1981, *The Languages of the Soviet Union*. Cambridge: Cambridge University Press.
ENCYCLOPAEDIA JUDAICA 1971, *Macropaedia* Vol.XII, pp. 948–51.
HETZRON, R. 1987, Semitic languages. In: B. COMRIE (ed.) *The World's Major Languages* (pp.654–63). London: Croom Helm.
ODDO, M. T. 1978, *Assyrian Dictionary*. Chicago: Assyrian Language and Culture Classes Inc.
PAULISSIAN, R. 1978, Preface to the Second Edition. In: M. T. ODDO (ed.) *Assyrian Dictionary*. Chicago: Assyrian Language and Culture Classes.
SARA, S. I. 1974, *A Description of Modern Chaldean*. The Hague: Mouton.

Bengali

Bengali is a member of the Indo-Aryan branch of the Indo-European family of languages (Nicholas & Oldenburg, 1972: 13). It is spoken in the Indian State of West Bengal, and in Bangladesh, formerly East Pakistan. As well, there are small numbers of Bengali speakers in the neighbouring Indian States of Assam, Bihar and Orissa (Zograph, 1982: 96).

The history of Indo-Aryan languages goes back to the arrival of the Aryan people in India probably sometime before 1500 BC (Chatterji, 1970: 23). By about the fourth century BC a literary form of Indo-Aryan had been standardised and its fundamental norms had been formalised and consolidated in grammatical works (Zograph, 1982: 10). This form, known as Sanskrit, became the language of culture and tradition throughout most of India, and it is still in use, virtually unchanged, to this day (Zograph, 1982: 11).

However, since the Aryan people entered northern India from the extreme west and since Bengal is situated at the extreme east of northern India, it was not until a considerable time after the Aryans first arrival that Bengal became completely Aryanised. Chatterji considers that even though there was a 'considerable Aryanisation' of Bengal by 300 AD, it was not until the fourth century AD that 'Bengal became finally and completely linked to Northern or Aryan India' in language and culture (1970: 76–7).

As with other Indo-Aryan languages, Bengali developed through a *Prakrit* and an *Apabhramsa* stage (Chatterji, 1970: 86ff; Sen, 1960: 1ff). (See the chapter on Hindi for further discussion of these stages.) According to Chatterji, Bengali emerged as a separate language in its own right in the tenth century (1980: 129).

The development of Bengali itself is usually divided into three stages: the Old or Formative Stage, the Middle Stage and the Modern Stage. It was in the Formative Stage, tenth to thirteenth centuries, that a Bengali literature began to develop. During the Middle Stage, thirteenth to nineteenth centuries, Bengali literature became firmly established and a literary language, based on West Bengali, was perfected by the sixteenth century. The Middle Stage was also a time of considerable influence on Bengali of Persian, the language of the Muslim rulers (Chatterji, 1970: 129ff; Nicholas & Oldenburg, 1972: 14ff; Sen, 1960: 4ff).

The influence of Persian was due to the fact that from the sixteenth to the nineteenth centuries Bengal was under Muslim rule. As a result of the Muslim rule, Persian was the official language of administration, law, and commerce till 1838 when it was replaced by Bengali and English (Sen, 1960: 6–7). According to Nicholas and Oldenburg, though, the Persian influence did not penetrate very deeply (1972: 14–15). They say:

> Linguistically, the situation did not change. The converts [to Islam] continued to speak Bengali; and even the non-Bengali Muslims were oriented toward the Bengali language, some of the rulers went so far as to commission Sanskrit and Persian classics to be translated into Bengali. (Nicholas & Oldenburg, 1972: 14–15)

The beginning of Modern Bengali is dated, it seems, from the time of the arrival of the English. The important factor appears to be the introduction of western style education and literary forms, rather than the English language itself. Chatterji notes that 'the advent of Western learning brought in a sudden demand for a prose style' (1970: 134). Sen says that

> modern Bengali prose possesses many idioms, turns and twists of expression which were undoubtedly induced by the thought-pattern of English. (Sen, 1960: 8)

And Nicholas and Oldenburg consider that 'western literary forms and values are an intrinsic and inescapable part of the intellectual life of Bengal' (1972: 15).

The influence of Western learning resulted in the adoption of a new form of literary Bengali. This form was based on the speech of the fifteenth century with a highly Sanskritised vocabulary and is known as *sadhu-bhasa* (Chatterji, 1970: 134–5). Grierson considered that *sadhu-bhasa* was adopting more and more Sanskrit vocabulary with each passing decade (1968: 16).

During the present century, however, another literary form grew up. This literary form was based

> on the cultivated form of the dialect (the standard colloquial) spoken in Calcutta by the educated people originally coming from districts bordering on the lower reaches of the Hooghly [river]. (Sen, 1960: 8)

This form is known as *calit bhasa*.

Sadhu-bhasa, though, is declining in use and is never used as a spoken language (Chatterji, 1970: 135). As Zograph puts it:

> Two very different styles have the status of literary norms: the 'classical' (*sadhu-bhasa*) based on the Western dialect and preserving an archaic structure, and the 'colloquial' (*calit bhasa*), which combines features of the contemporary Western dialect and of the Calcutta sub-dialect. The former, which was until the 1920s exclusively used in printed matter and in formal

oral communication, is nowadays still used for official purposes, special literature and certain areas of the press; but the latter has became the basic form used for modern literature. (Zograph, 1982: 98)

Bengali is written in the Bengali script which derives from the old Brahmi alphabet. It is related to, but differs from, the Deva-Nagari script used for Hindi (Sen, 1960: 9; Grierson, 1968: 9).

When East Pakistan was created by the partition of India in 1947, there was considerable controversy between East and West Pakistan over whether Urdu or Bengali should be the official language. In 1956 it was finally decided that Bengali should be the sole language of education and administration in East Pakistan (Hai, 1971: 190).

However, the separation of Muslim East Pakistan from the new Indian state of West Bengal led to some divergence in the literary language. As Nicholas and Oldenburg state:

> There were indications that dialect divergences were growing for lack of contact. And Muslim writers, largely in East Bengal [East Pakistan], were using increasingly more Perso-Arabic vocabulary and, naturally enough, treating more and more Muslim subject matter than their fellow writers in West Bengal. (Nicholas & Oldenburg, 1972: 16)

Houghton (1975) also notes divergences between the Muslim area of Bengal, now Bangladesh, and the Hindu West Bengal in India. She says that the differences are mainly confined to vocabulary choice, with few syntactic or phonological differences (1975: 144). Nevertheless, Houghton considers that an East Bengali, or Bangladeshi, standard form, based to some extent on the dialect of Dhaka, is evolving. She sees this form as 'a compromise standardisation of various East Bengali dialects and as a language spoken by the educated...' (1975: 131).

As far as the spoken language is concerned there are a large variety of dialects. According to Grierson the change from one dialect to the next is very gradual with slight variation occuring every few miles (1968: 17). And Zograph says:

> Local forms of speech change every few dozen kilometers, but not sufficiently to make them incomprehensible to close neighbours. As distances increase so too do dialectal variations... .(Zograph, 1982: 22)

However, scholars appear to disagree on the major groupings of dialects in Bengali. Grierson (1968: 17) and Zograph (1982: 98) consider that there are two major groups: western, with the central dialect spoken around the Hooghli river and Calcutta as the standard; and eastern, with the dialect of Dhaka as standard. Chatterji (1970: 138) and Sen (1960: 8), on the other hand, consider that there are four major groups, and Chatterji says that the dialect of Calcutta is the standard form (1970: 140).

It seems probable, though, that the population movement caused by the migration of Muslims to the east, into what is now Bangladesh, and of Hindus to the west, has produced dialect mixing and a breakdown, to some extent at least, of the old regional dialects.

As the distance between local dialects increases it is possible that problems of comprehension may occur. Dimock *et al.* (1976: x–xi) note that the dialects of the extreme west differ so widely from those of the extreme east that they are 'practically unintelligible to one another'. They point out though that

> the 'standard colloquial' or *calit-bhasa* [based originally on the educated speech of Calcutta], will be spoken and understood by educated people at both extremes. (Dimock *et al.*, 1976: xi)

For Bengali, therefore, there are two literary styles. *Sadhu-bhasa*, the archaic and heavily Sanskritised 'classical' form which is never used for speaking and, it appears, only rarely in writing nowadays, and *calit-bhasa*, the 'colloquial' form, which was originally based on the speech around Calcutta, and is used in formal speaking as well as writing. As well, there appears to be a standard East Bengali which is evolving, but which differs mainly in its use of Perso-Arabic vocabulary. The spoken language is characterised by considerable dialectal variation with possible problems of comprehension experienced as distances increase.

References

CHATTERJI, S. K. 1970, *The Origin and Development of the Bengali Language*. London: George Allen and Unwin.

DIMOCK, E. C. *et al.* 1976, *Introduction to Bengali: Part 1*. New Delhi: Mandiar.

GRIERSON, G. A. 1968, *Linguistic Survey of India* Vol. V Pt.1. Delhi: Motilal Banarsidass.

HAI, M. A. 1971, The development of Bengali since the establishment of Pakistan. In: J RUBIN and B. H. JERNUDD (eds) *Can Language be Planned* (pp.189–92). Honolulu: The University Press of Hawaii.

HOUGHTON, C. 1975, East Bengali language and political development in sociolinguistic perspective. In: J. R. MCLANE (ed) *Bengal in the Nineteenth and Twentieth Centuries*. Michigan: Michigan State University (Asian Studies Centre, South Asia Series No. 25).

NICHOLAS, M. and OLDENBURG P. 1972, *Bangladesh: The Birth of a Nation*. Madras: M. Seshachalam and Company.

SEN, S. 1960, *History of Bengali Literature*. New Delhi: Sahitya Akademi.

ZOGRAPH, G. A. 1982, *Languages of South Asia: A Guide*. London: Routledge and Kegan Paul (Languages of Asia and Africa, Vol. 3).

Bulgarian

Bulgarian is a South Slavonic language, a sub-division of the Slavonic branch of the Indo-European family (Comrie, 1987: 322). Bulgarian is spoken principally in Bulgaria, though there are quite a large number of Bulgarian speakers in the USSR (Comrie, 1981: 144). It should also be noted that there are no absolute breaks between one South Slavonic language and another. Rather, there is a dialect chain, or continuum, whereby language varieties shade gradually from one to another. Thus, as Crystal notes for Bulgarian and Macedonian:

> in the South Slavonic continuum, varieties spoken on the Yugoslav side of the border between Yugoslavia and Bulgaria are called dialects of Macedonian by the former country, but dialects of Bulgarian by the latter — as part of a claim to the territory. However, because there is a dialect chain in the area, linguistic criteria will never be able to solve conflicts of this kind. (Crystal, 1989: 25)

Slavs first arrived in the area which is today Bulgaria in the late fifth century AD, and in the seventh century the Slavs began to arrive in greater numbers. The seventh century also saw the arrival in this region of a group known as Bulgars, or Proto-Bulgarians, and under the military and political leadership of the Bulgars the first Bulgarian state was recognised by the Byzantine Emperor in 681 (Crampton, 1987: 2). The Bulgars were of Turkic origin and, according to Crampton, came from the region between the Urals and the Volga (1987: 2).

By the ninth century the Slav and Bulgar inhabitants of Bulgaria were all known as Bulgarians and a common Slav-based language was in use (Crampton, 1987: 3). De Bray notes that very few Bulgar words survived since the Bulgars were relatively few in number and were completely absorbed and 'Slav-ised' by the far more numerous Slav inhabitants (1969: 195). Crampton, though, considers that even though the Bulgars adopted the Slavonic language they did not fully amalgamate with the Slavs until they converted to Christianity in the late ninth century (1987: 3).

The adoption of Christianity also led to the adoption of a Slavonic written form. In the second half of the ninth century two monks, Constantine, who later assumed the name Cyril, and Methodius had begun translating the Gospels into Slavonic. The original alphabet used was Glagolitic, believed to have been invented by Cyril (Gardiner, 1984: 12). This early form of writing is known as

Old Church Slavonic which was first used in Moravia (now part of Czechoslovakia), but when the missionaries were expelled from that country in the late ninth century, they fled to Bulgaria and continued their writing in Bulgaria (Gardiner, 1984: 1ff).

Comrie notes that Old Church Slavonic has distinctive South Slavonic, and more specifically Bulgarian–Macedonian, features (1987: 322). Consequently, as Golab says,

> for the majority of Bulgarian linguists there is no doubt that Old Church Slavonic, usually called by them 'Old Bulgarian', represents the earliest attested stage in the development of their national language. (Golab, 1963: 485)

However, from a purely linguistic point of view it appears that Macedonian and Bulgarian exhibited only a very slight dialectal variation at the time of the creation of Old Church Slavonic (Golab, 1963: 486; Gardiner, 1984: 2). As well, as Gardiner points out, the language of the early texts may be rather artificial and not correspond exactly to any one spoken dialect (1984: 1–2). Golab considers, therefore, that Old Church Slavonic

> can be claimed with equal right by both the Bulgarians and the Macedonicans as the oldest historical stage in their national languages. (Golab, 1963: 486)

From the late ninth century, then, Old Church Slavonic served as the official language of the Bulgarian state. It was used for secular as well as religious works (Crampton, 1987: 23). The Glagolitic alphabet, though, was superceded by the Cyrillic, which, in a slightly modified form is still in use today (Comrie, 1987: 322; Gardiner, 1984: 12ff).

During the eleventh and twelfth centuries Bulgaria was under Byzantine rule, but its population retained its Bulgarian language and culture (Crampton, 1987: 5). During this period the characteristically Bulgarian features of the language established themselves and these features crept into the written language, due, according to De Bray, to the oversights and ignorance of the writers and scribes (1969: 193).

In the fourteenth century, though, the leader of the Bulgarian Church 'purified' the language, i.e. returned it to the model of Old Church Slavonic (De Bray, 1969: 193). But the end of the fourteenth century saw the conquest of Bulgaria by the Ottoman Turks (Crampton, 1987: 7), and the beginning of 'the dark days of decline under Turkish domination' (De Bray, 1969: 193).

Under the Turks the Bulgarian Church was placed under the authority of the Greek patriarch (Crompton, 1987: 7). As a result Greek became an important language in religion and education (Crompton, 1987: 14). Bulgarian language and culture was maintained, however, in the more remote villages where the impact of the conquest was less profound (Crompton, 1987: 14). From the sixteenth century popular works, such as almanacs, were translated from Greek into Bulgarian. Although these works often exhibited dialectal variation in translation, attempts to bring written Bulgarian closer to the spoken language 'were constantly countered by the influence and prestige of the church language which was regarded as the noblest and purest' (De Bray, 1969: 193).

A movement to bring the literary language closer to the spoken form and away from the archaic, stylised Old Church Slavonic began during the eighteenth century (Crompton, 1987: 9). By the early nineteenth century several grammars had been produced based on spoken Bulgarian dialects (De Bray, 1969: 194). As well, schools were being set up which taught in Bulgarian rather than Greek (Crompton, 1987: 12; 14).

Many of the early Bulgarian writers used a literary form based on the western Bulgarian dialects, but in the 1870s it was decided that the standard literary form should be based on the eastern dialects (De Bray, 1969: 194; Aronson, 1968: 13). Aronson, in fact, considers that the standard literary form was based on the north-eastern spoken dialect (1968: 13).

After Bulgaria became an independent state in 1878, there were attempts to rid Bulgarian of Turkish and other foreign borrowings, while looking to Russian and Church Slavonic for neologisms and as a source for the enrichment of the literary language (Aronson, 1968: 13). According to De Bray, in the twentieth century, at least up to the Second World War, language planners tried to keep Bulgarian as 'pure' as possible by banning words of Russian, Turkish, West European or other languages from the literary form (De Bray, 1969: 195).

Although the standard form of Bulgarian is based on the north-eastern spoken dialects, the move of the capital to Sofia in 1879 meant that there has been considerable influence from the western dialects (Aronson, 1968: 13). Aronson also says that language planners have often disagreed on specific points with the result that, 'it could be stated without much exageration that the major grammarians and their disciples established their own variants of the literary language' and that 'there are wide areas where two or more variants lay claim to the dignity of being the literary form' (Aronson, 1968: 14).

Consequently, the Bulgarian literary language is not identical to any particular dialect, and is in some ways an artificial creation (Aronson, 1968: 15). Nevertheless, the literary standardised form of Bulgarian is based on the eastern dialects and relatively fixed and codified. The orthography was reformed and greatly simplified after 1945 to bring it more into line with actual pronunciation (De Bray, 1969: 195–6).

The spoken dialects of Bulgarian are relatively homogeneous, presenting no problems of comprehension. They are usually divided into three major groupings: western, north-eastern, and south-eastern (De Bray, 1969: 200–1).

There is, in fact, a continuum of dialects in this region which also includes the areas of Yugoslav and Greek Macedonia. The Macedonian dialects, though, have features, which, while they occur in various spoken Bulgarian dialects, do not occur in literary Bulgarian, from which they are sharply differentiated (De Bray, 1969: 200).

Bulgarian, therefore, has a standard literary form developed during the nineteenth century. While this form is based on the eastern, or north-eastern spoken dialects, it is not identical to them since it also incorporates elements from other dialect groups, particularly western Bulgarian dialects. Language planners have attempted to keep Bulgarian as 'pure' as possible by replacing foreign words. There are several dialects which form a dialect continuum, though none of the dialects appears to cause any problems of comprehension. It is presumed that a standard spoken form, based on the literary form, is used in education, broadcasting and other formal situations.

References

ARONSON, H. I. 1968, *Bulgarian Inflectional Morphology*. The Hague: Mouton.
COMRIE, B. 1981, *The Languages of the Soviet Union*. Cambridge: Cambridge University Press.
COMRIE, B. 1987, Slavonic languages. In: B. COMRIE (ed.) *The World's Major Languages* (pp. 322–8). London: Croom Helm.
CRAMPTON, R. J. 1987, *A Short History of Bulgaria*. Cambridge: Cambridge University Press.
CRYSTAL, D. 1987, *The Cambridge Encyclopaedia of Language*. Cambridge: Cambridge University Press.
DE BRAY, R. G. A. 1969, *Guide to the Slavonic Languages*. London: J. M. Dent and Sons Ltd.
GARDINER, S. C. 1984, *Old Church Slavonic: An Elementary Grammar*. Cambridge: Cambridge University Press.
GOLAB, Z. 1963, Bulgaria. In: T. A. Sebeok (ed.) *Current Trends in Linguistics* Vol. 1 (pp. 477–98). The Hague: Mouton.

Byelorussian

Byelorussian, often spelt Belorussian and also known as White Russian, is a Slavonic language spoken in the Byelorussian SSR in the Soviet Union. Byelorussian is usually grouped with Ukrainian and Russian as a member of the East Slavonic group of Indo-European languages (Comrie, 1981: 144).

The three East Slavonic languages remained fairly homogeneous till at least the thirteenth century (Vlasto, 1986: 335ff). As well, a common written language had been in use in East Slavonic speaking areas since the tenth century. The written language was Old Church Slavonic, written in the Cyrillic alphabet, which had been adopted when Kiev, the centre of the first East Slavic state, became Christian (Shevelov, 1979: 213).

The form of Old Church Slavonic adopted by Kiev was based on Bulgarian, a South Slavonic language, and, although it was relatively fixed, it was nevertheless influenced to some extent by the East Slavonic spoken languages and consequently evolved into a number of different varieties (Shevelov, 1979: 215).

Byelorussian first appeared as a separate written form in the early fourteenth century when it was used by the Lithuanian state, which occupied Byelorussia, as their official language of administration (Comrie, 1981: 146; De Bray, 1969: 129). Comrie calls this language form 'West Russian chancellery language' (1981: 146), but Shevelov says this form was Ruthenian and incorporated some Ukrainian as well as Byelorussian elements (1981: 219). De Bray also notes that this early written form of Byelorussian incorporated some Ukrainian, though he notes that it was dominated by Church Slavonic (1969: 130). By the late fifteenth century, according to Shevelov, the written language used for administration in the Lithuanian controlled area was Byelorussian (1979: 401). In the sixteenth century, many important works, including a translation of the Bible, were produced in Byelorussian (De Bray, 1969: 130).

After the union of Lithuania and Poland in the late sixteenth century, Polish came to be the literary and prestigious language in Byelorussia. As Davies puts it 'a proper command of the Polish language became the mark of gentility and social accomplishment' (1984: 328). The use of Byelorussian as a literary language consequently began to decline (Matthews, 1951: 117).

Although the élite did not use Byelorussian, the mass of the people, the peasants, did (Gasinski, 1988).

According to Comrie it was during these centuries of foreign domination that the East Slavonic languages diverged from one another (Comrie, 1981: 145; 1987: 331ff). Innovations or changes in Byelorussian, and also in Ukrainian or Russian, were in general restricted by political boundaries to the area in which they occurred so that differences between the languages developed (Comrie, 1981: 145ff; 1987: 331ff).

With the partitions of Poland in the late eighteenth century, Byelorussia came under Russian rule. As a result, Russian took over from Polish as the language of the government and Byelorussian 'continued only as an amalgam of spoken dialects, without any developed written form, until after the Revolution' (Comrie, 1981: 146). In 1836 Russian was introduced as the language of instruction in Byelorussian schools (Wilson, 1986: 48). Polish, though, continued to be used for a time in the Catholic Church and was supported by most of the gentry (Katchan, 1980: 7).

During the eighteenth and nineteenth centuries Byelorussian literature was, to a fairly large extent, suppressed (Mayo, 1984: 51). In fact, from 1867 till 1905 printing in Byelorussian was forbidden by the Russian authorities (Wilson, 1986: 15).

However, De Bray considers that modern Byelorussian literature dates from the early nineteenth century (1969: 130). And Wilson points out that although Czarist Russia failed to recognise the national identity of Byelorussians, works of fiction were written in Byelorussian (1986: 15). McMillin also notes that literary works were produced in Byelorussian during the time Byelorussia was under Polish and Czarist Russian rule, though mostly in manuscript form (1984: 44ff).

The rebirth of Byelorussian literature in the nineteenth century is discussed at some length by Katchen (1980). She observes that during this period there were a considerable number of writers using Byelorussian, some of whom had their work printed outside Byelorussia and smuggled back for clandestine distribution. Katchen (1980) presents the view that in the nineteenth century Byelorussian literature, written in the Byelorussian literary language, was used for social protest and was one of the crucial factors in shaping Byelorussian nationalism.

By the late nineteenth century, then, a new generation of writers had appeared who were ready to promote the ideal of Byelorussia as a national entity (Katchen, 1980: 22–3). Wexler considers the 1890s as the real beginning of the Byelorussian linguistic revival, when strong efforts began to be made to develop the literary language by what he calls 'prescriptive intervention' (Wexler, 1979: 481).

According to Wexler, in the period from 1890 to 1918 language planning for the Byelorussian literary language favoured the use of forms based on the western dialects and opposed Russian or Polish elements (1979: 484). After the Bolshevik revolution and the founding of the Byelorussian SSR, Byelorussian was officially recognised as a separate written and spoken language (Comrie, 1981: 146).

Thus, this new form of the Byelorussian literary language, based more closely on the spoken language of the western regions and divorced from the old literary language used till the sixteenth century, gained official recognition and marked the resurrection of Byelorussian which for several centuries had been denied an existence of its own (Wilson, 1986: 27; Wexler, 1979: 484).

In the 1920s and 30s language planners continued to oppose Russian and Polish as sources of enrichment for the literary language. Rather, they sought elements from the dialects, now, according to Wexler, from the west central areas and those forms which were most widespread throughout the country (1979: 485). The modern orthography of Byelorussian was established by the Byelorussian Academy of Sciences in 1933 (Debray, 1969: 131).

However, from the 1930s Russian influence began to grow. Dialectal forms were now chosen from the eastern regions, particularly those forms shared with Russian dialects, and elements of vocabulary and grammar from the Russian literary language itself were also incorporated into Byelorussian (Wexler, 1979: 485ff). Russian is a co-official language in the Byelorussian SSR and so today, as Wexler puts it, 'Byelorussians have a choice of two literary languages — Russian or (Russianised) Byelorussian' (1979: 482).

Since the 1960s there has been some opposition to the Russification of Byelorussian, but even though there has been some opening of the literary language once more to western dialect forms, the Russification continues apace (Wexler, 1979). As Mayo notes, therefore, while there is a substantial indigenous dialectal base for the Byelorussian literary language, it has been heavily influenced by Russian (1984: 50ff).

The Russification of Byelorussia extends beyond the literary language itself. Russian, as a separate language, is making considerable inroads into the country. The 1970 census showed that 49% of Byelorussians used Russian regularly. This trend is, however, stronger in urban than in rural areas (Wexler, 1979: 501).

In 1987 in an open letter to the Soviet leader, Mr Gorbachev, well over a hundred members of the Byelorussian intelligentsia, including academics, teachers and writers, complained of the Russification of Byelorussia.

The letter states that the language of education and bureaucracy is almost exclusively Russian. The letter also states that although the number of titles published in Byelorussian, for newspapers and books, may be greater than the number published in Russian, the actual print run of Russian titles is many times greater. For example, in 1985 the six national Byelorussian newspapers printed 53 million copies while the five national papers in Russian printed nearly 350 million (Letter to Gorbachev, 1987: 15; 25).

In spoken Byelorussian Wexler distinguishes three forms. Firstly, the official spoken version of the literary language which is used for radio, television, formal speeches and so on. Secondly, an unofficial colloquial version of the literary language. And thirdly dialects which are mainly preserved in rural areas (Wexler, 1979: 496). In the first, the official spoken form, there is a considerable amount of Russification. In the unofficial form, there are also some Russian elements, though perhaps not as many. The extensive bilingualism, however, is tending to lead to language shift to Russian forms (Wexler, 1979: 496; 507).

The dialects show the greatest 'purity' since they are less influenced by Russian. It must be noted though, that the north-eastern dialects form a continuum from Byelorussian to Russian, while the south-western dialects are closer to Ukrainian (DeBray, 1969: 140). The differences between the Byelorussian dialects appears to be slight and there are no problems of comprehension between them. Also, as Wexler notes, 'speakers of dialect are being encouraged to acquire the spoken and written norms of the standard language' (1979: 504).

Byelorussian, therefore, had a literary language based on Church Slavonic from the fourteenth to the sixteenth or seventeenth century. Then Polish and later Russian came to dominate the area and Byelorussian declined as a literary language. In the nineteenth and especially the early part of the twentieth century Byelorussian literature was resurrected, but the new literary language was based on the spoken dialects. Initially western dialects were chosen, and Polish and Russian forms excluded, but after the 1930s the eastern dialects, being closer to Russian, and Russian literary forms were used to enrich the literary form. This has led to a considerable Russification of the Byelorussian literary language. Although there is now opposition to Russification, it appears to be continuing. As well, Russian itself is being used more and more in Byelorussia in education, the bureaucracy and printing. While dialect is still used in rural areas there is pressure on dialect speakers to acquire the spoken form of the literary language, which is used in the media, for formal speech and so on, and is also heavily Russified. There is also an 'unofficial' spoken version of the standard form which appears to be less heavily influenced by Russian. However, the extensive bilingualism in Byelorussia means that this form too has some Russian influence.

It is worth noting that, according to Wexler, outside of the USSR the form of the literary language developed prior to the late 1930s is still used. This form is based on the western or west central dialects and opposes the use of Russian elements (Wexler, 1979: 50 fn).

References

COMRIE, B. 1981, *The Languages of the Soviet Union*. Cambridge: Cambridge University Press.

COMRIE, B. 1987, Russian. In: B. COMRIE (ed.) *The World's Major Languages* (pp. 329–47). London: Croom Helm.

DAVIES, N. 1984, *Heart of Europe: A Short History of Poland*. Oxford: Clarendon Press.

DE BRAY, R. G. A. 1969, *Guide to the Slavonic Languages*. London: J. M. Dent and Sons.

GASINSKI, T. 1988, School of Modern Languages, Macquarie University, personal communication.

KATCHEN, O. 1980, 19th century: The rebirth of Byelorussian literature. Paper presented at the Humanities Research Centre Conference. Canberra: Australian National University.

LETTER TO GORBACHEV, 1987, New documents from Soviet Byelorussia Issue 2, London, The Association of Byelorussians in Great Britain.

MATTHEWS, W. K. 1951, *Languages of the USSR*. Cambridge: Cambridge University Press.

MAYO, P. J. 1984, Whither modern Byelorussian lexis? (Review Article). *The Journal of Byelorussian Studies* V (3–4), 50–7.

McMILLIN, A. B. 1984, The Baroque and enlightenment in Byelorussia: Towards a revision of the periodization of Byelorussian literature (Review Article). *The Journal of Byelorussian Studies* V (3–4), 44–9.

SHEVELOV, G. Y. 1979, *A Historical Phonology of the Ukrainian Language*. Heidelberg: Carol Winter Universitatsverlag.

SHEVELOV, G. Y. 1981, Evolution of the Ukrainian literary language. In: I. L. RUDNYTSKY (ed.) *Rethinking Ukrainian History* (pp. 216–31). Edmonton: University of Alberta.

VLASTO, A. P. 1986, *A Linguistic History of Russia to the End of the Eighteenth Century*. Oxford: The Clarendon Press.

WEXLER, P. 1979, The rise (and fall) of the modern Byelorussian literary language. *The Slavonic and East European Review* 57 (4), 481–508.

WILSON, S. 1986, *Belorussia and its Books*. Victoria, Australia: Monash University Department of Slavic Languages.

Cantonese

Cantonese is usually considered to be a dialect of Chinese, and Chinese to be an independent branch of the Sino-Tibetan family of languages (Chang & Chang, 1980: 6–7). Cantonese is spoken in Guandong (Canton) province in China, in Hong Kong and in many overseas Chinese settlements (Li & Thompson, 1979: 297–8).

Since there are many sub-dialects of Cantonese, scholars often consider Cantonese as a dialect group (Chao, 1976: 21).This dialect group is sometimes known as the Yue group (DeFrancis, 1984: 62). Li and Thompson, in fact, treat Cantonese as one dialect of the Yue group (1979: 296–8).

Cantonese may have begun to split from other Chinese dialects such as Mandarin as much as 3,000 years ago (So, 1987: 20). Forrest considers that Cantonese is 'the form which best preserves the essential traits of Ancient Chinese' (1965: 230). A consequence of this divergence is that Cantonese and other Chinese dialects such as Mandarin, Hakka, Fukienese and so on are all mutually unintelligible.

The history of the Chinese written language goes back to at least 1500 BC as is evidenced by the characters found on bones used for divination known as 'oracle bones'. These characters are, however, already so sophisticated that, as Chang and Chang note, writing probably began at least a thousand years earlier (1980: 50ff).

The Chinese writing system is not an alphabetic system. Instead of letters a system of characters are used to represent words. The characters began as pictographs but soon evolved beyond this stage and complex characters using semantic elements and semantic plus phonetic elements became the more usual forms (DeFrancis, 1984: 74ff).

The characters were first codified and standardised in about 200 BC (Forrest, 1965: 48; Chang & Chang, 1980: 61). And by about 200 AD in the Han dynasty, the system of characters still in use today had taken shape (DeFrancis, 1984: 83). According to DeFrancis, in the second century AD about 82% of Chinese characters were formed using the semantic–phonetic principle, and in the eighteenth century about 97% used this principle (1984: 84).

Since the Communist takeover of mainland China certain changes to the writing system have been introduced. A simplification of some of the characters has been undertaken; by 1964 some 2,000 had been simplified, and this process is still continuing (Li & Thompson, 1979: 329). The simplified characters are, for the most part, used only in mainland China and not in Hong Kong or Taiwan nor in many Chinese communities throughout the world (Hsu, 1979: 118). As well, a phonetic system for writing Mandarin using the Roman alphabet was officially introduced in 1958 (Seybolt & Chiang, 1979: 25). This system, known as Pinyin, is used in schools to teach the pronunciation of characters (Chang & Chang, 1980: 72), and, since 1979, has replaced all other 'Romanisations', such as the Wade–Giles system, which were in use; thus 'Peking' in an older system has become 'Beijing' and 'Mao Tse-tung' has become 'Mao Zedong' (Chang & Chang, 1980: 33).

It is important to note that written Chinese, in both characters and Romanised Pinyin, is based on the grammar and vocabulary of Mandarin. Speakers of all other dialects, though, use the same characters since there is only one written language. As Li and Thompson say:

> Since the initial appearance of the Chinese written system more than 4,000 years ago, the Chinese people have had only one written language. Thus, no matter how different the dialects are, literate Chinese people from different parts of the country have always been able to communicate with each other through writing, and they all have access to the same body of literature. (Li & Thompson, 1979: 326)

Literature in Chinese has a long history, but, as is often the case, the literary form of the language became divorced from the spoken language. As Chang and Chang put it:

> Like other tongues, the Chinese spoken language has also altered over the centuries. Yet while the speech of all classes of Chinese mutated as years passed, the written language used by scholars and bureaucrats diverged more and more from the spoken language, and developed at last into a unique literary style that came to be known as *wenyan*, or 'literary speech'. (Chang & Chang, 1980: 63)

In the early twentieth century a movement began to reform the literary language and bring it closer to the spoken language. This movement was helped by the end of imperial rule in 1911, but only really became effective after demonstrations in 1919. The new literary form encouraged people to write as they spoke and this form is known as *bai hua* 'plain language' (Chang & Chang, 1980: 68–9). It would appear that *bai hua* has now taken over from *wenyan* as the literary form of the language in mainland China, though *wenyan* is still in use to some extent. Chang and Chang note that:

> Enclaves of scholars and poets in Taiwan and other overseas Chinese communities still read and write in the old way. Middle school students in the People's Republic are taught to read *wenyan* through textbooks of

selected readings, but are not asked to compose or to read the original classics in their entirety; for reasons that are as much political as educational. (Chang & Chang, 1980: 74–5)

However, although the vocabulary and grammar of written Chinese are almost uniform throughout China, the pronunciation is not. That is, a written Chinese text read aloud by a Mandarin speaker would sound very different from the same text read by a Cantonese speaker since each would pronounce the characters according to the phonology of their own dialect (Light, 1980: 261).

Also, because the vocabulary and grammar of written Chinese are based on Mandarin, learning to read and write means, for speakers of dialects other than Mandarin, becoming virtually bilingual. Thus, an illiterate Cantonese speaker may have difficulty comprehending a passage of written Chinese being read aloud by a literate Cantonese speaker even though he or she would recognise the sounds as being Cantonese (Light, 1980: 261–2). However, it should be noted that although on purely linguistic grounds written Chinese is most closely akin to Mandarin, literate Cantonese speakers consider their written form to be Cantonese, albeit a special formal variety, and not Mandarin.

Spoken Cantonese has had some influence on the written language however, especially in Hong Kong. Hsu notes that there are several characters used in Hong Kong, derived from the spoken dialect, which are not used elsewhere, and that in some instances the syntax used in Hong Kong also differs (1979: 130–1).

Spoken Cantonese can be divided into several sub-dialects. DeFrancis notes that the differences between these sub-dialects can sometimes be considerable (1984: 64). It appears to be generally agreed among scholars, though, that the dialect of Guangzhou (Canton) is considered to be the standard (Li & Thompson, 1979: 296–8; Chao, 1976: 25). Chao, in fact, notes that, 'as the dialect of Canton city has considerable prestige, speakers of the sub-dialects all understand it and try to speak it' (1976: 25).

The dialect of Hong Kong is close to that of Guangzhou (Canton). Chao says that

it may be noted that, while the form of Cantonese changes more and more as one travels south from Canton down the Canton-Kowloon railway, the dialect in Kowloon and Hong Kong is nearer to that of metropolitan Canton than to those of neighbouring districts. (Chao, 1969: 6)

And Light considers that 'Cantonese as spoken in Guangzhou (Canton) and Hong Kong is usually accorded standard status' (1980: 260).

There is also a certain amount of 'vertical differentiation' within Cantonese. That is, there are quite substantial differences 'connected with the social position and mainly the educational background of individual speakers' (Kratochvil, 1968: 18). And Lehmann notes that there are a series of formal and informal dimensions within each dialect (1975: 11). These differences are mainly in vocabulary (Kratochvil, 1968: 18).

According to So,

Cantonese usage [in Hong Kong] spans the whole social spectrum, from discourse of highly academic and/or technical nature to that of a mundane, and personal nature'. (So, 1987: 22)

However, at the 'high' or formal end of this spectrum Cantonese has been heavily influenced by Mandarin forms mainly due to the fact that the written language is based on Mandarin. And as So notes, in Hong Kong Modern Standard Chinese (MSC), i.e. Putonghua, the new standardised form of Mandarin, is used in education for textbooks and for reading and writing (1987: 18–19). In consequence, 'there is a high degree of convergence between high Cantonese and MSC in lexis and syntax' (So, 1987: 22), but not in pronunciation.

Educated speakers using the 'high' or formal variety of Cantonese may, therefore, not be readily understood by Cantonese speakers who do not have access to the written form of the language.

References

CHANG, R. and M. S. CHANG 1980, *Speaking of Chinese*. New York: Andre Deutsch.

CHAO, Y. R. 1969, *Cantonese Primer*. Cambridge: Harvard University Press (Microfilm Facsimile).

CHAO, Y. R. 1976, *Aspects of Chinese Socio-linguistics: Essays by Y. R. Chao*. Selected by A. S. DIL, Stanford: Stanford University Press.

DEFRANCIS, J. 1984, *The Chinese Language: Fact and Fantasy*. Honolulu: University of Hawaii Press.

FORREST, R. A. D. 1965, *The Chinese Language*. London: Faber and Faber.

HSU, R. S. W. 1979, What is Standard Chinese. In: R. LORD (ed.) *Hong Kong Language Papers* (pp. 115–41). Hong Kong: Hong Kong University Press.

KRATOCHVIL, P. 1968, *The Chinese Language Today: Features of an Emerging Standard*. London: Hutchinson University Library.

LEHMANN, W. P. (ed) 1975, *Language and Linguistics in the People's Republic of China*. Austin: University of Texas Press.

LI, C. N. and THOMPSON, S. A. 1979, Chinese: Dialect variations and language reform. In: T. SHOPEN (ed.) *Languages and Their Status* (pp.295–335). Cambridge: Mass. Winthrop Publishers.

LIGHT, T. 1980, Bilingualism and standard language in the People's Republic of China. *Georgetown University Roundtable on Language and Linguistics*. (pp. 259–79).

SEYBOLT and CHIANG, (eds) 1979,

SO, W. C. 1987, Implementing mother-tongue education amidst societal transition from diglossia to triglossia: A sociolinguistic case study of Hong Kong. Paper presented at the 8th World Congress of Applied Linguists. Sydney.

Croatian

Croatian is a South Slavonic language spoken in the Croatian Republic of Yugoslavia. It is a member of the Slavonic group of Indo-European languages. The ancestor of the South Slavonic languages was brought to the Balkan region in the sixth and seventh centuries, and evolved, over time, into Croatian, Serbian, Slovene, Macedonian and Bulgarian (Corbett, 1987: 391). According to Corbett, the main linguistic divisions in South Slavonic were evident by the ninth century (1987: 391). It should be noted that Croatian and Serbian are often treated as one language with two varieties, or major dialects, but, as Corbett notes:

> The whole question of the status of the two varieties is very sensitive, because of the cultural and political implications. To the outside linguist, the numerous shared features between the varieties added to the case of mutual comprehension suggest one language with two varieties, and many Yugoslavs concur. But we must accept that some Yugoslavs feel it important, often for non-linguistic reasons, to recognise Croatian and Serbian as distinct languages. (Corbett, 1987: 396)

With the coming of Christianity in the ninth century the first Slavonic literary language was developed, based on the vernacular of Salonica in Macedonia. This language, Old Church Slavonic, was written originally in two alphabets, the Glagolitic and the Cyrillic. The Glagolitic, however, was soon ousted by the Cyrillic (Comrie, 1979: 129). (Though Jacobson considers that Glagolitic continued in use in parts of Croatia till at least the 16th century and is being revived at the present time 'for a new extension of the Slavonic liturgy' (quoted in Franolić, 1984: 143 note 2).)

The Cyrillic alphabet, based on the Greek alphabet, was used for religious and, after a time, secular writing by all the Slavic peoples. However, in the eleventh century the

> political rivalry between Byzantium and Rome ... led to conflict between the advocates of the Old Church Slavonic Orthodox liturgy and the Latin Roman Catholic liturgy. (Comrie, 1979: 130)

As a consequence, some western Slavonic languages, including Croatian, came under the influence of Rome and were written in the Latin alphabet, whereas other Slavonic languages, including Serbian, remained Orthodox and continued to use the Cyrillic alphabet. In the nineteenth century, though, both alphabets were reformed, and there is today an exact letter for letter correspondence between the Croatian form of the Latin alphabet and the Serbian Cyrillic. Also, it seems that the Latin alphabet is now being used to a certain extent in Serbia (Corbett, 1987: 392ff).

This division of religion and writing systems has important ramifications in the modern language. The different cultural orientation caused by the orthodox versus Catholic religions and Cyrillic versus Latin alphabets has led to 'substantial borrowing from Russian among the Serbs and from German and Czech among the Croats' (Franolić, 1984: 59). For example Serbian *spisak* (list) is *popis* in Croatian, and *ushit* (enthusiasm) in Serbian is *zanos* in Croatian (Franolić, 1984: 79). Religious terms are also different in many cases, e.g. *liturtija* the Serbian word for 'mass' is *misa* in Croatian (Franolić, 1984: 77).

A further cause of divergence in vocabulary is due to the influence of Turkish. In the fourteenth century Serbia was occupied by the Ottomans and consequently many words of Turkish, Persian and Arabic origin came into the Serbian lexicon but not Croatian. For example *kasapin* (butcher) in Serbian is *mesar* in Croatian (Franolic, 1984: 72ff).

Thus it can be seen that there are considerable differences in vocabulary between Croatian and Serbian. The differences cited above, moreover, do not include recent coinages for scientific and technical terms which also differ in Croatian and Serbian.

In Croatia and Serbia three main dialects are spoken. These are štokavian, kajkavian, and čakavian. In the nineteenth century the štokavian dialect was chosen as the standard literary language by both Croatia and Serbia. The štokavian dialect, though, has three variants based on the spelling and pronunciation of Old Slavonic *e*. These variants are ekavian, sometimes called što-e; ijekavian, što-ije; and ikavian, što-i; thus, 'a nice flower' is *lep cvet* in što-e, *lijep cvijet* in što-ije, and *lip cvit* in što-i (Babić, 1981: ix; Franolić, 1984). The Croatian standard literary language uses the ijekavian variant of the štokavian dialect (što-ije) whereas the Serbian standard literary language uses the ekavian variant (što-e) (Corbett, 1987: 395).

The što-ije form is, it appears, also the basis for the standard spoken language in Croatia. However, it is by no means the only form used, even though it may represent the most prestigious one.

In Zagreb, the capital of Croatia, the major local dialect form is kajkavian. Magner says that speakers in Zagreb are in a diglossic situation (i.e. having two codes), using their kajkavian speech for informal functions and their approximation of the standard što-ije form for formal functions (1978: 467).

Interestingly, while the dialect of Zagreb is kajkavian it also contains certain characteristics of što-e, the Serbian dialect (Magner, 1978: 467). The major difference, and the one from which the dialects got their names, is that in Zagreb the word for 'what' is *kaj* and in the 'standard' form in Croatia and Serbia it is *što*.

The Zagreb kajkavian form is not considered to be as prestigious as ijekavian though it is often used. As Magner notes:

> A university professor in Zagreb can hardly order a cup of coffee without hearing the sprightly sounds of Zagreb kajkavian. Generally he either filters it out of his consciousness or, if aware of it, classifies it as lower-class speech. (Magner, 1978: 466)

In Split a similar situation is present, but in this case the local dialect form is ikavian. Again, the speakers from Split tend to use the 'standard' form in formal situations and their local dialect elsewhere (Magner, 1978: 470). It should also be noted that as well as using a different local dialect the 'standard' form also differs. As Magner points out, 'the spoken [standard ijekavian] of Split with its italianate rhythms could hardly be confused with the clipped [standard ijekavian] of Zagreb' (1978: 473).

According to Albin and Alexander a further dialectal difference is found on the island of Vis. They say that 'the dialect of Vis is one of the most deviant from the [Croatian] literary standard of all the local dialects … spoken within Yugoslavia' (1972: 43).

Thus, it can be seen that while there is a 'standard' form there are regional variations within it and also many local dialects which differ considerably from the 'standard'. Radovanović points out that the different urban dialects tend to create their own specific features and thereby give rise to variants of the standard language (1983: 59).

As noted above, it is important to remember that the situation in Croatian and Serbian is not merely linguistic but social and political also. It is mainly for non-linguistic reasons that Croatian should be seen as a separate language. Dunatov (1978) argues that while there is 'no question' that the Croatian ijekavian and the Serbian ekavian are dialects of the same language in linguistic terms, there are sociolinguistic and political considerations which 'can equally well be used to argue for the autonomy of the Croatian standard vis-a-vis the Serbian' (1978: 265).

This problem is compounded, however, in Bosnia–Hercegovina where Croats, Serbs and Muslims live side by side and the majority of all speakers use the Croatian ijekavian form. In this case calling the language Croatian would alienate the Serbs, while calling it Serbo-croatian alienates the Croats. As well, as noted above, the Serbs write this form in the Cyrillic alphabet, while the Croats use the Latin alphabet (Dunatov, 1978: 261ff).

In sum, therefore, there are major differences in vocabulary between Croatian and Serbian, with Croatian borrowing mainly from German and Czechoslovakian. The writing systems also differ, Croatian using the Latin alphabet and Serbian the Cyrillic. The 'standard' dialect in Croatia is the ijeka-vian form of the što dialect but there are many local dialects, e.g. kajkavian and čakavian, and some of these are in fact closer to Serbian than to the 'standard' što-ije dialect, depending on the city or region that a speaker comes from. Though these 'standard' forms are all prestigious in their own area it is difficult to tell if one is more prestigious than any other.

References

ALBIN, A. and ALEXANDER, R. 1972, *The Speech of Yugoslav Immigrants in San Pedro, California*. The Hague: Martinus Hijhoff.

BABIĆ, S. 1981, *Serbo-Croatian for Foreigners*. Beograd: Kolariev Norodni Univerzitet.

COMRIE, B. 1979, Russian. In: T. SHOPEN (ed.) *Languages and their Status* (pp. 91–151). Cambridge, MA: Winthrop.

CORBETT, G. 1987, Serbo-Croat. In: B. COMRIE (ed.) *The World's Major Languages* (pp. 391–409). London: Croom Helm.

DUNATOV, R. 1978, A sociolinguistic analysis of the recent controversy concerning the Croatian/Serbian standard language(s). In: H. BIRNBAUM (ed.) *American Contributions to the Eighth International Congress of Slavists*. Vol. 1 (pp. 256–67). Columbus, Ohio: Slavica.

FRANOLIĆ, B. 1984, *A Historical Survey of Literary Croatian*. Paris: Nouvelles Editions Latines.

GAZI, S. 1973, *A History of Croatia*. New York: Philosophical Library.

MAGNER, T. F. 1978, City dialects in Yugoslavia. In: H. BIRNBAUM (ed.) *American Contributions to the Eighth International Congress of Slavists*. Vol 1 (pp. 465–81). Columbus, Ohio: Slavica.

RADOVANOVIĆ, M. 1983, Linguistic theory and sociolinguistics in Yugoslavia. *International Journal of the Sociology of Language* 44, 55–69.

Czech

Czech is a West Slavonic language, a member of the Indo-European family of languages (Comrie, 1987: 322ff). It is spoken in the Czech Federal Republic, part of the state of Czechoslovakia. Czech is also spoken in Romania, Yugoslavia, Hungary and Poland as a result of migration and the altering of political boundaries throughout history, and in several other countries around the world because of political and economic migration (Short, 1987: 367). Short notes, though, that the Czech spoken outside of the Czech Federal Republic may differ through physical separation and the influence of the dominant languages in other countries (1987: 367).

The Czech and Slovak Slavs may have arrived in what is now Czechoslovakia during the sixth century AD (Bradley, 1971: 1). The separate tribes formed into three major groups: in Bohemia in the west, Moravia in the central regions and Slovakia in the east (Bradley, 1971: 2ff). In the ninth century the most powerful group at that time, the Moravians, adopted Christianity in its Eastern form (Bradley, 1971: 4–5).

Writing in the Cyrillic alphabet was introduced along with Christianity (De Bray, 1969: 435). However, right from the early stages of Christianity in this region, the Western Church was also active in Bohemia and Moravia, and by the end of the ninth century the Eastern Church had been expelled from the area (Bradley, 1971: 6). Consequently, Latin and the Latin alphabet took over as the written form in Bohemia and Moravia (De Bray, 1969: 435; Short, 1987: 368).

By the tenth century the centre of power had moved to Prague in Bohemia and the Czech kingdom of Bohemia and Moravia was founded. It was at this time, too, that Slovakia was detached from the Czech lands and came under Hungarian rule. Slovakia only rejoined Bohemia and Moravia in the new Czechoslovakia in 1918 (Bradley, 1971: 6ff).

Czech, although previously used as a written language, began to replace Latin as the language of official and legal documents in the fourteenth century (De Bray, 1969: 436). And in the fifteenth century, Jan Hus, the religious reformer, made the first attempts at systematising the Czech orthography (Short, 1987: 368). De Bray notes that Hus,

introduced the living language of Prague as the literary language, purging it of archaisms and foreign, especially German, loan words. (De Bray, 1969: 436)

After the Reformation in the sixteenth century, the Bible and other religious works were translated into Czech (De Bray, 1969: 436). By this time, therefore, Czech was used as the literary language in all areas of life and fulfilled all of the functions previously filled by Latin (Salzmann, 1980: 41).

The Catholic Counter-Reformation resulted in the loss of Czech independence in 1620. As De Bray puts it,

> the final defeat of the Czechs at the battle of the White Mountain in 1620 ushered in the darkest period for Czech literature, a period of decay and stagnation which very nearly saw the final eclipse of the Czech language under the zealous persecutions of the Counter-Reformation. (De Bray, 1969: 436)

The Czech kingdom of Bohemia and Moravia came under Austrian Habsburg rule after 1620. Many of the Czech élite were killed or forced into exile, towns and cities were Germanised, and Latin and German became the officially recognised languages (Bradley, 1971: 94ff). Spoken and, to some extent, written Czech was maintained, though, amongst the peasantry (Bradley, 1971: 97). Auty says that during the seventeenth and eighteenth centuries Czech was used for writing and printing though only on a very small scale. He also notes that there was considerable variety in the form of the language used at this time which led to a lack of standards and, consequently, the Czech literary language occupied a marginal and unstable position, though it continued to be based on the Central dialects from around Prague (Auty, 1980: 83).

The Germanisation of Bohemia and Moravia continued through the eighteenth century. After 1774 German replaced Latin as the language used in schools (De Bray, 1969: 437), the bureaucracy was mainly German with an official policy of Germanisation (Bradley, 1971: 110-1) and most of the educated, urban Czechs spoke and wrote in German (De Bray, 1969: 437).

In the late eighteenth century, however, a reaction against the centralising and Germanising policies of the Austrian Habsburgs began in Bohemia (Bradley, 1971: 111; De Bray, 1969: 437). At first, because German was the only literary language available to the intellectuals, 'German was used to drive out German' (De Bray, 1969: 437); literacy in Czech, however, soon began to spread (Bradley, 1971: 112).

The revival of interest in the Czech nation and language led to work being done on the literary language. The first modern grammar was produced in 1809 and this is still the basis for the literary language (Short, 1987: 369). The models for this grammar were the old Czech writings of the middle ages, the Bible translation, and the spoken dialect from around Prague (Short, 1987: 369; De

Bray, 1969: 437–8). One consequence of using older Czech forms as models, though, was that the new literary language contained many archaic features (Short, 1987: 369).

The Czech literary language had been revived, codified, standardised and the orthography reformed by the end of the nineteenth century (Short, 1987: 369; De Bray, 1969: 437–8). Literature and literacy was expanding and Czech was officially recognised as a language of education after 1849 (Bradley, 1971: 121; 132). Czech also became the second language in provincial courts and administration, though there was considerable opposition to this from the German speakers (Bradley, 1971: 135).

With independence in 1918 Slovakia was re-integrated with Bohemia and Moravia into the new state of Czechoslovakia (Bradley, 1971: 147). Czechoslovak was declared the official and state language in the constitution (Salzmann, 1980: 42–3). Czechoslovak, though, was said to consist of two 'versions': Czech and Slovak, which were of equal legal status (Salzmann, 1980: 43). In the constitution of 1948, the individuality and equality of Czech and Slovak were, however, recognised (Salzmann, 1980: 46). Although Czech and Slovak are about 90% mutually intelligible (Short, 1987: 367), and television and radio broadcasts in Czechoslovakia 'make indiscriminate use of speakers of both languages' (Salzmann, 1980: 39), nevertheless

> the nature of the relationship between the Czechs and the Slovaks is complex and prickly, transcending the question of the two languages. (Salzmann, 1980: 40)

The form of the Czech written language used today has changed very little from that re-formed in the nineteenth century. In consequence, there is a concept of 'historical correctness' in the literary language (Auty, 1976: 85), and modern literary Czech therefore abounds in intentional archaic features (Kucera, 1961: 14; Short, 1987: 389). As a result, as Auty notes,

> little was done to narrow the gap which existed between normal, even educated, colloquial speech and the written language. (Auty, 1976: 85)

Literary Czech is taught in schools and is the language of most Czech writing. The spoken form of the literary language is used predominantly, but not exclusively, on radio and television, and in other mass media (Kučera, 1961: 13). Auty notes, however, that the 'rigidly puristic structure of the literary standard has been relaxed', and that this form is used only in the most formal of situations (1976: 86).

In spoken Czech four forms are usually recognised: dialect, Common Czech, Colloquial Czech, and the spoken form of the standard literary language (Short, 1987: 389; Auty, 1976: 85–6; Kučera, 1961: 13ff). The dialects are grouped into six major sub-groups, three Bohemian and two Moravian, with a transition group between them (De Bray, 1969: 445; Kučera, 1961: 12–13). The dialects, though, are tending to disappear, perhaps especially under the influence of Common Czech (Short, 1987: 390).

Common Czech probably existed prior to the re-formation of the literary language in the nineteenth century (Auty, 1976: 85–6). It is in effect a 'common denominator' of several local dialects and is sometimes known as an interdialect (Kučera, 1961: 15). What has occurred is that dialectal features which have only a local character have been replaced by features common to a whole group of dialects. For Czech there are, it seems, two forms of Common Czech, one based on the Central dialects around Prague and one based on Moravian dialects, known as Common Moravian Czech (Short, 1987: 390). Because of the prestige of the Prague dialects, the Common Czech based on them has spread well beyond the frontiers of that dialect area (Short, 1987: 390).

Colloquial Czech appears to be a compromise between the standard literary form and Common Czech (Auty, 1976: 85). It may have its beginnings in the mid-nineteenth century, shortly after the revival of the literary language (Belić cited in Auty, 1976: 85–6). There does not appear to be consensus among scholars as to exactly what the linguistic structure of Colloquial Czech is. Some scholars, e.g. Short (1987) see it as a 'version' of the literary language, while others, e.g. Kučera (1961) believe it to be the intermixing and combination of Common Czech elements with elements from the literary form. One of the problems with defining this form is that, by its nature, its character varies among different individuals, and even in the same individuals speech depending on the formality of the situation (Auty, 1976: 86; Kučera, 1961: 19).

It must be remembered, though, that there are no clear cut boundaries between the different forms of spoken Czech. As is usual with language there is a continuum. In this instance dialect, or, for urban educated Czechs perhaps Common Czech, will be at one end of the continuum and a close approximation to the literary standard, depending on level of education, will be at the other. Thus, as Auty says:

> no observer of the Czech speech-situation could deny that the normal educated speaker of Czech ranges over three different registers: Common Czech, used in completely relaxed, familiar, or emotionally coloured situations; Colloquial Czech, used in normal cultivated conversation; and literary Czech, used only in the most formal of utterances. It seems certain, too, that the influence of the literary language on Colloquial Czech has been gradually increasing during the last decades. At the same time the rigidly puristic structure of the literary standard has been relaxed. (Auty, 1976: 86)

For Czech, therefore, the literary standard form was developed in the nineteenth century on the basis of the older literary language and the dialect of Prague. The literary form is taught in schools and is used to a large extent in the media. There is a gap, though, between the literary language and the spoken forms. There are at least three, and possibly four, spoken forms of Czech depending on whether a speaker still maintains a local dialect or not. These forms are: dialect, slowly disappearing under the influence of Common Czech; Common Czech, which is replacing local features with features common to a whole dialect group, with the Common Czech based on the Prague region dialects appearing to be the most prestigious; Colloquial Czech, which is a compromise between Common Czech and the literary form; and the spoken version of the standard literary language. Between these different forms there are no clear cut divisions, but rather a continuum along which speakers move depending on the formality of the situation.

References

AUTY, R. 1976, Problems of the formation and development of the Czech literary language. In: T. F. MAGNER (ed.) *Slavonic Linguistics and Language Teaching* (pp. 82–8). Cambridge: MA: Slavonica Publishers.

BRADLEY, J. F. N. 1971, *Czechoslovakia: A Short History*. Edinburgh: Edinburgh University Press.

COMRIE, B. 1987, Slavonic languages. In: B. COMRIE (ed.) *The World's Major Languages* (pp. 322–8). London: Croom Helm.

DEBRAY, R. G. A. 1969, *Guide to the Slavonic Languages*. London: J. M. Dent and Sons.

KUČERA, H. 1961, *The Phonology of Czech*. The Hague: Mouton.

SALZMANN, Z. 1980, Language standardization in a bilingual state: The case of Czech and Slovak, two closely cognate languages. *Language Problems and Language Planning* 4 (1) 38–54.

SHORT, D. 1987, Czech and Slovak. In: B. COMRIE (ed.) *The World's Major Languages* (pp. 367–90). London: Croom Helm.

Danish

Danish is a Scandinavian language. The Scandinavian languages are offshoots of the Germanic branch of Indo-European. Up till about 800 AD all Scandinavian languages, Icelandic, Danish, Swedish, Norwegian and Faroese constituted a single language known as Common Scandinavian (Haugen, 1976: 91). This language was written in the Runic alphabet, the origins of which are unclear (Walshe, 1965: 27).

In the eleventh century Scandinavia was Christianised and the Latin alphabet was introduced, though the runes did not disappear till much later (Haugen, 1976: 191). At about the same time Common Scandinavian began to split and

> by 1350 the main characteristics of the various dialects [i.e. what we now know as Danish, Swedish, Norwegian etc.] had already emerged, and towards the end of the middle ages, around 1500, the linguistic diversification of Scandinavia was reaching its peak. (Kristensen & Thelander, 1984: 223)

During this period of linguistic diversification trade in Scandinavia was dominated by the German Hanseatic League. The German domination had a considerable effect on the language. As Haugen says:

> In ... cities and in their commerce with the Germans, many Scandinavians were forced to become bilingual in Low German. From this language they adopted quite literally thousands of words for the many and varied crafts that were introduced or dominated by the Germans.
>
> The borrowing of terms extended to the point where even German prefixes ... became part of the productive apparatus of the [Scandinavian] languages. Nor is it too improbable to speculate that the general breakdown of case and personal endings was due to the same bilingual influence. (Haugen, 1982: 14)

In the late 1300s the language of administration in Denmark was changed from Latin to Danish (Haugen, 1982: 13). Then, in the early 1500s the Reformation came to Denmark and the language of religion also changed from Latin to Danish. The translations of the Bible which followed the Reformation had more or less fixed the Danish written norm by 1550 (Haugen, 1976: 39; 247; 324).

The written norm, however, did not correspond to anyone's spoken dialect, rather it was 'a continuation and regularisation of the writing tradition of Copenhagen' (Haugen, 1976: 325). The written language was further normalised in the eighteenth century. In 1889 firm spelling rules were adopted, and in 1948 a minor orthographic reform was implemented which removed capital letters from nouns and brought Danish more into line with other Scandinavian orthographic systems (Haugen, 1976: 39).

In the sixteenth century, though, the spoken language was still far from standardised. Even in the élite circles there was no norm for the whole of Denmark (Haugen, 1976: 325). Furthermore, the isolation and inbreeding of the rural population was leading to a fragmentation of the spoken language rather than a homogeneity (Haugen, 1976: 323).

However, with the new Bible translations, and especially with the advent of printing, the written language became the basis of a supralocal speech norm. As Haugen puts it,

the spoken norm became one that adopted spelling pronunciations where the writing required it, ... but which elsewhere adopted the phonetic base of the local dialects, among which that of Copenhagen was the most prestigious. (Haugen, 1976: 326)

This developing spoken standard was for a considerable time restricted to the upper classes. The rural communities continued to speak their local dialects and in the cities a new form of urban speech was developing. The urban speech retained many traits of the surrounding rural areas, but interaction within the city tended to level out differences and thus create a new norm (Haugen, 1982: 3). But this new norm tended to be associated with the working classes and, therefore, was generally not considered prestigious (Haugen, 1976: 58).

In the nineteenth century with the spread of schooling, the prestigious written standard was disseminated throughout the population. But, as Haugen notes:

The new literacy did not at once mean a change in speech, only that a basis of passive knowledge of the written norm was established throughout the population. Everyone now knew that there was a norm which an educated, urbanised speaker could adopt ... . (Haugen, 1976: 360)

During this century the increasing mobility of the population, the advent of radios, television and other mass media as well as an increasing standard of education has caused a levelling of dialects within Denmark. This, however, has not led to the acceptance of one single standard speech form, but rather to the growth of several regional standards which compete with that of the capital, Copenhagen, and characterise their speakers without branding them as inferior (Haugen, 1976: 60).

The dialects of Denmark can be divided into two main groups; those of Jutland, divisible into western and eastern subgroups, and the central, or island, group. There is also a third group of dialects spoken in areas which were Danish till 1658 when they were taken over by Sweden. In these areas, e.g. Skane, Halland and the island of Bornholm there are dialects which are transitional between South Swedish and Danish. Skane and Halland are today Swedish provinces but the island of Bornholm reverted to Denmark (Haugen, 1976: 55–6; Walshe, 1965: 14ff).

In some areas of Denmark, particularly those areas farthest from the capital such as parts of Jutland, local dialects are still well preserved (Kristensen & Thelander, 1984: 223). These dialects are so different from the standard that they may cause problems of comprehension for outsiders (Haugen, 1982: 3). The dialect of the Island of Bornholm, being transitional between Danish and Swedish, may also cause problems.

Nevertheless, in many parts of Denmark, especially urban centres and their surrounding areas, dialects are gradually giving way to regional approximations to a standard form. According to Kristensen and Thelander:

> Dialect levelling has gone further in Denmark than in the other Scandinavian countries, due no doubt to the proximity to Copenhagen of any part of Denmark. The relative size and dominance of the capital (as compared to the rest of the country) may of course also account for the strong levelling of Danish dialects. Finally, it should be pointed out that local dialects are seldom influenced by the standard language, but rather by regional varieties of it, which in turn are influenced by the standard language itself, the closer to the capital the regional centre is situated, the stronger the influence. (Kristensen & Thelander, 1982: 224)

Dialects are, therefore, to a fairly large extent being replaced by regional varieties of the standard, at least outside of the home. Haugen notes that while speakers may use dialect at home and for informal purposes (1982: 3), they may be 'ashamed or unwilling' to use it when speaking to strangers or in more formal situations (1976: 57).

Thus, although 'there is no universally accepted standard speech norm' (Haugen, 1976: 59) for the whole of Denmark, there are a number of closely related regional varieties which act as the generally accepted prestigious forms. Some Danes, though, still speak dialects other than a regional standard which may be difficult for speakers from other regions to understand.

References

HAUGEN, E. 1976, *The Scandinavian Languages: An Introduction to their History.* London: Faber and Faber.

HAUGEN, E. 1982, *Scandinavian Language Structures: A Comparative Historical Survey.* Minneapolis: University of Minnesota Press.

KRISTENSEN, K and THELANDER M. 1984, On dialect levelling in Denmark and Sweden. *Folia Linguistica* 18 (1–2) 223–46.

WALSHE, M. O'C. 1965, *Introduction to the Scandinavian Languages.* London: Andre Deutsch.

Dutch

Dutch is a Germanic language, a member of the Indo-European family. The precursors of Dutch separated from Common Germanic, the ancestor of Dutch, English, German and the Scandinavian languages, sometime around 500 AD The language continued to evolve and the era of Modern Dutch is generally considered to have commenced in about 1500 AD (Donaldson, 1983: 128).

Dutch is spoken principally in Holland and the northern half of Belgium known as Flanders. There are some problems of terminology associated with Dutch and the area in which it is spoken which could lead to ambiguity and possibly misunderstanding and are, therefore, worth noting.

Firstly, the language of Flanders is generally known as Flemish and is often considered to be a separate language. However, Flemish dialects are closer to those of southern Holland than are the dialects of the north of Holland. Secondly, the official English and Dutch name for Holland is 'the Netherlands', but the Netherlands is also sometimes used to denote the whole area where Dutch is spoken, i.e. Holland and Belgian Flanders (Brachin *et al.*, 1976: viii). Thirdly, the name Holland more correctly refers to only two of the provinces of the Netherlands, i.e. North and South Holland in the west of the country. Although 'Holland' is used by people from these two provinces, as well as by most English speakers, as a synonym for the Netherlands, it reflects the 'economic might' of these provinces and is not used by people from the other provinces, nor is it used in any official contexts (Donaldson, 1983: 6). In this paper the conventions proposed by Brachin *et al.* (1976) for 'Dutch Studies' will be followed. Thus, the Netherlands will refer to the whole Dutch speaking area, and Holland and (Belgian) Flanders will refer to the two countries individually; Dutch will refer to the language of the Netherlands except when the Dutch spoken in only one of the countries is meant, in which case Northern Dutch and Flemish will be used to refer to the Dutch of Holland and Flanders respectively.

In the Netherlands there are several dialects which form a continuum of local speech. Although the transition from one dialect to another is gradual, Donaldson delimits 28 dialects which can be considered discrete (1983: 8).

Not all of these dialects are mutually intelligible. In the north of Holland Frisian is spoken and there is a debate among scholars as to whether Frisian is a dialect of Dutch or a separate language. It seems that it is usually considered to be a separate language (Pietersen, 1978) though it is also often included in dialect maps of Dutch (Donaldson, 1983: 8–9). Whatever the case may be, Frisian is not intelligible to the majority of Dutch speakers and has a separate written language (Donaldson, 1983: 11).

In the south-east of the Netherlands the Limburgs dialect is spoken. This dialect too causes problems of comprehension for the majority of Dutch speakers. The problem arises because Limburgs 'shares several features with High German' (Donaldson, 1983: 16). (Note that the word 'High' in High German originally denoted only the fact that this variety of German originated in the mountainous region of Southern Germany. The sociological interpretation came about as a result of this variety being the basis, at a later date, for 'standard' German.) In fact, as Donaldson notes:

> The overall effect of the factors [i.e. features of High German in the Limburgs dialect] is that Limburgs sounds more like German … . Applying purely linguistic criteria, one could probably more correctly classify it as a dialect of German. (Donaldson, 1983: 16)

The gradual transition of Dutch to German occurs all along the border between these two languages. As is usual with dialects, there is no precise border or definite transition point. Donaldson says:

> Those dialects spoken along the Dutch–German border are regarded as either Dutch or German dialects according to which of those two languages the speakers of those dialects regard as their standard written language … . The farmers on either side of the border in any given area speak virtually the same dialect in accordance with tribal settlement in the Dark Ages, but when they go to read a book or write a letter, the Dutch farmer will read and write standard Dutch, based on the language of the west of Holland, whereas the German farmer will read and write standard or so-called High German, based on the language of central Germany. Were they to exchange books or letters, they could not understand the other's language and yet in practice they speak the same dialect. (Donaldson, 1983: 11)

It would appear to follow, therefore, that speakers from the west of the Netherlands would have problems understanding the dialects on the Dutch–German border since it is the standard written variety which is taught in schools and not dialects. In other words, a speaker from the Dutch–German border dialect areas would be taught standard written Dutch but a speaker from the west would not be taught the border dialects.

Thus, it can be seen that even though the dialects of Dutch form a continuum there are significant differences between various dialect areas which can lead to mutual incomprehensibility. It is perhaps worth noting that the differences between the dialects from the north of Holland and those from the south of Holland are greater than those between the south of Holland and Flanders, with the exception of the Limburgs dialect from the south-east which, as noted above, is closer to High German. This is due to the fact that the northern dialects of Holland evolved from Old Frisian and Old Saxon whereas those of the south of Holland and Flanders evolved from Old Low Franconian. All three of these 'Old' forms split from Common Germanic, and then from each other, sometime between 500 and 1100 AD and evolved differently (Donaldson, 1983).

There is, however, a 'standard' form of Dutch known as *Algemeen Beschaaft Nederlands* (General Cultured Dutch) usually referred to as ABN. Although it is difficult to define exactly what this means, according to Donaldson,

> one can say that what the average speaker of Dutch in the Netherlands regards as ABN is the language of the provinces of North and South Holland with Utrecht. (Donaldson, 1983: 17–18)

Or the language of speakers from the cities in these provinces; namely, Haarlem, Amsterdam, Utrecht, Rotterdam, Delft, The Hague and Leiden (Donaldson, 1983: 18).

This does not mean, though, that all speakers from this region speak ABN. According to Donaldson, it is more common in these cities to draw a social distinction and to call the speech of the lower classes 'plat' (low), a derogatory term, even though their accent is similar to that of the upper classes. Conversely, it is possible to speak ABN with the accent of another dialect, though one could argue that perhaps it depends to what degree the accent is different (1983: 16–18).

Thus, ABN is not dependent purely on pronunciation. Other factors such as choice of vocabulary and aspects of grammar are also important in determining whether a speaker is using ABN or dialect. As a consequence, it is difficult to state categorically that there is a single standard form of spoken Dutch. As Koelmans puts it, 'ABN may one day become an entity but certainly is not that at the moment' (quoted in Donaldson, 1983: 18). And as Donaldson says, 'a standard form of the spoken language ... has, in some ways, still not been attained' (1983: 114).

In Flanders the position of ABN is perhaps somewhat weaker even than in Holland. This is because Belgium is linguistically divided into French speaking Wallonia and Dutch speaking Flanders. The French speakers, until very recently, were the political and social élite. In the nineteenth century the Flemish 'had no political power or social status' (Donaldson, 1983: 26). It was only in 1932 that Dutch speaking civil servants were no longer required to be proficient in French. In 1962 the language border between French and Dutch was fixed, and only then did Dutch become officially equal to French and used as the official language in the Dutch speaking region (Donaldson, 1983: 27–8). Even today, however, there is still a lingering feeling among many Flemish people that a knowledge of French is necessary for full social acceptance. (Donaldson, 1983: 33)

The problems, though, have still not been completely solved and it seems that 'linguistic friction will probably ... always be a fact of Belgian life' (Donaldson, 1983: 31).

As a result of the low status of Dutch in Belgium, and the fact that until recently it was not, or only rarely, used for official purposes, no standard form developed. Consequently most speakers of Dutch in Flanders were, and to a large extent still are, brought up speaking dialect only. In addition, the high status of French has led to borrowing from that language, principally items of vocabulary but also in some aspects of grammar (Donaldson, 1983: 33).

However, since Dutch gained more status in the 1960s 'Flanders has now clearly opted to follow northern practice ...' (Donaldson, 1983: 33), although the pronunciation may still reflect the region of origin of the speaker. This, however, is no impediment to standardisation and 'one must concede that a Flemish professor or lawyer for example speaks ABN' (Donaldson, 1983: 18).

It appears, though, that only a minority of Flemish Dutch speakers are moving to ABN. According to Van Coetsem, what is occurring is that they are

oscillating between a sort of purified dialect and, in a few cases, a Dutch that is to all intents and purposes pure 'northern' Dutch. (quoted in Donaldson, 1983: 18)

The attitude of the Dutch from Holland to the speech of the Flemish is, apparently, generally unfavourable. According to Donaldson, 'the average Dutchman regards him, his country and particularly his language as "quaint", to put it mildly' (1983: 33). He also notes that speakers of Northern Dutch often regard the vocabulary peculiar to Flemish speakers 'with disdain' (1983: 18).

In a study of the attitude of Flemish speakers to their dialect and ABN, Geerts et al. (1978) found that 74% felt their dialect was most appropriate in the home, 38% felt it was most appropriate at work, but nearly 86% felt that ABN was most appropriate in school and over 86% felt that ABN should be used in radio and television broadcasts. They conclude, however, that 'the Flemings do not regard "the Dutch of the Dutchmen" [i.e. ABN] as a self-evident norm' (1978: 44) and that they choose the language variety they use depending on the situation. It appears, also, from this report that many Flemish 'appear to accept a regional Flemish standard of Dutch' as being desirable since over 64% of the Flemish people surveyed did not want to speak like the Dutch from Holland (Geerts et al., 1978: 42–4).

As far as the written language is concerned there is considerable standardisation throughout the Netherlands. By the nineteenth century a standard form of written Dutch was already in existence due to the influence of printing and translations of the bible. Although there have been spelling reforms since then, the last one in 1947, the language of writing has not changed appreciably (Donaldson, 1983: 106ff). In Flanders too, the written form follows the usage in Holland. As Donaldson puts it,

> if a Fleming wrote his native tongue, he wrote [Northern] Dutch, as Flemish did not and does not exist as a written alternative to [Northern] Dutch. (Donaldson, 1983: 25)

Afrikaans, spoken in the Republic of South Africa, is descended from Dutch dialects. However, it is now generally regarded as a separate language (Kooij, 1987: 139).

References

BRACHIN, P. et al. (eds) 1976, Dutch Studies: An Annual Review of the Language, Literature and Life of the Low Countries. Vol. 2. The Hague: Martinus Nijhoff.

CLYNE, M. 1977, Nieuw-Hollands or Double-Dutch. In: P. BRACHIN et al. (eds) Dutch Studies: An Annual Review of the Language, Literature and Life of Low Countries. Vol. 3. The Hague: Martinus Nijhoff.

DONALDSON, B. C. 1983, Dutch: A Linguistic History of Holland and Belgium. Leiden: Martinus Nijhoff.

GEERTS, G. et al. 1978, Flemish attitudes towards dialect and standard language: A public opinion poll. International Journal of the Sociology of Language 15, 33–46.

KOOIJ, J. G. 1987, Dutch. In: B. COMRIE (ed.) The World's Major Languages (pp. 139–56). London: Croom Helm.

PIETERSEN, L. 1978, Issues and trends in Frisian bilingualism. In: J. A. FISHMAN (ed.) Advances in the Study of Societal Multilingualism (pp. 353–99). The Hague: Mouton.

Estonian

Estonian is a member of the Balto-Finnic sub-branch of the Finno-Ugric branch of the Uralic family of languages (Comrie, 1981: 94). Estonian has about one million speakers, mainly in the Estonian SSR, a part of the Soviet Union, but also, especially since the late 1940s, in migrant communities around the world (Crystal, 1987: 304; Birskys *et al.*, 1986: 126ff).

Birskys *et al.* note that archaeological evidence points to the arrival of Estonians on the Baltic coast several thousand years BC (1986: 111). According to Nirk, Estonian broke up early in its history into a number of dialects and local varieties, and by the first or second century AD the major dialectal divergencies between the north, south and west of the country were already evident (1970: 13–14). The differences between these dialects were mainly in the phonology and vocabulary, but also affected syntax and grammar (Nirk, 1970: 13–14).

Between 1208 and 1227 Estonia was invaded and conquered by German knights and by Danes on a crusade to Christianise the country (Collinder, 1960: 20; Birskys *et al.*, 1986: 112). The Danes sold their share of Estonia to the Germans in 1343 (Collinder, 1960: 20). However, as Birskys *et al.* put it:

> This conquest, which allegedly served the noble aim of bringing Christianity to the heathens, was actually an act of colonisation. The German crusaders remained and established themselves as a ruling class of feudal structure ... Eventually the local people were forced into serfdom, being completely dependent on their landlords and tied to their estate ... .
> (Birskys *et al.*, 1986: 112)

As a consequence of the economic and political power of the Germans,

> the Estonians were deprived of the possibility of achieving more developed forms of culture, including that of creating their own national literature. (Nirk, 1970: 34)

German, and to a certain extent, Latin, were the languages of the élite, and Estonian was restricted to the spoken language of the serfs (Comrie, 1981: 99; Nirk, 1970: 34).

In the sixteenth century, after the Reformation, some religious texts were produced in Estonian (Birskys *et al.*, 1986: 113). At about this time, though,

Estonia was divided. The north was annexed to Sweden and was Lutheran, while the south was under Polish rule and was Catholic (Nirk, 1970: 36). As a result,

> the same religious struggle which had caused [the religious texts] to be written brought about the destruction of most of them, and there is little evidence to suggest that they enjoyed any wide circulation among the people. (Nirk, 1970: 37)

When the whole of Estonia came under Sweden in the seventeenth century book production increased. However, because Estonia was divided between two bishoprics, one in the north and one in the south, and because of the marked dialectal differences between the north and the south of the country, books and texts were produced in two varieties (Voobus, 1974: 51ff). During this early period of writing in Estonian, the Southern dialect played a major role (Comrie, 1981: 99). And Nirk considers that the Southern dialect had the advantage over that of the north at this time (1970: 39).

Even though Estonia was under Swedish rule during this period, the German landowners still constituted the powerful élite (Collinder, 1960: 20). As well, the majority of the clergy were German and German speaking (Voobus, 1974: 54). Because most of the literature written in Estonian was produced for the German speaking clergy, the language used was very heavily influenced by German. As Voobus puts it,

> the publications were written in a curious and faulty language so seriously in conflict with the language of the people that they could not understand it. (Voobus, 1974: 54)

And Nirk says that these writings

> were mainly intended for the use of the clergy; their language is crude and unidiomatic, and their orthography is mechanically transferred from the German. (Nirk, 1970: 38)

Nirk also notes that the early grammars attempted 'to remould Estonian according to the rules of the German language' (1970: 38).

Towards the end of the seventeenth century, however, some writers, particularly those writing in the Southern dialect, standardised the orthography of Estonian and brought the literary language closer to the language of the Estonian people (Nirk, 1970: 39).

Due to the power of the northern Estonian clergy, the publications from the south were suppressed. Nirk says that:

> The fact that [the south] had begun to publish religious literature in the North-Estonian dialect, and even in an improved form ... roused the fierce

resentment of [the northern clergy] and gave rise to a prolonged conflict between the two dioceses that had the effect of retarding the publication of books in the Estonian language. As a result of the complaints of the North-Estonian clergy, the books published in [the south] — though markedly superior from the linguistic point of view — were sequestered and removed from circulation. (Nirk, 1970: 39)

When the Bible was published in the Northern Estonian dialect in 1739 the position of this form of Estonian was considerably strengthened (Voobus, 1974: 102). The language used, though, drew on some of the innovations of the writers from the south, such as their standardised orthography (Voobus, 1974: 101). Although the Southern dialect continued to be used for several years as a literary language, the northern dialect was eventually selected as the basis for the standard national written language of all of Estonia (Nirk, 1970: 46–7).

Comrie considers that the Northern dialect was adopted as the standard because of the

numerical preponderance of speakers of Northern Estonian, and the fact that the capital city, Tallinn, is in the Northern dialect area. (1981: 99–100)

Throughout the eighteenth and much of the nineteenth centuries, written Estonian was essentially religious in nature and mainly for the use of the German speaking clergy (Nirk, 1970: 47ff; Voobus, 1974). The language of the élite and of higher education remained German (Voobus, 1974: 213ff). The élite language was German despite the fact that Estonia had been taken over by Russia in 1710. In the 1880s, though, Russian was made the language of instruction in all schools, and a process of Russification was begun (Voobus, 1974: 241ff; Birskys et.al., 1986: 114).

The aboliton of serfdom in the late nineteenth century, and a rising sense of national identity, led to a sharp increase in the production of secular writing in Estonian, and provided a counter-current to the German élite and also to Russification (Nirk, 1970: 84ff; Birskys et al., 1986: 114). Comrie, in fact, notes that it was only in the nineteenth century that the name 'Estonian' gained wide acceptance in the country (1981: 99).

In the early part of the twentieth century a considerable amount of work was done on enriching, normalising and standardising the Estonian written language (Voobus, 1979: 19ff). Although the Northern Estonian dialect was the basis for the standard written form, elements of other dialects were incorporated, particularly vocabulary (Voobus, 1979: 21ff). Comrie says that standard Estonian, based on the Northern dialect, was developed during the late nineteenth and early twentieth centuries, and he notes that the influence of German on the vocabulary is still strong (1981: 99–100).

Estonia gained independence in 1920 and Estonian became the language of the state and of all levels of education (Birskys *et al.*, 1986: 116ff; Voobus, 1979: 134ff). Estonia was incorporated into the Soviet Union in the 1940s, and, according to Birskys *et al.*:

> there is strong pressure to adopt Russian as a teaching language in schools from year two onwards; the dissertations at the University of Tartu must be in Russian; and attempts have been made to convert the Estonian language from Roman to Cyrillic script. (Birskys *et al.*, 1986: 124)

In the spoken language, it seems that there are still considerable differences between the dialects in Estonia. Collinder notes that

> in many particulars, Southern Estonian (earlier, Dorpat-Estonian) deviates from Northern Estonian (earlier, Reval-Estonian), upon which standard Estonian is based. (Collinder, 1960: 20)

And Comrie points out that

> on purely structural grounds, one could argue that there are actually two Estonian languages, North Estonian (or Estonian proper) and South Estonian, with the former being closer to Finnish than it is to South Estonian. (Comrie, 1981: 99)

However, Comrie goes on to say that

> cultural and political factors have won out over structural similarity in defining language boundaries, so that Estonians as a whole have a feeling of unity among themselves and of a distinctness from speakers of other Balto-Finnic languages. (Comrie, 1981: 99)

It should also be noted that Estonian and Finnish are mutually unintelligible without special study (Collinder, 1960: 20).

As well as the division between the Northern and Southern dialects, there is also a North-Eastern dialect which differs from both the Northern and Southern dialects, though it is closer to the Northern (Comrie, 1981: 99). And Collinder also mentions a Western form spoken on the Islands off the coast of Estonia (1960: 20–1).

Estonian, therefore, has a standard form based on the northern dialect which was finally developed during the late nineteenth and early twentieth centuries. There are several dialects which differ considerably from each other, but it is probable that the influence of the standard form is gradually eroding these differences. As Comrie points out, peripheral dialects are tending to assimilate to the more central dialects (1981: 96). As with most Soviet Republics, Russian is an important language in Estonia for education and official purposes.

References

BIRSKYS, B. *et al.* 1986, *The Baltic Peoples in Australia.* Melbourne: A. E. Press (Australian Ethnic Heritage Series).

COLLINDER, B. 1960, *Comparative Grammar of the Uralic Languages.* Stockholm: Almquist and Wiksell (Handbook of Uralic Languages, Part 3).

COMRIE, B. 1981, *The Languages of the Soviet Union.* Cambridge: Cambridge University Press.

CRYSTAL, D. 1987, *The Cambridge Encyclopedia of Language.* Cambridge: Cambridge University Press.

NIRK, E. 1970, *Estonian Literature.* Tallinn: Eesti Raamat.

VOOBUS, A. 1974, *Studies in the History of the Estonian People 111.* Stockholm: E.T.S.E. (Papers of the Estonian Theological Society in Exile No.26).

VOOBUS, A. 1979, *Studies in the History of the Estonian People V.* Stockholm: E. T. S. E. (Papers of the Estonian Theological Society in Exile No.32).

Fijian

Fiji comprises about 500 islands, of which about one hundred are permanently inhabited, scattered over 650,000 square kilometres of the South Pacific Ocean (Lasaga, 1984: 1). Within this region there is considerable linguistic variation, though the question of how many languages or dialects there are is extremely problematic due to the lack of suitable linguistic criteria to use as a basis for decisions (Schütz, 1972a: 91). The linguistic diversity in Fiji also makes it difficult to determine the origins of Fijian forms and their genetic relationships to other language groups.

Archaeological evidence suggests that the Fijian islands were originally settled about 3,500 years ago (Geraghty, 1983: 388). It appears, though, that there were at least two subsequent migrations to the Fiji islands, and these may have had some effect on the development of the Fijian languages (Geraghty, 1983: 388ff). Although the Fijian languages are part of the Austronesian, or Malayo-Polynesian family (Schütz, 1972b: 6), there is debate among scholars as to whether they form part of the Polynesian or Melanesian sub-groups (Schütz, 1972a: 48ff; Geraghty, 1983: 348ff). Schütz appears to favour the arguments for the Fijian languages constituting a sub-group with Polynesian languages (1972a: 51–2), while Geraghty says that 'the Oceanic languages of Melanesia, like the Polynesian languages, show a complex relationship with the Fijian languages …' (1983: 389). Geraghty also points out that Western Fijian languages appear to be closer to Melanesian, but many Eastern Fijian languages appear to be related to Polynesian languages (1983: 389).

The development of an orthography and the first serious grammatical work on Fijian was done by two missionaries, David Cargill and William Cross, in the 1830s (Schütz, 1972a: 6ff; Schütz & Komaitai, 1971: xff). The orthography, based on the Latin alphabet, and grammar were developed for the language spoken on the island of Lakeba in the Lau group in the east of the Fijian Islands (Schütz & Komaitai, 1971: xii). The major reason for the development of the orthography and grammar was to 'fix' the language for translations of the Bible and other religious works to be carried out (Schütz, 1972a: 6).

However, it soon became clear that works written in Lakeba were unintelligible in many of the other islands (Schütz & Komaitai, 1971: xii). For a time the missionaries translated books of the New Testament into four Fijian languages, but 'this proved to be too great a burden' (Schütz & Komaitai, 1971: xii-xiii).

The choosing of a *lingua franca* for the missionaries' work consequently became inevitable (Schütz 1972a: 35). In the 1840s there was internal warfare in the Fiji islands and the political fortunes of Bau, a small island off the south-east coast of the large island of Viti Levu, were on the rise with the chief of Bau eventually becoming 'King' of all Fiji (Schütz, 1972a: 28ff; Schütz, 1972b: 16). The missionaries therefore chose Bauan as the language into which all works would be translated (Schütz, 1972a: 35).

A grammar and dictionary of Bauan were completed in 1850 by another missionary, David Hazelwood, and these remained the standard works for almost a century (Schütz & Komaitai, 1971: xiii; Schütz, 1972a: 42). Thus, Bauan became an important language of the Fijian Islands and has been used for religious, educational and central government activities since the mid 1800s (Schütz, 1972a: 107). The phrase 'Fijian Language', therefore, usually means the Bauan language (Schütz & Komaitai, 1971: xiii). According to Finegan, though, the sole official language of Fiji is English (1987: 78).

Since the mid-twentieth century, a few new grammars of Bauan (or Fijian as it is now usually called) have been written (Schütz, 1972a: 73ff). These grammars still use the orthographic system devised by Cargill in the 1830s.

Schütz notes that 'it seems safe to say that almost all adult Fijians today know Bauan' (1972a: 107). But Schütz and Komaitai point out that:

So far as we know, very little attention has been paid to the problems encountered by Fijians learning Bauan. It is likely that the main method of learning is merely by exposure. A child growing up in, say, Vanua Levu has an opportunity to hear Bauan spoken in his village during church services, in classes after a certain point, on the radio, and in situations in which Bauan is used as a common language between speakers of other languages. (Schütz & Komaitai, 1971: xxii-xxiii)

Also, Lasaga says that in many schools English is the medium of instruction (1984: 87), and that

it is a fact of life in Fiji that most people are fluent only in their mother tongue; a very small proportion of the total population is effectively trilingual, especially in Fijian, English and Hindi ... . (Lasaga, 1984: 191)

It is not clear, therefore, to what extent Fijian (or Bauan) is used in education, nor to what extent non ethnic Fijians, i.e. the Indian and European element of the population, are familiar with the Fijian language.

As far as spoken language is concerned, there is considerable linguistic diversity in the Fijian Islands. Geraghty discusses what he terms 'communalects', that is, the variety of speech used in a single, or a small number of villages in a geographically defined area (Geraghty, 1983: 17ff). The communalects may vary from area to area in one or more ways in phonology, vocabulary and/or grammar (Geraghty, 1983). However, as Geraghty points out:

> In fact, most Fijians are, at least passively, multilingual. Marriage customs are such that every village contains many women who speak a foreign [communalect] and visitors generally resort to Colloquial Fijian [i.e. Bauan] only in cases of difficulty in communication. (Geraghty, 1983: 64)

The problem of classifying Fijian spoken forms into languages and dialects is extemely complex due to the fact that different linguistic criteria do not show regularity of patterning. For example, if four areas are examined, it may be that area A and area B show similarities but differ from areas C and D on a particular phonological feature, while lexically areas B and C are very similar but differ from both area A and area D, and if a third criterion is chosen then areas A and C may appear similar and area B may be different from both areas A and C and area D. (See Geraghty, 1983 for a detailed study, also Schütz, 1972a: 96ff.)

It is, therefore, extremely difficult to be specific using the terms 'language' and/or 'dialect' for Fijian. As Schütz puts it:

> Thus, the only verifiable statements we can make are at the extremes of specificity: the first deals with the general grouping of languages into an eastern and a western type, and the second treats the distribution of a great number of specific features. Statements with a middle degree of specificity are impossible to make, since there are no non-arbitrary criteria that will allow us to count languages or to distinguish between 'language' and 'dialect'. (Schütz, 1972a: 102)

The division of Fijian speech forms into eastern and western types is, consequently, as specific as we can be in terms of 'language' or 'dialect' at this time. Geraghty, though, notes that eastern Fijian probably shows more internal diversity than western Fijian (1983: 313).

The use of Bauan as the literary form and as the *lingua franca* throughout the Fiji Islands has led to a certain amount of borrowing from Bauan into other languages. This, in turn, may well be leading to a certain amount of levelling, especially in vocabulary, of differences in the other Fijian varieties (Schütz, 1972a: 107–8). It is also worth noting that there does not appear to have been much cultural mixing between Fijians and the Indian population. Consequently, the Fijian languages have not been influenced by Indian languages (Schütz, 1972a: 109).

In one study, at least, of Bauan, four types of speech were distinguished. These are: colloquial Bauan; a form of Bauan used with non-native speakers; a formal type of Bauan used for public speaking; and church Bauan (Commack cited in Schütz, 1972a: 79). No information was available to us on how these types of Bauan differed from one another, except that church Bauan uses a different intonation system and 'is flavoured with archaisms from the Fijian Bible, parts of which are now well over a century old' (Commmack quoted in Schütz, 1972a: 79).

Fijian, therefore, is characterised by considerable linguistic diversity which makes the counting or specifying of languages and/or dialects extremely difficult and complex. Although there are continua of speech forms which may be mutually intelligible, there are also problems of comprehension between various areas where the speech forms may be mutually unintelligible. One form of Fijian, Bauan, was chosen by the missionaries in the mid-eighteenth century as the literary form and as a *lingua franca*. Bauan is now understood and spoken by most Fijians, though probably as a second language. There are four levels of Bauan: colloquial; that used with non-native speakers; Bauan for public speaking; and church Bauan. The use of Bauan may be levelling other Fijian forms, particularly in vocabulary. When people speak of 'the Fijian language' they are usually referring to Bauan.

References

FINEGAN, E. 1987, English. In: B. COMRIE (ed.) *The World's Major Languages* (pp. 78–109). London: Croom Helm.

GERAGHTY, P. A. 1983, *The History of the Fijian Languages*. Honolulu: University of Hawaii Press (Oceanic Linguistics Special Publications No.19).

LASAGA, I. 1984, *The Fijian People: Before and After Independence*. Canberra: Australian National University Press.

SCHÜTZ, A. J. 1972a, *The Languages of Fiji*. Oxford: Clarendon Press.

SCHÜTZ, A. J. 1972b, *Say it in Fijian*. Sydney: Pacific Publications.

SCHÜTZ, A. J. and KOMAITAI R. T. 1971, *Spoken Fijian*. Honolulu: University of Hawaii Press.

Filipino (Tagalog)

The Philippines is made up of approximately 7,200 islands, and many languages are spoken within this region. Most estimates appear to put the number of languages at between 80 and 150 (Llamzon, 1978: 18; Bautista, 1979: 2 among others). According to Llamzon,

> although the linguistic situation of the country is characterised by one of great diversity, this multiplicity of languages is considerably simplified by the fact that more than 90% of the population are speakers of eight languages, which have been traditionally regarded as 'major languages' (perhaps because they have the most number of speakers), namely Tagalog, Sebuano [often spelt Cebuano], Hiligaynon, Waray, Bikol, Iloko, Pampanggo and Pangasinan ... . (Llamzon, 1978: 18)

Bautista also says there are eight 'major languages' (1979: 2).

All of the Philippine languages belong to the Austronesian family of languages and probably came to the Philippines in two or three major waves of migration some hundreds of years BC. The Philippine languages are generally divided into three major groupings: northern, central and southern (Llamzon, 1978: 3 and 18).

Certain of the Philippine languages had a writing system which used a script which, according to Francisco, probably arrived in the Philippines from Sumatra around the tenth or eleventh century AD (cited in Llamzon 1978: 4). When the Spanish arrived and colonised the Philippines (the area was named after King Philip II of Spain) in the sixteenth century the use of the indigenous script was discouraged and the Latin alphabet introduced (Nelson, 1968: 109). The old script is, however, still used by the Mangyan of Mindoro and the Tagbanuas of Palawan (Nelson, 1968: 110).

The Spanish ruled the Philippines for more than three hundred years during which time the majority of the population adopted Catholicism. In the south, though, the Muslims resisted the advance of Catholicism and today these areas are still Muslim and Arabic is an important language. (The 1986 Constitution states that Arabic shall be promoted on a voluntary and optional basis in education and that the Constitution shall be translated into Arabic as well as other regional Philippine languages.)

The Spanish did not, however, succeed in imposing the Spanish language on the Philippine population, except for the élite. A census report taken just after the end of Spanish rule showed that only 10% of the Philippine population could speak Spanish (Llamzon, 1978: 5). The Spanish also gave considerable emphasis to the study of Tagalog, one of the 'major languages' of the Philippines, and attempted to set it up as a *lingua franca* for the whole region. But, according to Llamzon, they did not succeed in doing so, though Tagalog was used to quite a large extent by the end of the Spanish rule in the 1890s (1978: 5-6).

At the beginning of the twentieth century the Americans had ousted the Spanish and set up an American civil regime in the Philippines (Llamzon, 1978: 6; Nelson, 1968: 48ff). Very soon after they had arrived the Americans introduced English into the education system, to the exclusion of all other languages. As Smolicz puts it, under the Americans:

> a major effort was made to introduce the teaching of English to the country. This move was directed not only against Spanish, but against all the Filipino languages, which were outlawed from the school. (Smolicz, 1984: 53)

The emphasis on English, especially during the 1920s and 1930s 'undoubtedly helped to establish literacy in English among wide circles of Filipino population' (Smolicz, 1984: 54). Native languages continued to be used for domestic and extra-curricular activities, and pressure for recognition of the Philippino languages gradually increased (Smolicz, 1984: 54; Llamzon, 1978: 6).

An Institute of National Language was created in 1936 following the 1934 Constituional Convention, and in 1937, on the recommendation of this Institute, Tagalog was proclaimed as the basis of the national language of the Philippines (Yabes, 1981: 2–3; Llamzon, 1978: 6). There had been, though, and there continued to be, opposition to Tagalog as the national language (Yabes, 1981: 2–3; Smolicz, 1984: 54). The teaching of Tagalog was nevertheless introduced into all Philippino schools in 1940 (Yabes, 1981: 3–4; Llamzon, 1978: 6). Tagalog was also proclaimed an official language, along with English and Spanish, in 1940 (Llamzon, 1978: 6).

The occupation of the Philippines by Japan during the Second World War gave a boost to the spread of Tagalog, and after the War, in 1948, census data showed that over 30% of the population could speak Tagalog (Llamzon, 1978: 6).

In 1959 the name of the national language was officially changed from Tagalog to Pilipino (Bautista, 1979: 2). According to Cabrera *et al.* Pilipino is Tagalog 'enriched with officially recognised borrowings' (1965: v). Yabes notes that the grammar with which Tagalog, later Pilipino, was propagated represented 'a puristic form' (1981: 4). According to Llamzon the change of name was 'an attempt to extricate the national language from its ethnic ties and endow it with the properties of a national symbol' (1978: 19).

A further Constitutional Convention was convened in 1971 to revise the 1935 Constitution and at this convention there was considerable debate between the proponents of Tagalog/Pilipino and those who were against this language being the national language (Smolicz, 1984: 54; Llamzon, 1978: 7). The anti-Pilipino faction won and in the Constitution of 1973 Pilipino was no longer designated as the national language, though it remained an official language along with English, and also Spanish was later added as an official language by Presidential Decree (Llamzon, 1978: 7).

In place of Pilipino, the Constitution stated that 'the National Assembly shall take steps towards the development and formal adoption of a common national language to be known as Filipino' (quoted in Llamzon, 1978: 7; and Smolicz, 1984: 55). Filipino, it appears, was intended to be a synthetic language based not on any one Philippino language but on several of them, as well as incorporating words from foreign languages (Llamzon, 1978: 19; Smolicz, 1984: 55).

It would seem, however, that the development of a 'synthetic' Filipino did not eventuate. Rather, Pilipino continued to be used officially and in the mass media (Llamzon, 1978: 19). In 1974 the 'bilingual policy' was instituted which provided for the use of Pilipino and English in schools (Llamzon, 1978: 18, Smolicz, 1984: 56). Smolicz, in fact, suggests that this policy meant that

> all the other major Filipino languages were phased out from the curriculum and effectively banned from any kind of educational role in the school. (Smolicz, 1984: 56)

From the time of the 1973 Constitution, therefore, the national language question in the Philippines is somewhat unclear. Llamzon notes that:

> Some language experts think ... that the National Assembly, when it convenes, will merely change the name of the present Tagalog-based *Pilipino* to *Filipino* (following the injunction in the [1973] Constitution) and compel the Institute for National Language to hurry the pace and intake of elements ... into the language from other languages inside and outside the country. (Llamzon, 1978: 20)

And Smolicz says that:

> ... the implication has been drawn that in the meantime Pilipino will continue as the 'interim' national language. There appears to be no consensus as to what language 'Filipino' really is, except that it is generally assumed to be based upon 'Pilipino', but with the addition of some words and/or constructions from the other indigenous languages. Thus it would seem that Tagalog is now acting as the nucleus of 'Pilipino' and that in future 'Pilipino' will act as the nucleus for 'Filipino'. What is fairly clear, however, is that the national language,

irrespective whether it is spelled with a 'P' or 'F', is very close to Tagalog and the name 'Tagalog' and 'Pilipino' are often used interchangeably. (Smolicz, 1984: 53)

It would appear that these comments are in large measure correct. According to a representative of the Philippines government in the Philippine Consulate, Sydney, the relevant section of the 1986 Constitution promulgated by the new government in the Philippines says that:

The national language of the Philippines is Filipino. As it evolves it shall be further developed and enriched on the basis of existing Philippine and other languages.

It should be noted that the Constitution does not make clear whether Filipino is to be based on Pilipino, is the same language with a different spelling or is to be a new language developed by language planners. Schachter, however, notes that Filipino is Tagalog enriched with words from other Philippine languages (1987: 936). The Constitution does state, though, that a National Language Commission will be established to 'undertake, coordinate and promote researches for the development, propagation and preservation of Filipino'. This would tend to suggest that whatever Filipino is based on it has not been fully standardised.

The new Constitution proclaims Filipino and English to be the official languages of the Philippines to be used in official communication and education. However, regional languages are designated as 'auxiliary official languages' which 'shall serve as auxiliary media of instruction therein'. It would appear, therefore, that the 'bilingual policy' brought in in 1974 no longer has the effect of 'banning' other indigenous languages from the schools, though information on the extent to which English, Filipino and other indigenous languages are to be used in education was not available.

As far as actual language usage in the Philippines is concerned, it appears that many Philippinos use more than one language. Bautista, in a survey of language surveys, notes that in many cases the vernacular is used in the home, neighbourhood and community, whereas Pilipino (note that since most of our information is pre-1986 and since it is unclear what differences, if any, there are between Pilipino and Filipino, we shall continue to use the name Pilipino in this report) is used in more formal situations, in newspapers and books, in media programmes and more and more often as a *lingua franca*, especially among the younger generation. English is used in many of the same domains as Pilipino, as well as in the media, in most formal situations, and generally for 'official' speech (Bautista, 1984).

There would appear, therefore, to be a kind of continuum of language use with the regional vernacular at the informal end, Pilipino and English used, perhaps, interchangeably in the centre, and English tending to be used more as a speaker moves toward the formal end of the continuum. The new Constitution may affect the relative position of English on this continuum.

In Manila, which is situated in the Tagalog ethnic area, it appears that most speakers use Pilipino and English. This applies also to people from other language groups who migrate to Manila. According to Cruz, most non-Tagalogs shift to Pilipino and only rarely use their native language (1980: 73).

Pilipino, however, is not spoken by every Philippino. In 1970, just over 55% of the population were able to speak Pilipino, though the trend is for more people to learn Pilipino (perhaps now Filipino) every year. As Llamzon notes, 'if these statistical and sociological trends continue, the entire country may be Pilipino-speaking within a short time — perhaps within 20 to 30 years' (1978: 21).

According to Schachter, 'the dialect of Tagalog which is considered standard and which underlies Pilipino is the educated dialect of Manila' (1987: 936). It should be noted, though, that at least half of the Pilipino speakers have another language as their native tongue (Llamzon, 1978: 21). The way these speakers speak Pilipino, therefore, may be influenced by their native language and only approximate to the standard.

One result of the fact that most Philippinos are at least bilingual is the use of code switching, or shifting from one language to another within the same sentence or stretch of speaking. In the Philippines context this switching is known as 'mix–mix' (Bautista 1984: 101ff). According to Bautista mix–mix often combines Pilipino and English, though other Philippine languages are also used. Also, mix–mix is used, it appears, in all stratas of society, and is even used, at times, in writing (1984: 101–2). As noted previously for separate language use, it seems that as the situation tends towards the formal the amount of English in mix–mix increases (Bautista, 1984: 101–2).

In the Philippines, therefore, many languages are spoken by a large number of different ethnic groups. One of these languages, Tagalog, was chosen as the basis of the national language. The name of the national language was later changed to Pilipino. In 1974 the Constitution stated that Filipino, a language to be developed, would become the national language and Pilipino remained as an official language only, along with English. The 1986 Constitution states that Filipino now is the national language, but it is unclear what differences there are, if any, between Filipino and Pilipino (and, some argue, e.g. Yabes (1981) and Smolicz (1984), between Filipino, Pilipino and Tagalog).

Pilipino and English were both used in education and at least 55% of the population can now speak Pilipino with at least half this number speaking it as a second language. It seems that the educated Manila form of Tagalog underlies Pilipino, and possibly now Filipino. As well, code switching, or mix–mix, is apparently fairly common in the Philippines.

References

BAUTISTA, M. L. S. 1979, *Patterns of Speaking in Pilipino Dramas: A Socio-linguistic Analysis*. Tokyo: Tokyo University of Foreign Studies (Study of Languages and Cultures of Asia and Africa Monograph Series, No.13).

BAUTISTA, M. L. S. 1984, A survey of language use surveys in the Philippines, 1969–1983. *Philippine Journal of Linguistics* 15, 94–105.

CABRERA, N. C. *et al.* 1965, *Beginning Tagalog: A Course for Speakers of English.* Berkeley: University of California Press.

CRUZ, C. A. 1980, Sociolinguistic features of a selected Manila community. *Philippine Journal of Linguistics* 11, 64–74.

LLAMZON, T. A. 1978, *Handbook of Philippine Language Groups*. Quezon City: The Aleneo de Manila University Press (Published for UNESCO).

NELSON, R. 1968, *The Philippines*. New York: Walker and Company.

SCHACHTER, P. 1987, Tagalog. In: B. Comrie (ed.) *The World's Major Languages* (pp. 936–58). London: Croom Helm.

SMOLICZ, J. J. 1984, National language policy in the Philippines: A comparative study of the education status of 'Colonial' and indigenous languages with special reference to minority tongues. *Southeast Asian Journal of Social Science* 12, 51–67.

YABES, L. Y. 1981, Language policy and equality of opportunity for advancement. *Philippine Journal of Linguistics* 12, 1–10.

Finnish

Finnish, called Suomi by its speakers, is a member of the Baltic–Finnic sub-branch of the Finno–Ugric branch of the Uralic family of languages (Austerlitz, 1987: 570). It is one of two official national languages of the Republic of Finland where it is spoken by about 94% of the population. The other official national language is Swedish, which is spoken by about 6% of the population (Encyclopaedia Britannica, 1985: 172; Leino, 1986: 13).

According to Branch, scholars now believe that Finland has been continuously inhabited for at least 8,000 years (1987: 594). He also notes that speakers of Germanic and Baltic languages (e.g. Latvian and Lithuanian) probably arrived in the area about 3,500 years ago (1987: 594). Contacts between Baltic–Finnic languages and the Germanic and Baltic branches of the Indo-European family of languages consequently date from this time. Although the vocabulary and grammar of the Baltic–Finnic languages is very different to that of the Indo-European languages, contacts from these earliest times to the present have meant that there has been some lexical and grammatical borrowing from the Indo-European languages into Finnish (Branch, 1987: 594).

Modern Finnish did not evolve from one single dialect or dialect group. Collinder considers that separate tribes arrived in Finland from two directions: one from the south via the Gulf of Finland; and the other from the east via Karelia (1965: 10). And the Encyclopaedia Britannica says,

> Finnish as the common language of the Finns is not the direct descendant of one of the original Baltic–Finnic dialects; rather, it arose through the interaction of several groups in the territory of modern Finland. (Encyclopaedia Britannica, 1985: 705)

These original groups comprised a southern, a south-western and an eastern group (Encyclopaedia Britannica, 1985: 705).

Branch, however, believes that

> a number of dialects, from which present-day Finnish took shape, were probably being spoken in southern and western Finland in the early centuries AD. (Branch, 1987: 594)

And it was over succeeding centuries, as these people moved northwards, that influences from various directions caused an 'east–west distribution of linguistic, anthropological and ethnographical distinctive features' (Branch, 1987: 594).

Whatever the origins may be, it is generally accepted in the literature that Finnish, from a very early period, has been divided into two broad linguistic areas: an eastern and a western (the western area actually includes the north of Finland as well). There has always been a distinct linguistic boundary between these two areas, and the division is still reflected in the distribution of dialects to this day (Collinder, 1965: 10; Branch, 1987: 594). It would appear that the dialect groups are all mutually intelligible, even though the differences are quite marked.

In the twelfth and thirteenth centuries Finland came under Swedish rule after Crusades to Christianise the country (Leino, 1986: 16; Branch, 1987: 594). Rivalry between Sweden and the Russian Principality of Novgorod for control of the area, though, meant that the boundary between the Swedish and Russian spheres of influence was not drawn till 1323. Under this division all of Finland was under Swedish control (Encyclopaedia Britannica, 1985: 176).

Swedish rule resulted in considerable Swedish settlement in Finland, particularly in the coastal regions of the south and the west. A Swedish style administration was set up, and the clergy and nobility grew (Encyclopaedia Britannica, 1985: 176). Because the Swedes introduced centralised government for the first time in Finland, and demanded loyalty to a single ruler and faith in the Christian religion, the Finns, hitherto separate tribes, began to develop a sense of unity and drew together to form a Finnish nation (Branch, 1987: 594; Whitney, 1971: 20; Encyclopaedia Britannica, 1985: 176).

However, the administration and the nobility were almost entirely Swedish, and the clergy, although it contained a large Finnish element, was also predominantly Swedish (Encyclopaedia Britannica, 1985: 176; Leino, 1986: 17). The Swedish language, as a consequence, became the language of the educated classes, and of high culture as a whole (Whitney, 1971: 20–2; Leino, 1986: 17).

Although Finnish may have been used to some extent by the Catholic Church, it was not until the Reformation in the sixteenth century that Finnish became more widely used in church ceremonies (Whitney, 1971: 22). It was also after the Reformation that the first Finnish language literature began to appear (Leino, 1986: 17; Whitney, 1971: 22). There is evidence, however, that there was limited use of Finnish as a written language prior to this time (Branch, 1987: 595).

The development of the Finnish literary language is attributed to Mikael Agricola who produced, among other mainly religious works, a translation ot the New Testament which was published in 1548 (Branch, 1987: 595; Leino, 1986: 17; Whitney, 1971: 22ff). The basis of this literary language was the south-western dialects (Branch, 1987: 595). This form remained the literary language for

Finnish till the nineteenth century (Branch, 1987: 595). However, although literacy was widespread by the end of the seventeenth century, most of the literature in Finnish was religious or didactic works intended for the peasants (Leino, 1986: 17).

During the seventeenth and eighteenth centuries, in fact, the use of Swedish increased. As Korhonen points out, all important secular and ecclesiastical posts in government, education and the clergy were filled with Swedes from Sweden (1986: 16–17). He also says that

> at the end of the eighteenth century not only the civil service – excluding the Finnish speaking provincial clergy – but also the majority of the middle-classes in towns and the provincial nobility had become Swedified. (Korhonen, 1986: 17)

The seventeenth and eighteenth centuries also saw renewed rivalry between Sweden and Russia (now led by the Grand Duchy of Moscow) on the eastern frontier of Finland. Finland was even occupied by Russian forces between 1713 and 1721 (Encyclopaedia Britannica, 1985: 176). In 1809 Finland was ceded to Russia and became a Grand Duchy of the Russian Empire, and Swedish rule came to an end (Branch, 1987: 595; Collinder, 1965: 10). Shortly afterwards, the administrative capital of Finland was moved from Turku in the south-west to Helsinki in the south (Korhonen, 1986: 35).

The autonomy granted to Finland under Russian rule led to the awakening of a 'desire to cultivate a distinctly Finnish national identity rooted in the Finnish language' (Branch, 1987: 595). As a consequence, interest and debate on Finnish and its written form arose. The main difference of opinion was between supporters of the old literary language based on south-western dialects developed by M. Agricola, and those who wanted eastern dialects to be taken into consideration in the written norm. This debate came to be known as 'the dialect struggle' (Korhonen, 1986: 67–8).

The debate was settled around the middle of the nineteenth century with the development of a literary standard close to the spoken language which retained the base of the old literary form, but with its sentence structure and vocabulary revised and standardised to take account of eastern dialects (Branch, 1987: 595: Korhonen, 1986: 69). This was mainly due to the fact that the eastern dialects were brought to prominence and their position consolidated by the publication of epic poems, written in the eastern dialects, collected and edited by E. Lonnrot (Branch, 1987: 595; Korhonen, 1986: 69). This literary form was written in the Latin alphabet, and with it Finnish literature began to be produced (Leino, 1986: 17).

Although Finnish was developing rapidly in the nineteenth century, and attempts were made to improve the standard of Finnish spoken by public officials and priests, Swedish was still the dominant language (Korhonen, 1986:

72–3). Swedish was the only language allowed within the Finnish administration until the middle of the nineteenth century, and publications in Finnish other than of a religious or economic nature were prohibited between 1850 and 1860 (Encyclopaedia Britannica, 1985: 177; Korhonen, 1986: 72).

It was only in 1863 that a decree was passed granting Finnish equal status with Swedish. And this decree allowed for a twenty year period of transition before public departments and courts were obliged to provide documents in Finnish (Korhonen, 1986: 73), but it was not until 1902 that Finnish and Swedish were actually placed on an equal footing as official languages (Encyclopaedia Britannica, 1985: 177). However, from the 1860s literature in Finnish began to flourish.

In the early twentieth century there was some attempt at Russification of Finland, and the gradual imposition of Russian as the official language was ordered. However, in 1917 Finland issued a declaration of independence, and it was recognised as an independent nation in 1918 (Encyclopaedia Britannica, 1985: 178). Under the Finnish constitution both Finnish and Swedish were recognised as official national languages.

The official status of Swedish caused some controversy in Finland, and its position was progressively weakened as language laws were revised. However, it is still an official national language in Finland with certain guarantees under the law (Encyclopaedia Britannica, 1985: 178).

During the nineteenth and twentieth centuries many new words have been created to enable Finnish to express concepts of government, science and culture. And a lot of work on the development of the language has also been carried out (Korhonen, 1986: 73).

The spoken language is divided into five main dialect groups which form an eastern and a western area (Encyclopaedia Britannica, 1985: 705). The literary language, though, may well be levelling dialectal variation, particularly in phonology, i.e. the way words are pronounced. For the most part, each letter in the Finnish orthography represents one sound (Branch, 1987: 595), and so literary Finnish serves as a guide to a standardised way of pronouncing Finnish. Consequently, when Finns learn to read and write they also learn a standard pronunciation. It would appear, therefore, that a spoken form approximating to the written norm is considered standard. As Collinder notes, 'the reformed literary language ... soon became the spoken idiom of the educated classes' (1965: 10).

Finnish, or a Finnish dialect, is spoken in the Torne River Valley area of Sweden. According to Wande, there is some debate in this region as to whether this form of Finnish should be considered a language in its own right (1984: 235). Tornedal Finnish is apparently different from standard Finnish and Wande notes that speakers of this form do not feel at home with 'Finland' Finnish and have protested against the use of the standard form in local radio broadcasts (1984: 235).

Also, in the north of Finland other Finno-Ugric languages, known as Lappish or Saame are spoken. These languages are not mutually intelligible with Finnish, though most speakers can also speak Finnish and appear to be losing their native language in favour of adopting Finnish (Aikio, 1984).

For Finnish, therefore, there is a standard literary language which was developed in the nineteenth century after the separation from Sweden. This form has as its base the older literary form developed in the sixteenth century, but incorporates elements from the eastern dialects. There are five main dialect groups divided into an eastern and a western area, but the standard spoken form is more or less the same as the written form.

References

AIKIO, M. 1984, The position and use of the same language: Historical, contemporary and future perspectives. *Journal of Multilingual and Multicultural Development* 5 (3–4), 277–91.

AUSTERLITZ, R. 1987, Uralic languages. In: B. COMRIE (ed.) *The World's Major Languages* (pp. 567–76). London: Croom Helm.

BRANCH, M. 1987, Finnish. In: B. COMRIE (ed.) *The World's Major Languages* (pp. 593–617). London: Croom Helm.

COLLINDER, B. 1965, *An Introduction to the Uralic Languages*. Berkeley: University of California Press.

ENCYCLOPAEDIA BRITANNICA 1985, Finland. In: *Macropaedia* Vol. 19 (pp. 169–180).

ENCYCLOPAEDIA BRITANNICA 1985, Uralic languages. In: *Macropaedia* Vol. 22 (pp. 701–11).

KORHONEN, M. 1986, *Finno-Ugrian Language Studies in Finland 1828–1918*. Helsinki: Societas Scientiarum Fennica.

LEINO, P. 1986, *Language and Metre: Metrics and the Metrical System of Finnish*. Helsinki: Finnish Literature Society (Translated by A. Chesterman) *Studia Fennica* 31.

WANDE, E. 1984, Two Finnish minorities in Sweden. *Journal of Multilingual and Multicultural Development* 5 (3–4), 225–41.

WHITNEY, A.H. 1971, *Finnish Reader*. London: Teach Yourself Books.

French

French is a Romance language descended from Latin, a member of the Indo-European family. The Romans brought Latin to France, then known as Gaul, when they conquered the Celts and made the area a Roman colony. The whole area of present day France was under the domination of Rome by about 50 BC, but it was probably not until the fourth or fifth century AD that the Celtic language was finally displaced by Latin (Rickard, 1974: 11–12).

As the Roman empire declined, the territory of France was invaded by Germanic tribes, the Franks in the north and the Goths in the south, among others. By 536 AD one of these Germanic tribes, the Franks, had conquered all the others and reunited the whole of what is today France under one king. However, the Franks had earlier converted to Roman Catholicism and consequently Latin was adopted as the language of religion. Latin was also maintained by the Franks as the language of administration and law (Elcock, 1975: 247).

The Germanic speech brought by the invading tribes had a considerable influence on the spoken language of France. The name France, in fact, is derived from the name of the most important of these Germanic peoples, the Franks (Rickard, 1974: 22; Elcock, 1975: 226ff). However, the Germanic peoples did not manage to impose their language on the population of France. Rather it was Romance which eventually imposed itself upon the invaders (Wolff, 1971: 70). By the end of the tenth century German had virtually ceased to be spoken in French territory (Rickard, 1974: 43).

It was during this period of considerable political and social upheaval, from roughly the fifth century on, that the spoken language of France began to diverge from Latin. It did not, though, diverge uniformly; rather, several distinct forms began to emerge. In the north, the area most influenced by the Franks, a group of dialects collectively known as *Langue d'oil* evolved; in the south a group known as *langue d'oc* evolved; and in the eastern central region a third group called *Franco-Provençal* (Wolff, 1971: 150–1; Rickard, 1974: 25). Within each of these groups there was considerable variety (Rickard, 1974: 33).

Thus, by the late eighth century spoken French was made up of a considerable number of different dialects roughly classified into three major groups. The northern group, *langue d'oil*, was the one which showed the most significant changes. As Wolff notes, 'the most vigorous originality was shown by the northern dialects' (1971: 151).

Literature in French probably began around the ninth century (Rickard, 1974: 35), and by the twelfth century French had achieved widespread acceptance as a literary medium, side by side with Latin (Rickard 1974: 46). These early texts in French, though, did not adhere to a single literary form. As Pope puts it,

> throughout the twelfth and thirteenth centuries the local speech of all regions of northern France was freely used in literary productions. (Pope, 1952: 33)

In southern France, in the *langue d'oc* speaking areas, there was some attempt at standardisation during this period. According to Wolff,

> we owe the only real attempt at unification during the twelfth and thirteenth centuries to the troubadours: whether Provençals, Limousins, Gascons or even Catalans and Italians, they wrote in a common language from which dialectal peculiarities had been eliminated. (Wolff, 1971: 151)

However, during these two hundred years the speech of one area of northern France was gradually gaining prestige. When the Capetian kings established their capital in Paris in the region of Ile-de-France, that city became the centre for the Royal Court, the law-courts, the university and the Church. As a result,

> the language of Ile-de-France in general, and of Paris in particular, came to be accepted as the desirable norm of speech, and consequently as at least the basis for the desireable norm in writing. (Rickard, 1974: 47)

Thus, as the power of Paris grew, so did the prestige of its spoken language, a *langue d'oil* dialect of French known today as Francien. And as this dialect grew in prestige, so a written language which approximated to it also commanded prestige (Rickard, 1974: 52).

In the southern areas of France the standard literary language of *langue d'oc* suffered a severe setback when the political autonomy of the south was ended, in the early thirteenth century, by the fall of the Toulousain dynasty as a result of the Albigensian crusade. The south was thereafter politically subject to the royal authority of the kings in Paris, and Francien, the Paris dialect, began to be prestigious in this area too (Elcock, 1975: 400ff; Rickard, 1974: 54).

By the sixteenth century Paris French had attained such a dominant position as the language of literature that it was even used for documents intended only for local consumption in areas whose dialect was far removed from Francien (Rickard, 1974: 53). In fact, as Rickard puts it, '[Francien] ceased in effect to be a dialect and began to become a national language' (1974: 52), though this applied only to the written language. The spoken language was still characterised by considerable dialectal variation, though here too the prestigious form was based on the speech of Paris (Rickard, 1974: 87).

In the sixteenth century French was recognised as the official language of France to the exclusion of Latin and provincial languages or dialects (Rickard, 1974: 86). Latin also declined in favour of Paris French in the areas of science and theology, and printing, when not in Latin, was exclusively in Paris French (Rickard, 1974: 68, 91). In education, though, Latin remained dominant until the eighteenth century (Pope, 1952: 29).

Thus, by the end of the sixteenth century,

> it was understood that the norm, for the written as for the spoken language, was the usage of educated Parisians and of the educated citizens of major cities not too remote from Paris, yet this norm, in the absence of any further standardisation, still allowed very considerable latitude. (Rickard, 1974: 104)

The seventeenth and eighteenth centuries saw the standardisation and codification of the norm. The Academie Francaise was founded in 1635; and many grammars of French were produced during this period. In consequence, by the late eighteenth century 'the grammar of French had been codified to the last detail, and it was a codification which was to prevail, with very few modifications down to the present day. (Rickard, 1974: 104, 105ff)

This codification of French could perhaps more accurately be termed the codification of Francien, the dialect of Paris and its surrounds. French is from this point on, therefore, synonymous with Francien. This dialect, though it was undoubtedly the prestigous spoken form and virtually the only written form, was by no means the only spoken form. In 1790 a survey was conducted for the revolutionary government of the day by the Abbe Henri Gregoire into the linguistic state of the nation. This survey showed that out of a population of twenty-five million, only some three million could speak French well enough to converse in it, and considerably fewer could write it; while at least six million knew no French at all (Rickard, 1974: 123–4).

The vast majority of the population, therefore, spoke dialects other than Francien. In the north, in the *langue d'oil* area, the other dialects included, among others, Normandy, Picardy, Walloon; in the south, the *langue d'oc* dialects included Gascon, Provençal, Limousin; and in the east there were the Franco-Provençal dialects (Guiraud, 1971: 29). These dialects differed considerably from one another, though the differences between *langue d'oil*, *langue d'oc* and *Franco-Provençal* were greater than the differences within any one of the three major areas, though these too were quite marked (Guiraud, 1971). In fact, in many instances these dialects differed to the extent that they were mutually incomprehensible (Hoffman, 1988).

During the nineteenth century the use of dialects other than Francien began to decline as communications improved and speakers were exposed more and more to French. The decline became more rapid when primary education became compulsory in 1882 and the language of education was French (Rickard, 1974: 124–5).

According to Field, the social transformations caused by the First World War and national military service were another major cause of dialect loss, at least in the *langue d'oc* area (1981: 252). The almost exclusive use of French in the media has further eroded dialect use (Eckert, 1983: 294).

However, the use of dialect, or as they are sometimes nowadays called, *patois*, has not completely died out. According to Rickard, 'dialects are certainly still heard' (1974: 126), though it appears that this is true primarily of the *langue d'oc* dialects. In the territory where *langue d'oc* was spoken, often called Occitan in the more recent literature, there are still perhaps as many as two million people who speak a *langue d'oc* dialect in daily life (Field, 1981: 259). Rickard (1974: 126) puts this figure considerably higher. But, because French is seen as the language of the outside, the rich and the educated, the Occitan dialects have become more localised and are used 'only with natives of one's own village' (Eckert, 1983: 294). Eckert points out that:

> This localisation had several major effects on regional solidarity: it decreased awareness of the unity of the various varieties of Occitan, and the traditional pan-dialectal competence of the speakers throughout the region, and it quite simply transferred all extra-local communication into the French domain. (Eckert, 1983: 294)

In these Occitan dialect areas there are, however, several movements which are attempting to revive and reintroduce Occitan varieties and establish regional standards (Eckert, 1983).

In France, therefore, linguistic unification and standardisation are far advanced. The majority of the population nowadays speak only French, and even those who speak a different dialect, or patois, are almost certainly bilingual in French as well (Rickard, 1974: 127). What we know as French began as merely one among many dialects in France which, through the power of Paris, became the prestigious spoken and consequently written form of the language and eventually superseded the other dialects in all but the most local and intimate of domains, if not entirely.

However, even though the standardisation of French is far advanced there are still variations to be found from region to region. Rickard notes that there are regional differences in pronunciation and that vocabulary items may be used in different, local senses depending on the region (1974: 127). And Guiraud gives the example of a speaker from Marseilles who may command three varieties of French: cultivated, or standard French; a variety of 'popular' French; and

Marseilles French, which is influenced by certain features of the local Occitan dialect (1971: 9).

Paltridge and Giles, in a study on attitudes of French speakers to regional accents, concluded that educated Parisian French represents the standard accent and is prestigious, but that 'in many *informal* contexts and particularly outside Paris, the standard accent ... might well be devalued on "social appeal"' (1984: 79 their emphasis) since this way of speaking was seen as being 'too formal'. According to Rickard educated standard French varies little from region to region. He says:

> The popular, uninhibited, not to say uneducated level [of French] is much the same all over France, yet precisely because it is not the speech of the more educated classes, it is more liable to be affected by regionalisms which 'educated standard French' is better able to resist. (Rickard, 1974: 128)

French is also spoken in several other countries around the world. In Canada, a variety of French is spoken which differs both from the standard and from regional varieties within France. According to Deprez, this Canadian variety is often seen as 'bad' French by speakers from France, but Canadian speakers do not want to speak like the French from France (1982: 245, 257ff). In Belgian French, there are apparently many lexical items which are peculiar to Belgium, often known as 'belgicisms', although it seems that accent is not a major distinguishing trait. As Pohl puts it, 'above a very thick layer of common general or dialectal French, there are evident differences, mainly prosodical and lexical' (1978: 87).

In many of the islands where French is spoken, such as New Caledonia, Vanuatu, Mauritius, it seems that educated Parisian French is seen as the standard to be aimed at, and the variety expected in formal situations (Hoffman, 1988). In Mauritius, though, a type of Creole is the more usual form of communication in everyday situations (Hoffman, 1988).

It should also be noted that within France, French is not the only language spoken. In the west, Breton is spoken by some 750,000 people; in the east, German is spoken by well over a million people, and Flemish is spoken by about 100,000 in the north-east; in the south-west, about 70,000 speak Basque; and in the south, perhaps 200,000 speak Catalan (Rickard, 1974: 126).

References

DEPREZ, K. 1982, Belgian Netherlandic and Canadian French: A socio-linguistic comparison. *Language Problems and Language Planning* 6 (3), 241–70.
ECKERT, P. 1983, The paradox of national language movements. *Journal of Multilingual and Multicultural Development* 4 (4), 289–300.
ELCOCK, W. D. 1975, *The Romance Languages*. London: Faber and Faber.

FIELD, T. T. 1981, Language survival in a European context: The future of Occitan. *Language Problems and Language Planning* 5 (3), 251–63.

GUIRAUD, P. 1971, *Patois et Dialectes Francais*. Paris: Presses Universitaires de France.

HOFFMAN, P. 1988, Department of French Studies, University of Sydney, personal communication.

PALTRIDGE, J and GILES, H. 1984, Attitudes towards speakers of regional accents of French: Effects of regionality, age and sex of listeners. *Linguistische Berichte* 90, 71–83.

POHL, J. 1978, Communication field and linguistic field: The influence of the border (France and Belgium) on the French language. *International Journal of the Sociology of Language* 15, 85–90.

POPE, M. K. 1952, *From Latin to Modern French with Especial Consideration of Anglo-Norman*. Manchester: Manchester University Press.

RICKARD, P. 1974, *A History of the French Language*. London: Hutchinson University Library.

WOLFF, P. 1971, *Western Languages AD 100–1500*. London: Weidenfield and Nicolson (World University Library).

German

German is a member of the Germanic branch of the Indo-European family of languages. German, like Dutch, English, Frisian and the Scandinavian languages, evolved out of Common Germanic. By about the sixth century AD seven major dialect groups had developed in the area which today includes Germany, Switzerland, Austria, Belgium, Holland and Luxembourg. These dialect groups were: Bavarian in the south-east of Germany and Austria; Alemannic in the south-west of Germany and Switzerland; Franconian and Thuringian in central Germany and Luxembourg; Low Franconian in north-west Germany, Belgium and Holland; and Frisian in north-west Holland and northern Germany (Chambers & Wilkie, 1970: 17ff).

Within each of these dialect groups, of course, there was considerable variation and no absolute border existed between them. Also, Low Franconian as well as evolving into dialects which are today considered to be dialects of German was the precursor of Dutch, and, similarly, Frisian was the precursor of the modern Frisian language (Donaldson, 1983: 118ff).

In the sixth century certain consonants began to be pronounced differently in the dialects of the mountainous southern regions. This pronunciation change became known as the second, or, because it began in the mountains, the high German sound shift. The high German sound shift gradually moved north affecting all dialect groups, except Low Franconian and Saxon, to a greater or lesser extent. Those dialect groups which were affected became known as High German and those not affected as Low German (Donaldson, 1983: 123).

From about the thirteenth century German began to replace Latin as the language used for writing (Wells 1985: 103–4). However, because Germany did not, at that time, have one major political or cultural centre, but was composed of a large number of virtually independent kingdoms, states and cities (Detwiler, 1976), no one written form predominated. In other words, several written forms of German appeared in different areas of the country. As Wells puts it, 'lack of political unity in German-speaking lands and correspondingly strong local traditions impeded the development of a standard German language ...' (1985: 133).

In the early part of the sixteenth century one form of written German was widely disseminated through the writings of Martin Luther, particularly his Bible translation. The advent of printing made this dissemination possible. As

Wells notes, 'printing enabled Luther to reach vast audiences, making him the first German author to be read on a modern scale' (1985: 190). Luther's output was prodigious; between 1518 and 1522 approximately one-third of all German writings bore his name and between 1534 and 1584 one press in Wittenberg alone produced about 100,000 copies of his translation of the Bible (Johnson, 1972: 43–4).

The particular form of the language used by Luther was based on the written chancery language of Saxony in eastern central Germany. Interestingly, the written language of Saxony was not a 'pure' dialect but an amalgam of several dialects. According to Chambers and Wilkie it was 'a mixed colonial dialect containing northern, central, and southern features' (1970: 37). Nonetheless, it was in essence a High German dialect.

There is some controversy concerning the extent to which Luther can be considered 'the father of modern German'. He did not invent a new standard form of the language or lay down rules of correct usage (Chambers & Wilkie, 1970: 41; Johnson, 1972: 43). His own orthography, in fact, remained inconsistent throughout his life (Wells 1985: 192). But, as Wells points out,

> in a very general sense, Martin Luther could be credited through the Bible and the Reformation with having ensured that High German of an eastern central German type came to overlie the Low German dialects as a standard book or written language, even if the *form* ... was not his own. (Wells, 1985: 200–1)

Also, as Lockwood notes:

> In the Protestant parts Luther's language was authoritative. But his language only became familiar to the majority of his readers after they had learnt it. For the first time, Germans were beginning to feel that literary language was something to be acquired by study. (Lockwood, 1965: 113)

Between the time of Luther and the late eighteenth century several grammars were written which codified and standardised a literary language for use throughout Germany. The language form the grammarians tended to use as a base was the language used in Saxony, or East Central German, the same form as had been used by Luther. As Lockwood says, 'during the course of the eighteenth century, with the work of Gottsched and Adelung, both partisans of Saxon usage, the grammatical unity of the literary language was achieved' (1965: 115). This form was propagated by writers who 'used it with a clarity, eloquence and elegance which put paid to the chances of its rivals' (Johnson, 1972: 56). This standard literary language is to all intents and purposes the language employed today (Lockwood, 1965: 115).

In 1901 the governments of Germany, Austria and Switzerland called an 'orthographic conference' to recommend official rules for the orthography of literary German. The recommendations of the conference were accepted by most government authorities and were prescribed for use in schools in 1907 (Johnson, 1972: 57). Although these recommendations still form the basis of German orthography, discussion of possible reforms, for example of capitalisation of nouns, continues to this day (Clyne, 1984: 74ff).

The standard literary language has exerted considerable influence on the spoken language in German speaking countries. However, the situation with the vernacular is complex.

In the eighteenth century, although the literary language was well on the way to being standardised, the spoken language was mainly dialect and differed from region to region. According to Lockwood:

> Two hundred years ago, nearly all spoken German was dialectal. Only a small élite could actually speak the literary language and most of these could doubtless use dialect as well if required. Except in Saxony, the difference between the literary language and the ordinary spoken form was quite appreciable, in extreme cases (e.g. Switzerland, North Germany) the literary language was virtually a foreign tongue to those who spoke the local dialects. (Lockwood, 1965: 116)

As well as problems of comprehension between the dialects and the literary language, many of the dialects were also not mutually intelligible (Lockwood, 1965: 133). In other words, it was possible that a speaker of, for example, Low German from the north, would be unable to understand either the literary language or any of the dialects from the centre or the south of the country.

With the introduction of compulsory schooling in the latter half of the nineteenth century most Germans were taught the standard literary language, i.e. High German. The dialects, however, did not die out though they gradually became more restricted in the number of contexts in which their use was felt to be appropriate. As Wells puts it,

> dialect eventually became restricted to familiar, domestic, informal situations and to rural life and work ... or to certain regional but traditional occupations, like mining or fishing. (Wells, 1985: 356)

The variation in the dialects of German can be seen from the fact that a 1954 dialect atlas listed 374 forms of the word *Wort* (word) (Lockwood, 1965: 134–5).

With the spread of the High German literary language through education, it became the socially prestigious form of the spoken language and was consequently adopted by more and more speakers. The introduction of radio, television and other mass media has increased the speed of adoption of High German and has carried it into the smaller townships and rural areas where only dialect had been used previously (Lockwood, 1965: 116).

However, in adopting the literary language as a spoken form certain regional variations in pronunciation, vocabulary, idiom and, to a small extent, grammar
have been retained from the dialects. The form of language used by educated
speakers, therefore, differs from region to region even though it approximates to
the literary standard. This form is usually termed *Umgangssprache* by linguists.
Lockwood says:

> Standard German, as spoken, is called *Umgangssprache*. It is misleading to
> translate this term 'colloquial'; it is better to define it as 'non-dialect
> speech'. *Umgangssprache* is, however, far from uniform. It is far less
> homogeneous than the English spoken in England, for instance. It is not yet
> possible to speak of a national *Umgangssprache*, since the regional varia-
> tions are still so considerable. (Lockwood, 1965: 116)

It appears, though, that a non-regional form of German is used on radio
where, as Clyne notes, announcers from the south and west of Germany 'adopt
the same standards, and sound much the same, as their North German counterparts' (1984: 8). There is also a form of German established expressly for the
theatre   and   intended   to   be   non-regional. This   form, known   as
Bühnenaussprache, is sometimes used as an educated non-regional norm for formal speech as well as being the 'standard of the stage' (Johnson, 1972: 57;
Wells, 1985: 353ff).

The spoken language, therefore, forms a continuum from local dialect to
a non-regional norm with the term *Umgangssprache* used to cover everything
which is between the two extremes. However, as Clyne points out, the use of
only one term for any language form which is neither a 'pure' local dialect
nor a non-regional form obscures the multidimensionality of spoken German
(1984: 46). For example, in a study of Regensburg speech Keller (1976)
discusses five levels of spoken German. These are: the local city dialect, three
levels of *Umgangssprache*, and the 'standard' language of the radio and
television. He says that speakers unconsciously shift between the different
levels depending on who they are talking to and the situation (1976: 21). And
Clyne points out that most German speakers are able to switch between
multiple levels of spoken German in much the same way as multilinguals
switch between their languages (1984: 47).

It must be remembered, though, that there are no hard and fast demarcation
lines between these levels of the spoken language. Rather, as with dialects themselves, there is a continuum on which certain points can be considered different
enough to be treated as separate levels. Also, as Johnson notes, 'the amount of
success with which the standard or the regional dialect is realised fluctuates
from individual to individual' (1972: 59).

Clyne discusses the particular levels used by different social strata. He says,

working class people gravitate between dialect and a 'mixture' of dialect and standard German; the middle class often vacillate between this 'mixture' and standard German. (Clyne, 1984: 51)

However, the important point is that there appears to be no stigmatisation attached to a particular level of language in itself, but rather it is the appropriateness of the level used to the given situation which counts. In Regensburg and other Bavarian cities, for example, Keller reports that practically everyone can and does use dialect but they switch to a level of *Umgangssprache* or, in the case of the higher educated, a close approximation to the written standard depending on the context and/or the situation (1976: 37ff).

The north of Germany is perhaps an exception in that dialect is used far less there than in the rest of Germany. This is due to the fact that in the north Low German was to a large extent superseded by the High German form from the centre and south of the country. As Wells puts it:

Historically, this reflects the imposition of the High German language on Low German speakers whose colloquial language then strove to conform to the overlying standard language ... Northerners, therefore, lacking the dialectal basis of the standard language, tend to be particularly critical of *Umgangssprache* and to view it as substandard or non-standard. However, in the south the regional colloquial languages were rooted in dialect and never lost touch with it ... . (Wells, 1985: 369)

And as Clyne notes:

A myth continuing to the present day is that the 'best' German is spoken in Hanover. Because the north (including Berlin) was originally Low German speaking, and once used High German as a second language, the High German spoken there tended to accentuate a close relationship between phonemes (sounds) and graphemes (written letters), giving the semblance of 'greater correctness. (Clyne, 1984: 8)

In Germany at the present time a paradoxical situation regarding dialect use appears to be evident. It seems that dialect use is both declining and enjoying a regional resurgence. According to Clyne, dialects are declining due to the disappearance of closed rural communities, the increase in commuting to large towns and cities for work, and the levelling-out of class differences; whereas the regional resurgence is due to a desire on the part of speakers to identify with their own region, or ethnic minority. The latter trend appears to be most pronounced among the younger generation (1984: 57ff).

In Austria, as in Germany, there is a continuum of the spoken language from dialect to 'standard'. However, the difference between the two extremes is not as great as in Germany (Gal, 1979: 69). According to Braverman in a survey of the speech of Salzburg, 'no standard German is spoken in Salzburg by the native population' (1982: 28). And Clyne notes that the 'highest' variety used in Austria is not 'standard' High German but rather a variety which corresponds to a South German regional variety or *Umgangssprache*. This form constitutes the Austrian standard (1984: 9–10).

Braverman also notes that dialect is widely used and is not generally considered stigmatised. She says:

> Survey figures indicate the widespread use of dialect and the value placed upon its existence in all segments of Salzburg society. Although standard German serves as a model, not much effort seems to be made toward attaining or generally using it. (Braverman, 1982: 128)

Nevertheless, in more formal situations a level of language close to the Austrian 'standard' is considered necessary, and this form has connotations of higher social class and education and consequently is prestigious (Clyne, 1984: 10; Braverman, 1982: 126–7).

In Switzerland dialect use is far more widespread than in Germany or Austria. The majority of the dialects are descended from Alemannic. There is no social stigma attached to the use of dialect in Switzerland, nor does the use of dialect indicate educational levels. As McRae says:

> In all areas of German Switzerland the regional dialects are the usual means of informal oral communication, without distinction of educational or social status. While every Swiss–German child is taught standard High German in school and uses it in his normal written language, it is not used in normal conversation between dialect speakers. (McRae, 1983: 69)

Most of the Swiss dialects are mutually comprehensible even though the total number of different dialects may run into the hundreds (McRae, 1983: 68). There are also levels of dialect ranging from local to regional, and, as Clyne notes,

> communication at the inter-regional level is based on slightly adapting your own regional (rather than local) dialect to that of your speech partner, often by taking over lexemes (words) and other features from Swiss Standard German. (Clyne, 1984: 14)

He also notes that most German Swiss are now bi- or polydialectal (1984: 14).

In Switzerland, standard German is used primarily as the written language. It is used to a fairly large extent in education,the national parliament and the media, though in the cantonal, and increasingly in the national, parliaments dialect is used, and dialect is also making inroads into radio and TV (Clyne, 1984: 15; McRae, 1983: 69; Hughes, 1975: 63). In other words the domain of High German is gradually decreasing and dialect use is increasing. As Hughes puts it, 'dialect is annually making new empires' (1975: 63). And as Clyne remarks, 'dialect is making inroads into *informal* speech in *formal* domains, and even into *formal* speech' (1984: 15).

The attitude of Swiss German speakers to standard High German is, according to Steinberg, that:

> Swiss Germans suspect any fellow Swiss who uses High German too well and are embarrassed by anyone who uses it too badly. A native German speaker will recognise at once that radio announcers on Swiss radio have accents, but to the Swiss they sound too German to be real Swiss. (Steinberg, 1976: 105)

The form of High German spoken in Switzerland, therefore, differs from that spoken in Germany. Clyne notes that there are differences in phonology, vocabulary and to a certain extent in the grammar (1984: 16ff). Clyne, in fact, refers to a 'Swiss Standard German' which, while based on the High German of Germany, is an independent form peculiar to Switzerland (1984: 16).

References

BRAVERMAN, S. H. 1984, *The City Dialect of Salzburg: A Definition of Dialect in its Social Reality*. Goppingen: Kummerle Verlag.

CHAMBERS, W. W. and WILKIE, J. R. 1970, *A Short History of the German Language*. London: Methuen and Co.

CLYNE, M. G. 1984, *Language and Society in the German-Speaking Countries*. Cambridge: Cambridge University Press.

DETWILER, D. S. 1976, *Germany: A Short History*. Carbondale: Southern Illinois University Press.

DONALDSON, B. C. 1983, *Dutch: A Linguistic History of Holland and Belgium*. Leiden: Martinus Nijhoff.

GAL, S. 1979, *Language Shift: Social Determinants of Linguistic Change in Bilingual Austria*. New York: Academic Press.

HUGHES, C. 1975, *Switzerland*. London: Ernest Benn.

JOHNSON, L. P. 1972, The German language. In: M. PASLEY (ed.) *Germany: A Companion to German Studies*. London: Methuen and Co.

KELLER, T. L. 1976, *The City Dialect of Regensburg*. Hamburg: Helmut Buske Verlag.

LOCKWOOD, W. B. 1965, *An Informal History of the German Language*. London: Andre Deutsch.

McRAE, K. D. 1983, *Conflict and Compromise in Multilingual Societies: Switzerland*. Waterloo: Ontario, Wilfrid Laurier University Press.

STEINBERG, J. 1976, *Why Switzerland?* Cambridge: Cambridge University Press.

WELLS, C. J. 1985, *German: A Linguistic History to 1945*. Oxford: The Clarendon Press.

Greek

Greek forms, by itself, a separate branch of the Indo-European family of languages. The Greek language probably came to the Aegean area during the second millenium BC (Joseph, 1987: 410, 412). The political and social organisation into city states led to a plethora of different dialects being spoken. However, it seems that these dialects can be sorted into a small number of major dialect groups. Thomson puts the number at five (1972: 32) whereas Palmer says there were four (1980: 57).

The earliest writing in Greek dates from about 1400 BC in the Mycenaean Greek documents found on Crete, and from somewhat later on the Greek mainland. Since that time Greek has been in almost continuous use as a written language, though it has passed through several stages of evolution, e.g. Mycenaean Greek, Classical Greek and Modern Greek (Joseph, 1987: 410ff).

A variety of writing systems have been used for Greek, but the most enduring has been the Greek alphabet. The Greek alphabet is adapted from the old North Semitic alphabet and was introduced into Greece in the tenth or ninth century BC. According to Greek tradition, the alphabet was transmitted through the Phoenicians (Joseph, 1987: 415–6).

In the fifth century BC Athens rose to power and its dialect, Attic, became the official language of all Greek speakers (Tsirpanlis, 1970: 14). Attic thus became the literary language of Greek, and most writing since, right up to the twentieth century, has been based on it as writers tended to emulate Classical Attic (Joseph, 1987: 414–5).

During subsequent centuries, however, the vernacular, or spoken language, continued to evolve. First there was what is known as 'the Koine', based on Attic, which was the official language of the Empire of Alexander (approximately 330–150 BC) which stretched to the borders of India. Then the Romans came and Greek was influenced by Latin (approximately 150 BC–600 AD). The conversion to Christianity (approximately 300 AD) and the growth of the Byzantine culture (approximately 600–1453 AD) had considerable effect on the spoken language. And finally the Ottoman Empire (1453–1821) imposed Turkish as the official language, and again the Greek vernacular was influenced by this (Tsirpanlis, 1970: 14–17; Browning, 1982: 49–52).

However, in intellectual, religious, and official circles the vernacular had been looked down on from about the first century AD, if not before, and was 'referred to with expressions of contempt' (Browning, 1982: 50). As a consequence, as noted above, the vast majority of literature, whether secular or religious, was written in an archaising imitation of Attic (Tsirpanlis, 1970: 15–16). Thus, the spoken and written forms of Greek began to diverge nearly 2,000 years ago, and have continued to diverge virtually to the present day.

After the end of the Ottoman rule in Greece in the 1820s a movement arose to introduce a new written language based on the speech of the south of Greece, which would have brought the written and the vernacular forms closer together. This movement did not succeed since, as Karanikolas points out, 'the roots of Atticism [i.e. the literary language based on 5th century BC Attic] had taken too firm a hold' (1979: 81).

The spoken language, called Demotic, was considered too impoverished and adulterated by centuries of foreign influence to become the standard language. On the other hand, though, the Attic form was unintelligible to the majority of Greeks. Consequently, a compromise, which heavily favoured the Attic form, was arrived at. The vocabulary was purified of all foreign words and these were replaced with Attic words if they existed, or new forms were coined in the Attic style. The grammar which was imposed on this 'pure' vocabulary was also based on the Attic dialect (Browning, 1982: 53; Karanikolas, 1979: 81; Tsirpanlis, 1970: 18). The resulting language was called Katharevousa, which means 'purifying' according to Hawkins (1979: 175) or 'pure language' according to Karanikolas (1979: 82).

The differences between Katharevousa and Demotic appear in all aspects of the language; phonology, morphology, syntax, and, perhaps most noticeably, in vocabulary.

The important fact is that

there are no native speakers of [Katharevousa], and descriptions of it are based partly on a body of literature, and partly on the grammarians own prejudices ... . (Hawkins, 1979: 175)

Despite the fact that for all Greeks it was at best a second language and at worst unintelligible, Katharevousa was made the official language of the newly independent state of Greece in 1830.

Browning sums up the effects of the introduction of Katharevousa when he says:

The whole public communication of the state, from speeches in the Chamber of Deputies to instructions for filling in a form in the post office, followed the pattern set by literature and became more and more unintelligible to the mass of Greeks, and more and more imprecise. And in every school in the country children were taught that the language they had learned at their mother's knee, and which everyone used, was unworthy and antinational. It was a recipe for national schizophrenia. (Browning, 1982: 54)

And Mandilaras remarks that

a movement of this kind [i.e. the introduction of Katharevousa] undermined education and national culture, made difficult the popularisation of scholarship, made religious teaching remote, and made the functions of the state ... seem strange. (Mandilaras, 1972: 95)

In the late nineteenth century some authors began to use Demotic in their novels and one author translated the bible into Demotic (Browning, 1982: 55). This caused a political storm and 'the language question' [i.e. the struggle between Demotic and Katharevousa] became a political issue.

In 1917 Demotic was officially introduced into the education system but only in elementary schools. All secondary education was carried out in Katharevousa. But, as Karanikolas puts it:

Unfortunately, successive political and constitutional changes did not allow Demotic to prevail as the only language of the elementary school, nor was it allowed to extend to the other school levels ... . No other cultural issue in Greece has been so closely linked with politics as the language. During [this] period, linguistic educational policy would favour first Katharevousa, then Demotic, and back again to Katharevousa. (Karanikolas, 1979: 82).

In political terms, Katharevousa 'has, in some way, been identified as "conservative" while Demotic is deemed "progressive"' (Diamessis, 1982: 167). The supporters and users of Demotic have also at times been deemed antinational, communist, slavophile [at the time of troubles with the Slavs], ignorant, and other derogatory terms simply because of the way they spoke or wrote (Browning, 1982).

By the middle of this century, however, the actual language situation was not a simple split between Katharevousa on the one hand and Demotic on the other. It was considerably more complex. Browning denotes five 'states of the language' which were in use. These were:

(i)   Katharevousa, the official language which was no-one's mother tongue and existed in its pure form only in writing. It enjoyed great prestige.
(ii) The mixed language, known as '*mikte*' which used the structure of Katharevousa but avoided its more complex and difficult aspects, and drew terms from the spoken language. It was used in much journalism, speeches, radio, technical writing, and by those who tried to use Katharevousa but couldn't manage to.

(iii)   Kathomiloumene, basically the spoken language, Demotic, but drawing many 'learned' terms from Katharevousa. It was favoured by the middle classes and some types of journalism.

(iv)   Demotic, the spoken language of the mass of people, and of all people in informal situations. It is the result of the historical development of Greek since about the third century BC. The implications of its use were often political rather than social.

(v)   Purist Demotic, a systematised and codified form of Demotic used by many novelists. Unlike Demotic, though, it was no-one's mother tongue.

These 'states of the language' were used in different situations. For example, in newspapers, editorials would be in (iii), most news reporting in (ii), official announcements in (i), and short stories etc, in (iv); on radio, plays would be in (iv), news bulletins in (ii) and talks would vary between (ii) and (iii) (Browning, 1982: 60).

In 1976 a law was passed which made Demotic the official Greek language. As Diamessis, the Minister's Counsellor on Education and Research at the Greek Ministry of Education in 1982, says, 'Demotic is and will be, henceforth, the official and only version of Greek' (1982: 162).

However, as Sotiropoulos remarks:

The linguistic guidelines [i.e. use of Demotic only] are not accepted or applied uniformly. For example, the bureaucracy of the Greek army completely ignores the recent linguistic innovation, while the bureaucracies in scores of other ministries apply it lukewarmly. (Sotiropoulos, 1982: 7)

Browning considers that what is, in fact, becoming the 'normal language of public communication' would better be called Standard Modern Greek rather than Demotic (1982: 58). This is because, he says, many Katharevousa elements are incorporated in Demotic for various purposes. For example, cliches and tags are often in Katharevousa e.g. 'ok' and 'be that as it may'; if no Demotic term exists then Katharevousa is used, such as in scientific, technical, political, and religious discussions, which were originally in Katharevousa, where terms and even whole phrases have been taken directly from Katharevousa. As well, Katharevousa may be used to show group solidarity, e.g. between doctors or lawyers, and to add a certain emotional colouring to what is said, e.g. to show irony, indignation, jocularity, and so on (Browning, 1982: 63–4).

Thus, although Demotic has taken over from Katharevousa as the official language,

this linguistic pattern [i.e. Katharevousa] is still deeply ingrained in the writing and even speaking habits of lawyers, military men, and civil servants, and it will not be easily erased overnight. (Sotiropoulos, 1982: 15).

Browning sums up the situation in Greek today when he says:

Old habits are not easily lost. Greeks are still keenly interested in their language and ready to argue about it. Sometimes they give the impression of being more interested in how something is said than in what is said. But it is no longer possible, as it was until recently, to draw sweeping conclusions regarding a speaker's social status or political affiliations from the manner in which he declines third-declension nouns. The language question has been diffused. (Browning, 1982: 67)

The situation in migrant communities is unclear as far as the use of Katharevousa and Demotic is concerned. However, since many migrants left Greece prior to 1976 it must be presumed that any secondary education they received would have been in Katharevousa. Also, many classes in Greek schools outside Greece are taught by priests (Tsouris 1975: 59) and, as Bardis notes, the Greek Church tends to retain the use of Katharevousa (1976: 42). Further, a member of the Modern Greek Department at Sydney University pointed out that when he gives public lectures in Demotic there are always some members of the audience who feel that the language used should be Katharevousa.

As far as dialectal variation is concerned, there is certainly considerable variation within Greece. Tsirpanlis says that 'the total result of the political history of modern Greece is a complex and interesting dialect picture' (1970: 20). He goes on to enumerate six major dialect groups (1970: 21). Newton also considers that there are a small number of 'core' dialects [he says there are five] which provide 'a rough classificatory scheme' for an indeterminate number of different dialects some of which vary only slightly from others, while some are considerably different (1972: 13). According to Joseph, since Demotic has been made the official form of Greek, the now-standard language is based generally on the southern (i.e. Peloponnesian) dialect (1987: 415).

References

BARDIS, P. D. 1976, *The Future of the Greek Language in the United States*. San Francisco: R. and E. Research Associates.
BROWNING, R. 1982, Greek diglossia yesterday and today. *International Journal of the Sociology of Language* 35, 49–68.
DIAMESSIS, S. E. 1982, The introduction of the new Greek language. *Multilingua* 1 (3), 167–8.
HAWKINS, P. 1979, Greek diglossia and variation theory. *General Linguistics* 19 (4), 169–87.
JOSEPH, B. D. 1987, Greek. In: B. COMRIE (ed.) *The World's Major Languages* (pp. 410–39). London: Croom Helm.
KARANIKOLAS, A. S. 1979, The evolution of the Greek language and its present form. *Georgetown University Round Table on Languages and Linguistics* (pp. 78–85).
MANDILARAS, B. G. 1972, *Studies in the Greek Language*. Athens: N. Xenopoulos Press.

NEWTON, B. 1972, *The Generative Interpretation of Dialect: A Study of Modern Greek Phonology*. Cambridge: Cambridge University Press.

PALMER, L. R. 1980, *The Greek Language*. London: Faber and Faber.

SOTIROPOULOS, D. 1982, The social roots of modern Greek diglossia. *Language Problems and Language Planning* 6 (1), 1–28.

THOMSON, G. 1972, *The Greek Language*. Cambridge: W. Heffer and Sons.

TSIRPANLIS, C. N. 1970, *A Short History of the Greek Language*. Thessaloniki.

TSOURIS, M. P. 1975, Greek communities in Australia. In: C. PRICE (ed.) *Greeks in Australia* (pp. 18–71). Canberra: A. N. U. Press (Immigrants in Australia, Series 5).

Gujarati

Gujarati is a member of the Indo-Aryan branch of the Indo-European family of languages (Grierson, 1968: 326). It is the official language of administration in the north Indian state of Gujarat where it is spoken by over 25 million people (Zograph, 1982: 29, 65). The state and its language came to be called Gujarat and Gujarati after a tribe known as the Gurjars, or Gurjaras, who conquered the area between the fifth and sixth or seventh centuries AD (Grierson, 1968: 323, 327; Jhaveri, 1978: 1).

Like other Indo-Aryan languages, Gujarati evolved from the original Aryan language, Vedic, which was brought to India about 4,000 years ago (Zograph, 1982: 9ff). The next stage in the development of the Indo-Aryan languages was Sanskrit which had been standardised and codified as a literary language by about the fourth century BC. Literary Sanskrit still represents an important language in India today in virtually the same form (Zograph, 1982: 10–11).

Although Sanskrit remained fixed, the spoken languages of northern India did not. Gujarati, and the other Indo-Aryan languages continued to evolve, and passed through the two major evolutionary stages: the Prakrit and Apabhramsa stages (see the chapter on Hindi for a fuller discussion of this point). According to Grierson, Gujarati evolved from the Nagara form of the Saurasena Apabhramsa (1968: 327), but Jhaveri says 'its immediate predecessor is Gaurjara Apabhramsa' (1978: 2). Zograph notes that the Nagara Apabhramsa was extensively used in the area of Gujarat (1982: 14). The Prakrits and Apabhramsas were also used for literary purposes and had developed literary forms (Zograph, 1982: 14).

Although Zograph considers that in Gujarat and other north Indian regions the spoken languages evolved into the New Indo-Aryan forms about 1000 AD, he notes that literature in Gujarati did not begin until the fifteenth century (1982: 16, 66). It seems that Apabhramsa continued to be used as a literary language even though it was no longer spoken (Grierson, 1968: 327; Jhaveri, 1978: 2–3).

According to Jhaveri, Gujarati, as a separate literary form, began to be used in the fourteenth or fifteenth century, and the modern form in use today had evolved by the eighteenth or nineteenth century (1978: 3). The spelling system for Gujarati was standardised in the 1930s (Pandit, 1969: 114–5).

Gujarati is written in the Gujarati alphabet which is similar to the Devanagari script. It can also be written in the Devanagari script (Zograph, 1982: 70; Grierson, 1968: 338).

Gujarati, Grierson notes, is unique among Indo-Aryan languages in that its development can be traced in texts from the original Vedic language, through the Prakrit and Apabhramsa stages, and on to the modern form used in literature today (1968: 327). As Grierson puts it, 'no single step is wanting. The line is complete for nearly four thousand years' (1968: 327).

Gujarati is closely related to Western Hindi, and especially to Rajasthani (Grierson, 1968: 328). And Jhaveri says that 'till about the sixteenth century, both Gujarat and Western Rajasthan had, barring some inevitable dialectal differences, a common language' (1978: 2).

Dialectal variation within Gujarati is apparently relatively slight. Zograph says that 'the language is noteworthy for its relative homogeneity, showing little dialectal or local variation' (1982: 65). And Grierson notes that 'the only true dialectic [sic] variation of Gujarati consists in the speech of the uneducated and that of the educated' (1968: 326).

However, this applies to what are termed by Jhaveri 'the dialects of the plains' (1978: 4). The dialects of the hilly areas, known as Bhili, are sometimes considered as dialects of Gujarati, but are sometimes treated as separate languages (Zograph, 1982: 65; Jhaveri, 1978: 4; Grierson, 1968: 326). The Bhili dialects are 'structurally an intermediate stage between Gujarati and Rajasthani' (Zograph, 1982: 66).

The 'dialects of the plains' are divided by Zograph into four major subdivisions (1982: 4). According to Pandit, however, nothing significant has so far been published on Gujarati dialects (1969: 114). And Zograph notes that the Gujarati dialects 'have not been described in sufficient detail' (1982: 65). It is difficult, therefore, to say with any certainty what the dialectal variation in Gujarati is at the present time.

The standard form used by educated speakers, Grierson notes, is that found in grammars (1968: 326). Both Zograph (1982: 65) and Jhaveri (1978: 2) say that the present day standard for both written and spoken Gujarati is based on the form used by educated speakers from the Ahmedabad region. It should be noted, however, that deviations from the standard reflect both regional and social variation (Jhaveri, 1978: 2). That is, different castes and different professions may exhibit dialectal variation, principally in vocabulary, as well as dialectal variation peculiar to a particular region (Jhaveri, 1978: 4).

Gujarati has been heavily influenced, especially in its vocabulary, by several other Indian languages, and also by foreign languages, such as Persian, Arabic, Portugese and Dutch (Jhaveri, 1978: 5). English has had a considerable influence on Gujarati too. As Jhaveri says, 'English has touched the very vitals of the language and changed its face' (1978: 5).

Gujarati, therefore, is a New Indo-Aryan language which evolved from Vedic and Sanskrit through the Prakrit and Apabhramsa stages. It has a recorded history dating back nearly 4,000 years. The present standard is based on the educated speech of the area around Ahmadabad. There are a few dialects, both regional and social, though these differ only slightly from the standard. There is another group of dialects, known as Bhili, which differ more considerably from the Gujarati standard, but these are sometimes considered separate languages as they are intermediate between Gujarati and Rajasthani.

References

GRIERSON, G. A. 1968, *Linguistic Survey of India*. Vol. IX, Pt. 11. Delhi: Motilal Banarsidoss.
JHAVERI, M. 1978, *History of Gujarati Literature*. New Delhi: Sahitya Akademi.
PANDIT, P. B. 1969, Gujarati. In: T. A. SEBEOK (ed.) *Current Trends in Linguistics* Vol. 5, (pp. 105–21). The Hague: Mouton.
ZOGRAPH, G. A. 1982, *Languages of South Asia: A Guide*. London: Routledge and Kegan Paul (Translated by G. L. Campbell).

Hebrew

Hebrew is a Semitic language, a member of the Afroasiatic family of languages (Hetzron, 1987a: 648). Weinreich believes that originally Hebrew was a fusion language (i.e. the mixing together of elements of different languages to form one new language) of several Semitic formations (1980: 55). It was the spoken language of the Jews and was the language in which the Torah was mostly written.

During the sixth century BC the Jews were exiled to Babylonia. On their return to Palestine towards the end of the sixth century BC they brought Aramaic, a related Semitic language which had replaced Hebrew, with them, and 'thus began the decline of Hebrew as a spoken language' (Weinreich, 1980: 56). However, Weinreich notes that it is possible that Hebrew continued to be spoken by at least some of the population of Palestine till the fourth century AD (1980: 56). Aramaic, though, penetrated the later parts of the Torah written in the fifth century BC, and also the Talmud. The Talmud is the name given to the special body of sacred knowledge used to interpret and explicate the Torah; it was originally oral but began to be written in the sixth century AD partly in Hebrew and partly in Aramaic (Rosten, 1968: 528–30).

Despite the fact that Hebrew had ceased to be a spoken language in Palestine by the fourth century AD (and considerably earlier among those Jews who had migrated to other areas of Europe), it remained in use as a written language. As Rabin says,

> soon after [200 AD], the written use of Hebrew, and especially its use in religious activities and the highly prized study of religious literature, reasserted itself in Palestine and spread over large parts of the diaspora [i.e. Jews living outside of Palestine]. (Rabin, 1983: 43)

And Birnbaum states that:

> Hebrew functioned as the real literary medium and as the general means of written communication, its role being similar to Latin in relation to European vernaculars. However, among the Jews this state of affairs continued for a much longer time, until fairly recently. (Birnbaum, 1979: 34)

The use of Hebrew as a written language was, for the most part, confined to male Jews. Women were only rarely taught it (Rosten, 1968: 540). Not all males mastered Hebrew either, as Fishman points out:

Jewish communities carried with them the ideal of universal public education, dedicated to the mastery of basic Hebrew texts (usually via oral instruction, commentary and translation ...) but this ideal was often incompletely realised. Women generally and the poorer classes particularly, commonly learned only enough Hebrew to laboriously but uncomprehendingly follow the Hebrew prayer book. (Fishman, 1965: 4)

Nevertheless, the important fact is that Hebrew, or, perhaps more correctly, Hebrew and Aramaic, have been in almost constant use since the time of the Torah. Since the language of the Torah was sacred and unalterable, and since Hebrew was used mainly for religious purposes, it remained static for a considerable number of centuries.

In the mid nineteenth century a movement began in Eastern Europe, among the Ashkenazic Jews, to make Hebrew once again the spoken language of all Jews. Although the movement failed in Europe it took Hebrew out of the mainly religious sphere and a large amount of secular literature began to appear (Goldsmith, 1976). The movement, however, succeeded in Palestine.

In the late nineteenth and early twentieth centuries many Jews migrated to Palestine from various parts of the world. At that time, the majority of Jews who were already settled in Palestine were Yiddish speaking. (Weinreich, 1980: 303). This migration:

> ... brought to Palestine people who not only knew Hebrew and considered it the national language of the Jewish people, but who also so *willed* Hebrew [sic] that they crashed the barrier between written and spoken language and revived Hebrew as their vernacular in the home, in the schools, and in public life. (Weinreich, 1980: 303–4)

The situation in Palestine at that time, however, was extremely complex as far as language use was concerned. Immigrants from many parts of the world brought their own language or dialect with them. Ben Yehuda comments on the linguistic situation when he says,

> this was truly a 'Babel Generation', groups speaking various languages, each group in the language of the country it had come from, and these languages have caused these groups to feel almost alien to each other. (Quoted in Nahir, 1983: 268)

The problems of multilingualism were recognised, as Nahir says:

> It was precisely their linguistic fragmentation that brought many to the realisation that, if national unity was to be achieved, a state of multilingualism could not be allowed to continue, or that unification had to be both national and linguistic. In addition, the very existence of societal multilingualism brought about the need for a single communicative vehicle. (Nahir, 1983: 269)

In 1890, in Palestine, the council of Hebrew Languages (CHL) was formed by the intellectuals of Jerusalem. The aim of the council was to diffuse the Hebrew language and Hebrew speech among all classes of the people (Fainberg, 1983: 14). As late as 1904, though, only a few families in Jerusalem spoke Hebrew, and, in the settlements, languages other than Hebrew were predominant (Zuta, quoted in Nahir, 1983: 269). Also, throughout the first decade of the twentieth century the debate between the proponents of Hebrew and the proponents of Yiddish continued. This debate, however, was mainly centred in Europe and only to a much lesser degree in Palestine (Nahir, 1983: 273). In Palestine most of the immigrants 'strongly resented the necessity to use [Yiddish], as it constantly reminded them of their people's prolonged exile' (Nahir, 1983: 271). They also viewed Yiddish as a 'vulgar language' (Nahir, 1983: 271).

The revival of Hebrew was eventually successful and it became the national language. Two major problems remained, however. Firstly, a severe shortage of modern terminology in what had, till then, been a language used mainly for religious purposes; and secondly the difficulty of teaching in a language which most students did not know sufficiently well (Nahir, 1983: 277).

The CHL endeavoured to provide new words (neologisms) based on the Hebrew of the Torah and the Talmud where possible or else from Semitic, especially Aramaic, roots (Fainberg, 1983: 15). As well,

> neologisms created in any place in Israel and even abroad were addressed to the CHL in Jerusalem and its decisions were binding on all those who wished to use Hebrew. (Fainberg, 1983: 14)

The second problem was eventually overcome as Hebrew became the mother tongue of more and more children.

In 1953, a few years after the State of Israel was proclaimed, a law was passed to set up The Academy of the Hebrew Language (AHL). The AHL continued the work begun by the CHL and is still the formal body concerned with the needs of the Hebrew language. Its responsibilities cover Hebrew vocabulary, grammar, spelling and terminology and its decisions are to be adhered to by all government departments and educational and scientific institutes (Fainberg, 1983: 16). The decisions and neologisms from the AHL are published in the government gazette and distributed on posters to government offices, public buildings, schools and the mass media for dissemination to the public (Fainberg, 1983: 18).

According to Rabin (1983) there is a strong tendency in Israel towards normativism. By normativism Rabin means a set of rules for the usage of language based mainly on ancient sources. However, normativism is almost exclusively confined to the written language. As Rabin says, 'there is ... little effect of normativism upon the spoken language' (1983: 50). He also notes that even though 'correct Hebrew' (i.e. Hebrew spoken according to normative rules) is desired it is usually only found in formal speech and not in everyday use (Rabin, 1983: 50–1). It is perhaps worthy of note that Rabin considers that radio announcers use 'the most regimented form of Israeli speech' (1983: 46), that is, the most normativised form of speech.

One factor which may contribute to the normative aspect of Hebrew is that most migrants who do not speak Hebrew on arrival usually learn it formally in special courses called 'ulpan' courses (Rosenbaum, 1983). Also, since 'revived' Hebrew is comparatively young and since only about half of the Israeli population today are native speakers of Hebrew, the question of language is still important.

According to Cooper & Danet, there is little regional variation in Israeli Hebrew (1980: 5). Also, even though migrants from different parts of the world spoke Hebrew with different accents when they arrived, 'these differences appear to be disappearing in the second generation' (Cooper & Danet 1980: 6). And Rabin states that

> Hebrew does not have a language variety resembling the educated colloquial of most Western languages, and although there exist of course marked differences between the speech of the educated and the uneducated, both use largely the same non-normative grammatical colloquialisms. (Rabin, 1983: 50)

According to a study of Melbourne Jews by Klarberg, modern spoken Hebrew should be called 'Ivrit'. He says, 'Ivrit as a variety of Hebrew is not only distinct phonetically [from Classical Hebrew], it also has identifiable items of vocabulary and syntax' (1985: 58). Hetzron also notes that the differences between Modern Hebrew and the Hebrew of the Talmud are great enough to make it impossible for the person who knows one to understand the other without special study (1987b: 686). However, he adds that

> a partial understanding is indeed possible and the similarities are so obvious that calling them separate languages or two versions of the same tongue would be an arbitrary, only terminological decision. (Hetzron, 1987b: 686)

References

BIRNBAUM, S. A. 1979, *Yiddish: A Survey and a Grammar*. Manchester: Manchester University Press.
COOPER, R. and DANET, B. 1980, Language in the melting pot: The sociolinguistic context for language planning in Israel. *Language Problems and Language Planning* 4 (1), 1–28.
FAINBERG, Y. A. 1983, Linguistic and sociodemographic factors influencing the acceptance of Hebrew neologisms. *International Journal of the Sociology of Language* 41, 9–40.

FISHMAN, J. A. 1965, *Yiddish in America: Socio-Linguistic Description and Analysis*. Bloomington: Indiana (Indiana Research Centre in Anthropology, Folklore and Linguistics Series, No. 36).

GOLDSMITH, E. S. 1976, *Architects of Yiddishism at the Beginning of the Twentieth Century: A Study in Jewish Cultural History*. London: Associated University Presses.

HETZRON, R. 1987a, Afroasiatic languages. In: B. COMRIE (ed.) *The World's Major Languages* (pp. 645–53). London: Croom Helm.

HETZRON, R. 1987b, Hebrew. In: B. COMRIE (ed.) *The World's Major Languages* (pp. 686–704). London: Croom Helm.

KLARBERG, M. 1985, Hebrew and Yiddish in Melbourne. In: M. CLYNE (ed.) *Australia, Meeting Place of Languages* (pp. 57–62). Canberra: Pacific Linguistics (Series C. No. 92).

NAHIR, M. 1983, Sociocultural factors in the revival of Hebrew. *Language Problems and Language Planning* 7 (3), 263–84.

RABIN, C. 1983, The sociology of normativism in Israeli Hebrew. *International Journal of the Sociology of Language* 41, 41–56.

ROSENBAUM, Y. 1983, Hebrew adoption among new immigrants to Israel: The first three years. *International Journal of the Sociology of Language* 41, 115–30.

ROSTEN, L. 1968, *The Joys of Yiddish*. London: Penguin Books.

WEINREICH, M. 1980, *History of the Yiddish Language*. Chicago: The University of Chicago Press (Translated by S. Noble).

Hindi

Hindi is an Indo-Aryan language, a branch of the Indo-European family. Along with English, Hindi is the official language of India. It is also the state language of Bihar, Haryana, Himachal Pradesh, Madhya Pradesh, Rajasthan and Uttar Pradesh in northern India (Kachru, 1987: 470). Note: Hindi and Urdu are linguistically very similar, differing mainly in their learned vocabulary and script; therefore, the chapters on Hindi and Urdu overlap to a significant degree.

The Indo-Aryan languages have their origin in the migration of the Aryan peoples into India which began around 2000 BC. As Zograph notes,

> it would seem that the groups of Aryans who entered India were neither ethnically nor linguistically homogeneous, and that they brought with them not one single language but rather a collection of related dialects. (Zograph, 1982: 9)

The most ancient form of the Aryan's language which was written down was Vedic. Vedic, though, appears to reflect the spoken dialects of that time and, consequently, was not unified in its form (Zograph, 1982: 10).

During the first millenium BC a form known as Sanskrit evolved, and by about the fourth century BC a written form of Sanskrit had been standardised and codified, particularly in the work of the grammarian Panini (Zograph, 1982: 10–11). Once Sanskrit had been standardised it remained fixed and is still in use today in virtually the same form. The constitution of India lists Sanskrit as one of the most important languages of the country (Zograph, 1982: 11).

The spoken language, however, was not fixed and continued to evolve. Two major stages in the development of the Indo-Aryan languages from Sanskrit to the modern languages are usually discussed by scholars: these are the Prakrit and Apabhramsa stages. The Prakrits, meaning 'natural' or 'ordinary speech', are attested in several forms in different regions of northern India. These Prakrits were also used for literature, and one of them, Pali, became the language of Buddhism (Zograph, 1982: 12ff). The Prakrit known as Sauraseni, spoken in the western part of northern India is considered by Grierson to be the ancestor of Hindi (1968, Vol. IX: 2).

The Apabhramsas, meaning 'corrupted language', also developed different-ly in different regions. They formed the transition between the Prakrits and the modern Indo-Aryan languages (Zograph, 1982: 14). Like the Prakrits, the Apabhramsas were also used for literature (Zograph, 1982: 14).

The modern Indo-Aryan languages, often called New Indo-Aryan, evolved from about 1000 AD (Kachru, 1987: 470). These New Indo-Aryan languages did not evolve identically or discretely. The linguistic situation in northern India thus became, and has remained, complex. The distinction between language and dialect is often difficult to draw in this area (Kachru & Bhatia, 1978; Rai, 1984: 287ff). And as Zograph says:

> Local forms of speech change every few kilometers, but not sufficiently to make them incomprehensible to close neighbours. As distances increase so too do dialectal variations, until the actual transition to another language is made. Thus, from the Panjab to Bangladesh, there is not one single sharply defined linguistic boundary, although, according to the [Linguistic Survey of India], six languages represented by dozens of dialects merge, one into another, across this vast territory. (Zograph, 1982: 22)

Several of these New Indo-Aryan languages, such as Braj, or Brajbhasa, Rajasthani, Maithili, and Awadhi, were used for literature and developed into standardised literary forms (Kachru & Bhatia, 1978; McGregor, 1974: 62). The Devanagari script was usually used for this literature (McGregor, 1981: 4).

At about the same time that the New Indo-Aryan languages were evolving out of the Apabhramsa stage, i.e. the eleventh to thirteenth centuries, India was invaded by Persian Muslims (Rai, 1984: 284). Under the Muslims Persian, with a heavy admixture of Arabic, the language of Islam, became the language of law, administration and élite culture throughout most of northern India (Kachru & Bhatia, 1978: 48).

The name 'Hindi' originated with the Persians. McGregor says:

> The term 'Hindi' ... is not strictly a name of any of the chief dialects con-cerned, but rather an adjective, Persian in origin, meaning 'Indian', or more precisely, 'connected with north India' ... it was used from an early date by the Indian Muslims to refer to forms of speech which they encountered in north India. (McGregor, 1974: 62)

The question of whether the forms of speech and literature subsumed under the name 'Hindi' represented different languages or dialectal variations of a sin-gle language is problematic, and scholars do not appear to agree on this issue. Grierson, for example, divides Hindi into Eastern and Western and also consid-ers such forms as Bihari, Marathi, and Rajasthani among others as separate lan-guages (1968, Vol. VI, Vol. IX). Chatterji also considers Eastern and Western Hindi to be distinct, but classifies other forms differently from Grierson

(Chatterji cited in Zograph, 1982: 25ff). Whereas McGregor says, 'the Hindi literature of the centuries preceding 1800 is composed in *various related dialects*' (1974: 62, our emphasis). And Rai considers that 'it is imperative ... that we see the various local, dialectal forms of Hindi speech, quite incipient then, as one Hindi language' (1984: 123).

Whatever the classification, the important point to note is that the term Hindi, up to the nineteenth century was used to denote the forms of speech used by Indians and written in the Devanagari script, as opposed to Persian with a considerable admixture of Arabic, used as the language of law, administration and by the ruling Muslims, and written in the Perso-Arabic script.

Most of these New Indo-Aryan forms subsumed under the name Hindi were used by Indians living outside of urban areas and were both relatively local in area of usage and relatively free of cultural and linguistic influences from the Indo-Persians (McGregor, 1981: 4). However, one of these forms, variously known as Hindustani, Khari Boli, and also as Hindi, had evolved as a kind of *lingua franca* throughout northern India, particularly in the towns and cities (McGregor, 1974: 62; Kachru, 1987: 471).

This form of New Indo-Aryan was the dialect (or perhaps language) spoken around Delhi, where the Muslims had their first main area of settlement (McGregor, 1974: 62). It gradually adopted Persian and Arabic vocabulary, and came to be written in the Perso-Arabic script (McGregor, 1974: 62). In the eighteenth century this form of New Indo-Aryan was adopted by the Muslim court as their language of literature and the influx of Persian and Arabic vocabulary intensified (Zograph, 1982: 32; McGregor, 1981: 3). The literary form which developed was, according to Rai, 'purified' of Sanskrit elements (1984: 285), and continued to be written in the Perso-Arabic script. The name 'Urdu' was applied to this form (Kachru, 1987: 471; Mobbs, 1981: 205). The British, who took over northern India in the nineteenth century, gave Urdu the status of official legal and administrative language, while introducing English for higher government business and in the higher law courts (Kachru & Bhatia, 1978: 48; McGregor, 1974: 70).

However, Urdu was associated with Muslims, and, consequently, Hindus began using a version of Hindustani, or Khari Boli, written in the Devanagari script as a reaction to Urdu (Mobbs, 1981: 205). Although many of the New Indo-Aryan forms could have been used, the currency of the Hindustani, Khari Boli, form meant that 'it was inevitable that this should become the basis of the new style' (McGregor, 1974: 63).

Thus, from the same base as Urdu, a literary form known as Hindi, or High Hindi, developed in the nineteenth century. High Hindi was written in the Devanagari script, eschewed Persian and Arabic vocabulary, and looked to

Sanskrit, Prakrits and Apabhramsas for vocabulary and literary conventions (Kachru, 1987: 471). By 1900 Hindi had also gained official recognition in parts of northern India (Kachru & Bhatia, 1978: 48).

The association of Hindi with Hindus and Urdu with Muslims led to rivalry and antagonism between supporters of the two forms (Rai, 1984: 285–6; Kachru & Bhatia, 1978: 49). As a result, Hindi and Urdu came to be seen by some as two different languages (Mobbs, 1981: 205). On religious, social and political grounds there may be a case for considering Hindi and Urdu as different languages (Rai, 1984: 287ff), but on purely linguistic grounds there is far less of a case. As Zograph says, 'such grammatical differences as exist between Hindi and Urdu are insignificant' (1982: 33). The major differences are found in the vocabulary, and even here it is in the 'high' or literary forms that these differences are mostly manifest (Zograph, 1982: 33).

In their spoken forms Hindi and Urdu differ very little. As Mobbs puts it,

Urdu and Hindi may differ, in the spoken mode, in the selection of lexical items for certain word classes [e.g. nouns]; but the majority of words and all the grammatical elements in a text are common to both styles. (Mobbs, 1981: 209)

Also, many words of Persian origin were naturalised in Khari Boli before Hindi and Urdu split and still remain in the base form of both styles (Mobbs, 1981: 210, fn10).

In colloquial speech the inter-regional *lingua franca*, also based on Khari Boli, and usually called Hindustani, was in use till recently, if it is not still used. This form did not make use of either Persian/Arabic or extensive Sanskrit vocabulary (Zograph, 1982: 32; Kachru & Bhatia, 1978: 49). In the early twentieth century an attempt was made to use Hindustani as a bridge between the rival Hindi and Urdu camps. This attempt failed, however, because Hindustani was seen as merely a colloquial variety which could not fulfil the functions of a national language (Kachru & Bhatia, 1978: 49).

In the early part of this century, therefore, Hindustani, or colloquial Khari Boli, was in use as a *lingua franca* throughout most of northern India. Urdu, based on Khari Boli, written in the Perso-Arabic script and heavily influenced by Persian and Arabic vocabulary, was used by most Muslims. Hindi, also based on Khari Boli, written in the Devanagari script, eschewing Persian and Arabic influence in favour of Sanskrit borrowings was used by Hindus.

It must, however, be noted that the term Hindi as applied to the literary language developed since the nineteenth century refers to one specific, codified form of the New Indo-Aryan languages. Thus, Hindi, sometimes called High or standard Hindi, in this sense was developed as a reaction to Urdu in the nineteenth century, and with the gradual spread of education from mid-century and the ensuing growth of social and cultural consciousness and of patriotic feeling it [was] available as a vehicle for an increasing proportion of literary activity, and public use in general. (McGregor, 1974: 63)

The term Hindi also has another meaning. It is used as the collective term for a variety of related dialects (or languages) used in northern India (Zograph, 1982: 33). This is much the same sense as the term had when it was first used by the Persians to describe the speech forms which they encountered in northern India. It is in this sense that McGregor, for example, notes that

the more purely traditional literature which continued to be composed in Brajbhasa and other Hindi dialects in the nineteenth century is seen as an extension of the preceding period ... . (McGregor, 1974: 63)

When India gained independence in the 1940s Urdu became the official language of Pakistan, and Hindi, or rather High Hindi, became the official national language of India, alongside English. Hindi also became the state language of most of the states of northern India (Kachru, 1987: 470).

The use of High or Standard Hindi as the national and state language is, according to Sinha (1979), 'leading to a diglossic situation in the state of Bihar'. Sinha notes that Bihari Hindi differs from Standard Hindi in phonology, vocabulary and grammar, though the two are mutually intelligible (Sinha, 1979). Bihari Hindi is used in all colloquial situations, whereas Standard Hindi, learnt in school, is used for all writing and for formal speeches and so on (Sinha, 1979: 310). This is quite possibly also the case in other states such as Rajasthan (Kachru & Bhatia, 1978).

Sinha also points out that the form of Hindi used on All-India Radio, although it follows the written form in grammar and is therefore standardised, does not have any standardised form of pronunciation (1979: 302). It would appear, therefore, that Standard Hindi has a codified grammar and is used in writing and for formal situations, but many other dialects (or languages) are used in colloquial situations. And the pronunciation of Standard Hindi may be influenced by the particular mother tongue variety of a speaker, such that 'one can effortlessly know the linguistic background of a Hindi speaker of Bihar (i.e. whether he is a speaker of Bhojpuri, Bajjika, Maithili, etc). (Sinha, 1979: 302)

For Hindi, therefore, there are two senses in which this term is used. Firstly, as the name of the standardised literary language developed on the base of Khari Boli in the nineteenth century, and now the official national language of India and the state language of many states in northern India. Secondly, as the collective term for a variety of northern Indian dialects (or languages), such as Rajasthani, Maithili and so on, which differ from standard Hindi in pronunciation, vocabulary and grammar, and some of which have a literary form dating back hundreds of years. Kachru and Bhatia, in fact, consider that now that the

Hindi-Urdu rivalry has ended, there will emerge a 'dialect' conflict since 'some of the so-called dialects have begun to seek higher status' (1978: 50). The standard literary form of Hindi has a codified grammar, but not, apparently, a standard pronunciation. For most standard Hindi speakers, this form is learnt as a second 'high' language.

References

GRIERSON, G. A. 1968, *Linguistic Survey of India* Vol. VI and Vol. IX Pt. 1. Delhi: Motilal Banarsidoss.

KACHRU, Y. 1987, Hindi-Urdu. In: B. COMRIE (ed.) *The World's Major Languages* (pp. 470–89). London: Croom Helm.

KACHRU, Y. and BHATIA, T. K. 1978, The emerging 'dialect' conflict in Hindi: A case of glottopolitics. *International Journal of the Sociology of Language* 16, 47–58.

McGREGOR, R. S. 1974, *Hindi Literature of the Nineteenth and Early Twentieth Centuries*. Weisbaden: Otto Harrasowitz (Vol. VIII of J. Gonda (ed.) *A History of Indian Literature*).

McGREGOR, R. S. 1981, *A New Voice for New Times: The Development of Modern Hindi Literature*. Canberra: The Australian National University Press.

MOBBS, M. C. 1981, Two languages or one? The significance of the language names 'Hindi' and 'Urdu'. *Journal of Multilingual and Multicultural Development* 2 (3), 203–11.

RAI, A. 1984, *A House Divided: The Origin and Development of Hindi/Hindavi*. Delhi: Oxford University Press.

SINHA, P. 1979, Some linguistic features of Bihari Hindi. *Indian Linguistics* 40 (4), 301–11.

ZOGRAPH, G. A. 1982, *Languages of South Asia: A Guide*. London: Routledge and Kegan Paul (*Languages of Asia and Africa* Vol. 3).

Hungarian

Hungarian, or Magyar as it sometimes known, is a member of the Uralic, or Finno-Ugric language family (Austerlitz, 1987: 567). The Hungarians originally came from an area of what is today the USSR between the Volga River and the Ural mountains (Volgyes, 1982: 1). They settled in the area they now occupy towards the end of the ninth century AD (Macartney, 1962: 8; Volgyes, 1982: 1). Outside of Hungary the name 'Hungarian' is generally used to denote the language and people, whereas within Hungary and by Hungarians the name 'Magyar' is more often used (Hajdu, 1975: 111).

When the Hungarians arrived in what is now Hungary, it is probable that there were several tribes each of which spoke a slightly different dialect (Deme, 1972: 260). However, none of these dialects would have caused problems of comprehension for speakers of any of the other dialects (Imre, 1972: 309).

Up to the middle of the sixteenth century almost all religious and state affairs were conducted in Latin. This seems to have applied to both oral and written language since Hungarian was not considered to be a suitable language for any official usage (Deme, 1972: 264–5). However, there was a flourishing tradition of orally transmitted literature at the lower levels of society (Deme, 1972: 265).

With the advent of printing and the Reformation practice of translating the Bible and other religious works into the vernacular, more and more works began to appear in Hungarian. However, the printers did not set up a standard; they tended, instead, to let their personal usage prevail (Deme, 1972: 269).

According to Deme, the major influence towards a standard form came not from the religious or secular élite, but rather from scribes who were recruited from the lower as well as the higher levels of the population (1972: 271).

The political situation in Hungary also had an effect on the development of a standard form. The centre and south of the country was under Turkish rule from 1526 till the end of the seventeenth century. The east was under Austrian control, and therefore German was the prestigious language. It was only in the north-east and Transylvania that Hungarian was extensively used in writing. Of these two, it was the north-eastern form which came to predominate and was used as the basis for the first grammars of Hungarian (Deme, 1972: 270ff).

However, although Hungarian was used for literature, the influence of Latin and German was still considerable. Latin was the language of state administration and public service until 1830 (Macartney, 1962: 134). And German, due to Austria having assumed control of all of Hungary after the expulsion of the Turks, was the language of the urban, educated élite (Deme, 1972: 274). Nevertheless, by the early twentieth century the literary language based on the north-eastern variety had become the standard for all of Hungary. Its vocabulary had been enlarged and the spelling codified (Deme, 1972: 283ff). The separation of Hungary from Austria in 1920 meant that this form took over from German as the prestigious variety (Deme, 1972: 285)

The literary form also influenced the spoken language. From the sixteenth to the nineteenth century population movement caused by war and occupation had brought about considerable dialect mixing. This mixing had, in turn, led to the levelling out of marked dialectal features and the growth of regional vernaculars (Imre, 1972: 305). During the nineteenth century the literary language began to assume the position of a supra-regional variety which acted 'in the direction of a uniform standardisation of the common language' (Imre, 1972: 306).

However, the standardisation applied mainly to urban populations and not so much to the rural population. It is only in recent years that the spread of education, radio and television, and the industrialisation of rural areas has led to the diminishing use of dialect and an increase in the use of the standardised norm (Imre, 1972: 309).

In the urban centres, therefore, use of 'standard' Hungarian is the norm and in rural areas a situation has appeared where dialect is used in informal situations and the 'standard', or at least a close approximation of it, is used in more formal situations (Imre, 1972: 310). It should be remembered, though, that there are no problems of comprehension either between dialects themselves or between dialect and 'standard' Hungarian. According to Hajdu, the Hungarian language area can be divided into eight dialect regions. As he says, though, 'none of these is far removed from the standard literary language' (1975: 109).

The use of dialect at present seems to be taken as representing 'more backward, more conservative, and more under-developed social groups' (Deme, 1972: 290).

In 1920 certain areas of Hungary were ceded to Czechoslovakia, Romania and Yugoslavia. These areas contained a sizeable number of Hungarian speakers. However, according to Deme, these Hungarian speakers 'are doing their best to keep in step with the Hungarian standard' (1972: 293). Consequently, no major divergence in language is present although it appears that certain regional variations are evident (Deme, 1972: 293).

References

AUSTERLITZ, R. 1987, Uralic languages. In: B. COMRIE (ed.) *The World's Major Languages* (pp. 567–76). London: Croom Helm.

DEME, L. 1972, Standard Hungarian. In: L. BENKO and S. IMRE (eds) *The Hungarian Language*. The Hague: Mouton.

HAJDU, P. 1975, *Finno-Ugrian Languages and Peoples*. London: Andre Deutsch (Translated by G. F. Cushing).

IMRE, S. 1972, Hungarian dialects. In: L. BENKO and S. IMRE (eds) *The Hungarian Language*. The Hague: Mouton.

MACARTNEY, C. A. 1962, *Hungary: A Short History*. Edinburgh: Edinburgh University Press.

VOLGYES, I. 1982, *Hungary: A Nation of Contradictions*. Boulder, CO: Westview Press.

Indonesian

Indonesian, or Bahasa Indonesia as it is often called, is a language based on and developed from Malay (Anwar, 1980: 1). According to Henderson *et al.* it is based on a Sumatran variant of Malay (1970: 49). It is, therefore, a member of the Malay-Polynesian family of languages. Indonesian is used throughout the Indonesian archipelago though it is not the first language of the majority of Indonesians (Anwar, 1980: 1).

Within Indonesia there are many different ethnic groups and many different languages. Estimates of the number of distinct languages vary. The Indonesian Department of Information (1980) puts the number at between 150 and 250; while Henderson et.al. say there are between 250 and over 400 (1970: 87). Whatever the number may be, the fact is that most Indonesians have a language other than Indonesian as their mother tongue and the number of different languages is considerable.

Because of the multiplicity of languages a form of Malay was used for centuries, especially, but not exclusively, by sailors and traders, as a *lingua franca* (Alisjahbana, 1976: 32ff). Malay continued to be used as the *lingua franca* under the Dutch, who took control of the archipelago in the early seventeenth century. The Dutch used Malay for communicating with the Indonesian population and also within the governmental apparatus, though Dutch was the language of power and prestige (Alisjahbana, 1976: 35ff).

In the second half of the nineteenth century and the beginning of the twentieth the Dutch established primary and secondary schools, mainly in Java, for some of the Indonesian population. Many of these schools taught in Malay, though other indigenous languages such as Javanese, and Sundanese were also used. Dutch became a compulsory subject in the schools in the early 1900s. There were, however, special schools for the children of the élite where Dutch was first taught as a subject, and then, after 1914, Dutch was used as the sole medium of instruction (Alisjahbana, 1976: 35–6).

However, the Indonesian intelligentsia realised that Dutch, which was only fully accessible to the élite, could not be used to unify the mass of the people and thereby generate a force strong enough to challenge the colonial power. Thus, as Alisjahbana notes:

With the growing development of a consciousness of Indonesian nationality, and the rapid advances made by movements striving for Indonesian unity under the stimulus of this new consciousness, the use of Malay became increasingly widespread. (Alisjahbana, 1976: 39)

A literary form of Malay, written in the Arabic script, had been in use at the Sultan's court in Malacca and later at Riau-Johore from the sixteenth century (Prentice, 1987: 915–6). This form, nowadays known as 'Classical Malay', remained the standard for written Malay among a small élite till the first quarter of the twentieth century in Indonesia and until the 1950s in Malaysia, and it formed the basis from which Indonesian and Malaysian were developed (Prentice, 1987: 916).

By the 1920s mass political parties were using Malay; books on science and literature were being published in Malay; and many newspapers in Malay were available. In 1928, at the Second Congress of Indonesian Youth,

> the Youth of Indonesia took an oath to the effect that they belonged to one nation, the Indonesian nation, had one mother-country, Indonesia, and one language, the Indonesian language. (Alisjahbana, 1976: 39)

The name of the language was thus changed from Malay to Indonesian and in 1933 a magazine appeared which was designed to promote the Indonesian language and its literature (Alisjahbana, 1976: 40). The first Indonesian Language Congress was held in 1938 where it was decided that an institute and a faculty for the study of Indonesian had to be created to decide on technical terminology, to create a new orthography, and to codify a new grammar. However, under the Dutch none of these decisions could be carried out (Alisjahbana, 1976: 40).

When the Japanese landed in 1942 and seized power they abolished the use of Dutch. In consequence, since few, if any, Indonesians knew Japanese, Indonesian began to be used as the language of government, all education and the law, as well as the language of communication between different ethnic groups. A Commission on the Indonesian Language was set up to provide the language with new terminology and to compose a grammar to enable Indonesian to develop (Alisjahbana, 1976: 40–1). Also, according to Palmier it was during the Japanese occupation that the structure of the education system which is still in place today was established (1985: 67).

With the declaration of independence in 1945 the constitution stipulated that Indonesian would be the official language, thereby ratifying what had effectively been the case since 1942. However, the Dutch refused to hand over sovereignty and a war of independence began which lasted till 1949 (Anwar, 1980: 52ff). The Indonesian language became a symbol of nationalism, and, as Anwar notes,

> it was during the period of guerilla warfare that the spread of Indonesian into the villages took place more significantly. (Anwar, 1980: 62)

The rapid expansion of the use of Indonesian caused its own problems, however. In 1952 one Indonesian writer noted:

> Bahasa Indonesia today is facing enormous problems of various kinds. Each ethnic group has been giving a certain characteristic to the unitary language. This is not limited to the vocabulary but also involves the morphology, the phonology as well as the syntax of Indonesian. As a result, the language is becoming a confusing language. (Nasution quoted in Anwar, 1980: 113)

The situation was further complicated by the fact that many journalists, writers and public figures had had little or no formal training in Indonesian. In consequence, 'everybody tended to use his local variety of Indonesian in the absence of a satisfactory standard language' (Alisjahbana, 1976: 78).

However, the efforts of the language planners and the introduction of a new grammar into the education system has meant that the standard is now being disseminated more. As Alisjahbana says:

> The whole education in Indonesia from primary school to university has been conducted in the Indonesian language since the Japanese occupation. A whole generation has thus studied the language in school. This is the reason why (although the deviating forces are very strong; for the great majority of the Indonesians the Indonesian language is not their mother tongue) it can be said that gradually the Indonesian language has been satisfactorily transformed from a pidgin-like *lingua franca* into an official modern language, which is steadily developing in richness as well as in standardisation. (Alisjahbana, 1976: 106)

Indonesian in its written form is now fairly well standardised. Henderson *et al.* note that

> what may be called 'literary Indonesian' or 'standard Indonesian' as it appears in written materials — newspapers and books — and in formal speeches, is much the same everywhere, though with some regional differences in vocabulary. (Henderson *et al.*, 1970: 108)

But in some areas standardisation has yet to be achieved. According to Anwar:

> In practice in higher education practically every lecturer produces and uses his own Indonesian terminologies for his own field which are not necessarily acceptable to other professors in the same field. Sometimes attempts are made to standardise terminologies in use in one particular university but again these terminologies are not necessarily acceptable to or even understood by colleagues in other universities. (Anwar, 1980: 101)

For the written language several spelling reforms have been proposed and adopted since 1942. The last, and the spelling system currently in use, was adopted and made official in 1972. The writing system makes use of the Latin alphabet and this has caused some problems for the spelling of words of Arabic origin (Anwar, 1980: 82ff). The majority of Indonesians learn to read and write primarily, if not entirely, in Indonesian rather than their ethnic language, and are, therefore, 'more at ease when reading and writing in Bahasa Indonesia ...' (Isman, 1981: 199).

While the written language has attained a fairly high degree of standardisation this does not appear to be the case for the spoken language. In 1974 the director of the Institute of Language Development in Jakarta wrote:

> Observation of Bahasa Indonesia reveals that written Bahasa Indonesia differs from spoken Bahasa Indonesia to such an extent that an attempt to account for both by a single unified approach would be extremely complex, if not impossible. (Halim quoted in Anwar, 1980: 146–7)

However, as Anwar remarks:

> From the point of view of language use the differences in the varieties of Indonesian pose no difficult problems ... . It stands to reason that the majority of speakers use the national language with a trace of interference from their regional languages and this phenomenon is more pronounced among less-educated Indonesians ... . Non-educated speakers tend to use more words and grammatical elements borrowed from their regional languages when called upon to talk in Indonesian, but this practice in general is perfectly acceptable. It is also acceptable to talk in mixed languages using some sentences or part of a sentence in one language and others in another. As a matter of fact, even educated speakers, no matter from what ethnic background, are used to conversing among themselves in mixed languages. (Anwar, 1980: 147)

Indonesian, as a spoken language within any particular ethnic group, has restricted areas of use. In general it is used only in the more formal situations. For example, Walker notes that in a town in Irian Jaya Indonesian is used only for public information in formal settings, school, and government relations (1982: 85); Kumanireng says that 'Bahasa Indonesia ... is used in matters which are academic, philosophical and professional in nature' (1982: 132); and McGinn says that in southern Sumatra Indonesian is used for speeches and social functions of any formality (1982: 1). In other situations the regional language or a form of Malay, i.e. the language used previously as a *lingua franca* before Indonesian was developed and standardised, will be used.

However, as a vehicle of inter-ethnic communication Indonesian is extensively used. It is also used in government circles and as the medium for radio, TV, films and stage productions (Isman, 1981: 200). It is possible, though, that there will be a certain amount of variation from region to region, especially perhaps in vocabulary, though also in grammar as noted above.

The fact that younger Indonesians tend to have greater facility in Indonesian is shown by a study conducted by Sutomo. The study found that Javanese teachers in the 25–35 age group tended to have a better knowledge of Indonesian terminology and structure than teachers in the 45–55 age group (Sutomo, 1982: 116–7). These findings would appear to support the view that knowledge of a standardised form of Indonesian is increasing.

As far as a standardised spoken form of Indonesian is concerned, Anwar says:

> The use of Indonesian by educated people living in big towns such as Jakarta, Bandung, Medan, etc, has brought about the establishment of modern colloquial prestige Indonesian. The 'standard' variety of this colloquial Indonesian is undoubtedly connected with the speech prevalent in the capital, but this should not be confused with what has been generally called Bahasa Jakarta, Jakarta Indonesian. The real Jakarta speech ... is now regarded as rural speech and not a prestigious colloquial Indonesian. (Anwar, 1980: 154)

But Muhadjir says that the Jakarta dialect is becoming more important and prestigious than it used to be and is beginning to be used in newspapers, on the radio, and in films, though mainly in more informal situations. Also, according to Muhadjir, many young people from other regions are beginning to use the Jakarta dialect (1981: 6).

Also, Alisjahbana notes that there are still problems of standardisation to be overcome. He says:

> It is the dialect of Jakarta, the spoken language in daily life and the language of the press, which are the strongest impediments to a stricter standardisation of the official language ... The spoken language and the language of the press are not yet fully standardised since so many officials and editors still do not have a good command of the language. (Alisjahbana, 1976: 122)

The full standardisation of the language, therefore, appears to be some way off, though it is possible that as more Indonesians complete their education solely in Indonesian this situation may gradually change. At the present time it appears that it is the speech of the educated Indonesians in the capital city which is accepted as the model of the language which people in other areas try to imitate (Anwar, 1980: 185).

Although the speech of the urban educated population is seen by many as the standard to be aspired to, it is perhaps the case that the linguistic diversity of the population as a whole will make this difficult to achieve. As Henderson *et al.* note:

> Spoken ... Indonesian differs from place to place, as would be expected in

the multilingual environment of the islands. There is a tendency for non-Malays to translate directly from their native speech into Indonesian. The practice rarely leads to misunderstanding, but it does make for noticeable differences in grammar and in the selection of words. Such differences are often a source of arguments concerning what constitutes correct Indonesian. (Henderson *et al.*, 1970: 108)

It should be noted that the Indonesian language and the official language of Malaysia are very similar. They both used Malay as the basis for the official language and the 1972 spelling reform was adopted by both countries to bring their orthography together. The major differences are in coining new terms, Indonesia borrows from Arabic, Sanskrit, English and Dutch, whereas Malaysia borrows principally from Arabic and English (Alisjahbana, 1976: 42ff, 80ff). The Malaysian form of the language is also used in Singapore and Brunei.

References

ALISJAHBANA, S. T. 1976, *Language Planning for Modernization: The Case of Indonesian and Malaysian*. The Hague: Mouton.

ANWAR, K. 1980, *Indonesian: The Development and Use of a National Language*. Yogyakarta: Gadjah Mada University Press.

DEPARTMENT OF INFORMATION 1980, *Indonesia: An Official Handbook*. Indonesia: Directorate for Foreign Information Services.

HENDERSON, J. W. *et al.* 1970, *Area Handbook for Indonesia*. Washington: US Government Printing Office.

ISMAN, J. 1981, The role of the national language in fostering national identities in Indonesia. In: A. HALIM (ed.) *Bahasa Dan Pembangunan Bangsa* (pp. 185–210). Jakarta.

KUMANIRENG, T. Y. 1982, Diglossia in Larantuka, Flores. In: A. HALIM, L. CARRINGTON and S. A. WURM (eds) *Papers from the Third International Conference on Austronesian Linguistics* (pp. 131–6). Canberra: The Australian National University (Pacific Linguistics, Series C. No 76).

McGINN, R. 1982, Outline of Rejang syntax. *NUSA Linguistic Studies in Indonesian and Other Languages in Indonesia* 14.

MUHADJIR 1981, Morphology of Jakarta dialect, affixation and reduplication. *NUSA Linguistic Studies in Indonesian and Other Languages in Indonesia* 11.

PALMIER, L. 1985, National integration. In L. PALMIER (ed.) *Understanding Indonesia* (pp. 66–81). Aldershot, England: Gower.

PRENTICE, D. J. 1987, Malay (Indonesian and Malaysian). In: B. COMRIE (ed.) *The World's Major Languages* (pp. 913–35). London: Croom Helm.

SUTOMO, I. 1982, Some sociocultural factors as determinants of language proficiency. In: A. HALIM, L. CARRINGTON and S. A. WURM (eds) *Papers from the Third International Conference on Austronesian Linguistics* (pp. 115–22). Canberra: The Australian National University (Pacific Linguistics, Series C. No 76).

WALKER, R. 1982, Language use at Namatota: A sociolinguistic profile. In A. HALIM, L. CARRINGTON and S. A. WURM (eds) *Papers from the Third International Conference on Austronesian Linguistics* (pp. 79–94). Canberra: The Australian National University (Pacific Linguistics, Series C. No 76).

Irish Gaelic

Irish Gaelic, more commonly known as Irish, is a Celtic language. At one time Celtic peoples occupied virtually the whole of Europe. However, they were gradually displaced or assimilated by the territorial advances of other peoples, such as the Nordic and Germanic tribes from the north and the Romans from the south (Gregor, 1980: 1ff).

By about 300 BC the Celtic language had split into two main dialects: Brythonic and Goidelic. Brythonic speakers were the first to arrive in the British Isles and, according to Gregory, they imposed their language on most of the area, including Ireland (1980: 21).

However, when Caesar invaded Gaul between 58 and 50 BC, Goidelic speakers fled from there to Ireland where they displaced the Brythonic speakers. It is from the Goidelic branch of Celtic, therefore, that Irish is descended (Gregor, 1980: 23, 704ff).

Irish evolved an alphabet of its own prior to the fifth century AD. This alphabet, known as Ogham, was used for writing on stone and probably also on wood (Greene, 1972: 8–9). However, Greene believes that Ogham was 'in fact only a sort of cipher based on the Latin alphabet ...'(1972: 9).

In the fifth century the coming of Christianity brought Latin and the Latin alphabet to Ireland. Writing in Irish, though, began in earnest in the seventh century (Greene, 1972: 10), and by the ninth century the learned classes, based mainly in monasteries, had brought about a standardisation of the language. The standard form from this time is known as Old Irish (Greene, 1972: 12). The 'Gaelic script' used for writing Irish was based on the Latin alphabet, but contained only 18 letters. This script was used to write Irish till well into this century (O Cuív, 1973: 7, 20).

This form of the language received a setback when Ireland was invaded by the Norwegians and Danes in the middle of the ninth century, and many Irish scholars were forced to flee (Gregor, 1980: 108).

However, the works produced during this period were used as the basis of traditional learning until at least the twelfth century. As O Cuív notes

> Old Irish ... regarded as an important element of Irish traditional learning, was studied down to the twelfth century, and probably even

later. (O Cuív, 1973: 2)

Greene, though, says that

> The Middle Irish period (900–1200) represents the struggle between the
> evolving speech of the people and older standards upheld by scholars
> who had neither the knowledge nor the authority to enforce them.
> (Greene, 1972: 12)

The Irish literary language, therefore, appears to have undergone a period
of transition between 900 and 1200 AD. By about the beginning of the
thirteenth century a new form of the literary language, known as Early
Modern or Classical Irish had evolved (Greene, 1972: 12; O Cuív, 1973: 3).
This standard literary form was maintained by a group of 'learned laymen'
who earned their living by writing and selling poetry in praise of the
aristocracy (Greene, 1972: 12).

The spoken language, at this time, had begun to change considerably.
According to O Cuív, the pronunciation, grammar, and vocabulary of the spoken
language began to change from the twelfth century on. The changes were not
uniform throughout the country, though; rather, 'dialectal differences became
more marked since the developments did not take place at the same time or in
the same way in all areas' (O Cuív, 1973: 4).

As a consequence, the spoken language diverged more and more from the
standard literary language (O Cuív, 1973: 23) till eventually anyone who wished
to write in Irish would have to undertake special study to learn the literary language. According to O Cuív:

> The amount of detail [a writer] would have to assimilate before he could
> claim to know the standard language at all well was considerable. His
> course of training would include matters pertaining to phonetics, phonolo-
> gy, morphology, syntax, vocabulary and metrics. (O Cuív, 1973: 4)

According to O'Rahilly, the professional writers who maintained the literary language with all of its 'archaic and obsolete' features 'belonged exclusively
to the upper classes' (1972: 251–2).

When, in the seventeenth century, the Irish aristocracy was destroyed by the
English the literary language also began to decay. As O'Rahilly puts it,

> deprived of their remaining patrons, the literary class succumbed also, and
> with them the old literary language, both in prose and verse, may be said to
> have come to an end. (O'Rahilly, 1972: 254)

Or, as Greene says,

> after the battle of Kinsale in 1601, the Irish aristocracy was ruined and with
> it the scholars who had maintained the standard language; from that point

onwards the classical language begins to decay, and the dialects of the people to take its place. (Greene, 1972: 12)

The form of the language used for literature, therefore, moved closer to the
spoken language. According to O'Rahilly:

> in the seventeenth century, especially in its second half, we see the speech
> of the people beginning to leave its mark on the literature, especially in the
> South. Of prose-writing there was little after the Cromwellian epoch; but in
> verse the change to the new order was very striking. (O'Rahilly, 1972: 255)

However, as O'Rahilly also notes,

> in the greater part of the country the cultivation of Irish literature soon fell
> into complete neglect, or at best was left to an isolated individual here and
> there. (O'Rahilly, 1972: 254)

Thus, in the seventeenth century Irish literature declined, and the literary
language fragmented into forms influenced by the various dialects. At that time
there were probably three major dialect groups; one group in southern Ireland
and two in the north. These groups, though, were characterised by considerable
variety in actual usage (O'Rahilly, 1972: 259ff).

The seventeenth century also marked the beginning of the introduction of
English into Ireland and the decline in the Irish language generally. Edwards
says,

> between 1600 and 1800 English grew in influence, and became the lan-
> guage of regular communication for about half the population; increasingly,
> it became the language of status and power. (Edwards, 1984: 269)

And O Domhnallain notes that:

> the English language was introduced, and with such success that by the
> year 1851 ... only one and a half million people, 23% of the total popula-
> tion, were recorded as Irish speakers. From that time forward, under the
> influence of English rule and of an English-medium education system
> which entirely excluded the Irish language, the decline in the use of that
> language continued. (O Domhnallain, 1977: 84)

There were no doubt many reasons, social, political, and religious, for the
rapid decline in the use of Irish. However, in the late nineteenth century a movement for the revival of Irish began. The Society for the Preservation of the Irish
Language was formed in 1876, and in 1880 the Gaelic Union was formed
(Edwards, 1984: 269). But Edwards considers that it was in 1893, with the
founding of the Gaelic League, that the revival effort really began (1984: 269).

By this time, as noted above, the number of native Irish speakers was relatively small. Also, it appears that the majority of these speakers resided in areas

on the west and south coasts of Ireland known as the Gaeltacht (Gregor, 1980: 293ff). Even in the Gaeltacht, the Irish speaking areas, literacy in Irish was almost non-existent (MacAodha, 1972: 27).

The Gaelic League attempted to alter this state of affairs by providing Irish language classes in non-Gaeltacht areas and by providing reading material and literacy classes in both the Gaeltacht and non-Gaeltacht areas (MacAodha, 1972: 22ff).

With the revival of interest in literature in Irish, it was necessary to provide the language with a new literary form. Some scholars argued for a return to the old Classical language while others advocated a literary language based on the natural speech of the time. The debate was won by the proponents of a language based on the natural speech of the people. However, this led to works, especially schoolbooks, being published in different dialect versions and it is only in the last thirty years that an official standard for the whole of Eire has been imposed (Greene, 1972: 13ff).

After the establishment of the Irish Free State in 1922 the state took over much of the work of the Gaelic League in attempting to revive Irish. One of the first acts of the new national government was to adapt the primary education system into a vehicle to bring about the restoration of the Irish language (O Domhnallain, 1977: 85). As well, Irish was made the first official language of the state with English as the second official language (MacNamara, 1971: 76).

Irish, therefore, was made the medium of instruction in all primary schools, a compulsory subject in secondary schools, and all civil servants were required to have a knowledge of Irish (MacNamara, 1971). In the Gaeltacht areas, though, all schooling both primary and secondary was, and still is, conducted through the medium of Irish and English is taught only as a subject (O Domhnallain, 1977: 88).

Despite these efforts Irish has continued to decline. A survey carried out by the Committee on Language Attitudes Research found that only 9% of the population have 'high verbal competence' in Irish, though 30% have a 'moderate ability'. Also, the 1971 census records that

> the number of Irish speakers recorded as living in Irish speaking areas [the Gaeltacht] was given as 55,440, that is approximately 1.9% of the total population. (O Domhnallain, 1977: 84).

The Gaeltacht today occupies three non-contiguous areas, mainly on the west coast. But, as Howell notes, 'each of Ireland's three Gaeltacht areas is a separate subculture with its own distinctive Gaelic dialect' (1982: 41). The three dialects are: Ulster, in the north west; Connemara in the center; and Munster in the south. The dialects are mutually intelligible, the major differences being certain vocabulary items and pronunciation. The radio broadcasts in these areas in

Irish are tending to ensure, however, that speakers of one dialect are familiar with the vocabulary of the others. There is also minor variation within each dialect (Coll, 1987).

Thus, in Ireland today Irish is still spoken in the three Gaeltacht areas as a native language, but the majority, if not all, Irish speakers are bilingual with English as their second language. Throughout the rest of Eire, Irish is taught as a school subject and a knowledge of Irish is required for certain positions, such as the civil service.

There is now a standardised written form of Irish based on all three of the surviving dialects and used throughout the education system. In the spoken language there is no standard form, nor is there a prestigious dialect; all of the three dialects are apparently equal in status. It is possible, though, that the use of a standardised written form in schools may lead to this form being seen as the standard spoken form as well. What prestige there is in Irish appears to attach to speakers who speak Irish as a native language as opposed to those who have learnt it as a second language even though they may be fluent (Coll, 1987).

References

COLL 1987, Department of English, University of Sydney, personal communication.

EDWARDS, J. 1984, Irish: Planning and preservation. *Journal of Multilingual and Multicultural Development* 5 (3–4), 267–75.

GREENE, D. 1972, *The Irish Language*. Cork: Mercier Press (The Cultural Relations Committee of Ireland).

GREGOR, D. B. 1980, *Celtic: A Comparative Study*. Cambridge: The Oleander Press.

HOWELL, J. W. J. 1982, Bilingual broadcasting and the survival of authentic culture in Wales and Ireland. *Journal of Communication* 32 (4), 39–54.

MACAODHA, B. S. 1972, Was this a social revolution? In: S. O'TUAMA (ed.) *The Gaelic League Idea* (pp. 20–30). Cork: The Mercier Press.

MACNAMARA, J. 1971, Successes and failures in the movement for the restoration of Irish. In: J. RUBIN and B. H. JERNUDD (eds) *Can Language be Planned?* (pp. 65–94). Honolulu: The University Press of Hawaii.

O CUIV, B. 1973, *The Linguistic Training of the Mediaeval Irish Poet*. Dublin: Dublin Institute for Advanced Studies.

O DOMHNALLAIN, T. 1977, Ireland: The Irish language in education. *Language Problems and Language Planning* 1 (2), 83–96.

O'RAHILLY, T. F. 1972, *Irish Dialects Past and Present*. Dublin: Dublin Institute for Advanced Studies.

Italian

Italian is a Romance language, a member of the Indo-European family of languages. Although it is common practice to use the name 'Italian' for the linguistic entity used by Italians, the linguistic situation in Italy is in fact extremely complex. As Vincent puts it:

> While there is now, almost a century and a quarter after political unification, a fair measure of agreement on the grammar and the morphology and, to a lesser extent, on the phonology and lexis of the standard language as used in the written and spoken media and as taught in schools and to foreigners, it is still far from being the case that Italians speak only, or in many instances even principally, Italian. (Vincent, 1987: 279)

Italian is descended from Latin. However, after the fall of the Roman empire, the spoken Latin of everyday use, often called Vulgar Latin, evolved into a series of related but different varieties. Some of these varieties, especially those in the north-west of what is today Italy, are actually closer to those of southern French forms than to what is today known as Italian (Vincent, 1987: 279).

These varieties, generally called 'the Italian dialects', continued to evolve and some of them had developed their own literary traditions by the thirteenth century (Vincent, 1987: 280). In the fourteenth century, one of these varieties, or dialects, Tuscan, was used by Dante and other major writers and this 'ensured that literary, and thus linguistic, pre-eminence should go to Tuscan' (Vincent, 1987: 280).

The history of what is today known as Italian, though it should perhaps be called 'standard Italian', thus begins in the fourteenth century with the Tuscan–Florentine dialect. The supremacy of Tuscan was, however, not conceded without considerable debate. Debate over what came to be called 'the language question' continued for several centuries, but the prestige of Tuscan meant that most literature was written in that dialect (Vincent, 1987: 280–1).

After the unifiction of Italy in 1861, Tuscan was chosen as the linguistic standard to be used in the new national school system (Vincent, 1987: 280–1). This 'standard' language, though, was at this time limited to the élite. As Devoto says up to the middle of the nineteenth century the Italian literary language had not been the language of a nation, but rather that of a caste of 'litterati' or an oligarchy. (Devoto, 1978: 278)

The 'dialects' were still the major means of communication between people. As Clivic remarks:

As far as language is concerned, it has been calculated reliably that, about 1861, no more than two and one-half per cent of the population could speak Italian. This corresponds to little more than 600,000 people out of a total population that was then in excess of 25 million. The extent to which Italian was actually unknown in Italy is evidenced even more strikingly by the fact that, of those who could speak the national language, only 210,000 lived outside of Tuscany (70,000 of them in Rome). (Clivic, 979: 38)

With the spread of secondary schooling, conscription into the armed services, and the increase in mass media, the literary language began to be diffused among the people of Italy. However, it is still the case that Italians learn a dialectal variety as their first language and 'standard' Italian as a second language. Mioni and Arnuzzo-Lansweert say 'that a recent poll shows that about 25% of Italians claim to be fluent in Italian only, 7% in dialect only, and the remainder in both Italian and dialect' (1979: 95). In 1982, though, opinion polls recorded that over 50% of those interviewed claimed that their first language was 'standard Italian' rather than a dialect (Vincent, 1987: 281).

In Italy today, therefore, there is an opposition between 'standard' Italian and the dialects. The linguistic situation, however, is more complex than a simple dichotomy. Cardona, for example, differentiates four codes used in Italy today. These are: a purely dialectal level, e.g. Sardinian or Piedmontese among others; what he terms 'dialectal Italian', which is essentially a regional dialect but incorporating features of 'standard Italian'; regional Italian, basically 'standard' Italian but with many features from the dialects; and common, or 'standard' Italian, which has minimal or no peculiar regional features (Cardona, 1976: 3). And Vincent discusses 'popular Italian', 'a kind of national substandard, a language which is neither the literary norm nor yet a dialect tied to a particular town or region' (1987: 281).

It should be noted, though, that these codes, or types of Italian, are not discrete entities with clearly defined boundaries. Rather, as Vincent puts it,

for most speakers it is a question of ranging themselves at some point of a continuum from standard Italian through regional Italian and regional dialect to the local dialect, as circumstances and other participants seem to warrant. (Vincent, 1987: 281)

It is also worth noting that some of the local varieties may cause problems of comprehension for speakers of other varieties.

As well, as Cardona points out, though, common (or standard) Italian may be uniform in its written form but in the spoken form,

> owing to its recent spreading and to the fact that it is the mother tongue of only a minority of Italians, Standard Italian is by no means uniform throughout the country. (Cardona, 1976: 4).

This point is made somewhat more forcefully by Andreoni who says:

> In Italy today, almost everyone speaks the national language with his own regional accent, with differences in pronunciation and vocabulary that do not create serious communication problems. Teachers ... who believe that the correct Italian pronunciation is that of a certain 'well-to-do' class in Florence should spend a few hours in a Roman school, or listen to lectures at Naples University or turn on the radio or television in Bologna. The range of spoken varieties belies the existence of an agreed standard. (Andreoni in Introduction to Leoni, 1981: ix)

The linguistic situation in Italy, therefore, is somewhat complex. The dialects continue to hold sway as the first language of many Italians. Most people, though, learn 'standard' Italian as a second language and speak it with a greater or lesser degree of regional variation. There would also appear to be a considerable intermediate area where dialectal features impinge on the 'standard' language.

In English speaking countries to which Italians have emigrated the situation is further complicated by the influence of English. In a survey conducted for the Austalian Department of Immigration and Ethnic Affairs it was found that of the Italians surveyed, 9% used formal (or 'standard') Italian most often, 24% used dialect only, 26% used dialect and English, 34% used what the report calls 'new idiom' (i.e. English words incorporated into Italian grammar), and 7% used English most often (Vasta, 1985: 24).

The high use of dialect and even higher use of 'new idiom' would appear to be important factors in understanding Italian in migrant communities. In the Australian situation Bettoni considers that

> Australian Italian, at present characterised by a base of Italian dialects, popular Italian and Standard Italian and by different kinds and amounts of transference from English, is doomed precisely because of its characteristics. (Bettoni, 1981: 113)

Leoni, on the other hand, in discussing 'Austral-Italian', i.e. Italian grammar and syntax but with lexical, morphological and phonetic borrowings from English, says that this form is '... a phenomenon of no mean size, it is indeed a vivacious and robust linguistic reality' (1981: xxii).

Bettoni and Gibbons recently surveyed the attitudes of Italians in Australia to different types of Italian commonly used by Australian Italians. They found that dialects (in this study Sicilian and Venetian were used) and speech forms which mixed dialect and numerous English elements were viewed negatively by their respondents, whereas the variety they call 'regional Italian', i.e. a form close to the written standard, but still revealing a speakers' region of origin, was considered prestigious (Bettoni & Gibbons, forthcoming).

In Italy, therefore, there is a standard form, based on the Tuscan regional dialect which is used as the literary language throughout the country, and as the standard spoken form. In its spoken form, though, standard Italian differs from region to region. As well as the standard form there are also regional dialects (such as Venetian, Sicilian, Piedmontese) which developed during the same period as Tuscan but, although some developed literary forms, they did not gain the same prestige as Tuscan and are now used mostly as spoken forms. Many Italians still have one of these regional dialects as their first language, and learn standard Italian as a second language. The linguistic situation is further complicated by the fact that most speakers can range along a continuum between their local variety of a regional dialect and an approximation to the standard, though it appears that 'pure' standard Italian exists only as a written language. In English speaking countries to which Italians have migrated, the intrusion of English has made the linguistic forms used by Italians even more complex.

References

BETTONI, C. 1981, *Italian in North Queensland — Changes in the Speech of First and Second Generation Bilinguals.* Townsville: James Cook University.
BETTONI, C. and GIBBONS, J. Forthcoming, Linguistic purism and language shift. *International Journal of the Sociology of Language.*
CARDONA, G. P. 1976, *Standard Italian.* The Hague: Mouton.
CLIVIC, G. P. 1979 The development of the Italian language and its dialects. In: S. B. CHANDLER and J. A. MOLINARO (eds) *The Culture of Italy — Medieval to Modern* (pp. 25–41). Toronto: Griffin House.
DEVOTO, G. 1978, *The Languages of Italy* Chicago: The University of Chicago Press (Translated by V. L. Katainen).
LEONI, F. 1981, *Vocabolario Australitaliano.* Armidale: The University of New England.
MIONI, A. M. and ARNUZZO-LANSWEERT, A. M. 1979, Sociolinguistics in Italy. *International Journal of the Sociology of Language* 21, 81–107.
VASTA, E. 1985, *If You Had Your Time Again, Would You Migrate To Australia? — A Study of Long-Settled Italo-Australians in Brisbane.* Canberra: Australian Government Publishing Service (Dept. of Immigration and Ethnic Affairs).
VINCENT, N. 1987, Italian. In: B. COMRIE (ed.) *The World's Major Languages* (pp. 279–302). London: Croom Helm.

Japanese

Several hypotheses have been presented which attempt to assign Japanese to a variety of language families (Shibatani, 1987: 856). None of these hypotheses, though, appears to be very persuasive, but it is possible that Japanese is related to the Altaic family of languages and is probably remotely related to Korean (Shibatani, 1987: 856–7; Encyclopaedia Britannica, 1985: 750). Crystal, however, considers that Japanese is an isolate language; that is, it forms a language family with only a single member (1987: 439). Japanese is spoken principally in Japan, though there are some migrant communities, particularly in North and South America, which have maintained Japanese (Encyclopaedia Britannica, 1985: 750).

The origins of Japanese are also uncertain. One hypothesis posits that the ancestor of Japanese was brought from the Asian mainland to Kyushu, one of the Japanese islands, by the Yayoi culture about 2,000 years ago, and quickly spread through the other islands. A second, and more probable, hypothesis is that Japanese separated from Korean at least 5,000 years ago and that the Proto-Japanese form spoken by the Yayoi culture was merely one of a number of early forms, but one which gradually absorbed or squeezed out all the other forms as it spread outwards from Kyushu (Encyclopaedia Britannica, 1985: 750). Nevertheless, Japanese was, according to some of the earliest writings, and still is characterised by considerable dialect diversity (Encyclopaedia Britannica, 1985: 750–1; Shibatani, 1987: 860).

From about the fifth or sixth century, and possibly even earlier, Chinese culture began to be studied in Japan, including Chinese philosophy and Buddhism (Habein, 1984: 7–8). According to Inoue, interest in things Chinese took root in the first century AD when Confucianism was taught by Korean scholars, and Buddhism was introduced in the sixth century (1979: 243–4).

Along with other things Chinese, the Japanese also adopted the Chinese system of writing, using characters. The earliest Japanese written works dating from the eighth century were written in Chinese characters, known in Japanese as *kanji*, and often in the Chinese style using Chinese syntax (Habein, 1984: 8; Shibatani, 1987: 857). The Chinese style of writing remained the official Japanese system of writing for the Japanese court for several hundred years (Habein, 1984; Encyclopaedia Britannica, 1985: 753).

The use of Chinese characters, or *kanji*, and the practice of reading them by using a Japanese approximation of the way they were pronounced in Chinese led to a considerable amount of borrowing of vocabulary from Chinese (Shibatani, 1987: 857; Inoue, 1979: 244). In other words, when a character was introduced into Japan it was given a reading which imitated the pronunciation used in Chinese, and consequently many Chinese words were introduced into Japanese. The reading of a character in imitation of the original Chinese pronunciation is known as the *on* reading (Chaplin & Martin 1969: 2).

However, the *kanji* could, and usually did, also have a reading using the native Japanese word with the same, or a similar, meaning as the Chinese word. That is, the same character could be read in two ways: one using an imitation of the Chinese word, the *on* reading, and the second, called the *kun* reading, using a native Japanese word with the same meaning as the Chinese borrowing (Shikatani, 1987: 857; Chaplin & Martin, 1969: 2).

As well, very shortly after their introduction to Japan, the Chinese characters began to be used phonetically to write Japanese. In this case a *kanji* was used for its sound value only, ignoring its meaning (Shikatani, 1987: 857; Habein, 1984: 22ff). When a *kanji* is used as a phonetic symbol only it is called a *kana* (Miller, 1986: 11).

During the ninth century two forms of *kana* were developed. One of them, called *katakana*, was developed primarily by priests as an aid to reading Chinese texts (Habein, 1984: 22ff). Originally the priests used complete characters but this was found to be inconvenient and they therefore began to develop their own personal simplified characters (Habein, 1984: 23). By the tenth century, though, a uniform set of simplified characters was in use, and these were used alongside the *kanji* to show the particles, verb and noun endings and so on, which are part of Japanese but do not form part of Chinese (Habein, 1984: 23; Encyclopaedic Britannica, 1985: 753–4).

The other *kana* system, *hiragana*, was also developed in the ninth century. This system also uses simplified characters but in a different form to *katakana*. *Hiragana* was used principally by women, who were excluded from the study of Chinese at this time, and was originally known as *onnade* 'women's writing' (Habein, 1984: 25). Because it was used by women, who did not have access to *kanji*, *hiragana* was used on its own and not mixed with *kanji* (Shibatani, 1987: 857).

Both *katakana* and *hiragana* are often called syllabaries since the simplified characters are used to represent, in nearly all cases, a combination of a consonant plus a vowel. Thus, there are symbols, in both *katakana* and *hiragana* for, for example, *ka, si, tu, ne* and so on, though the symbol in *katakana* differs from that in *hiragana* (Shibatani, 1987: 858).

By the tenth century, therefore, the Japanese writing system was fairly complex. As an example, the symbol for 'mountain' could be read as *san*, the *on* Chinese form, or as *yama*, the *kun*, or Japanese semantic equivalent; alternatively 'mountain' could be written using either the *katakana* or *hiragana* system of simplified characters used for their phonetic value only (Shibatani, 1987: 857).

From the tenth to the nineteenth century *kanji*, *katakana*, and *hiragana* were all used; sometimes alone and sometimes in combination (Habein, 1987). Although the spoken language changed quite considerably during this period, particularly perhaps with the rise of the warrior classes after the thirteenth century, the written language remained essentially unchanged. The pronunciation of both *kanji* and *kana* was based on the speech of the court élite from the tenth century imperial capital around the Kyoto-Osaka region (Habein, 1984; Encyclopaedia Britannica, 1985: 754).

In the late nineteenth century, after the Meiji restoration, a movement began to bring the written language closer to the spoken language (Encyclopaedia Britannica, 1985: 754; Habein, 1984: 97ff). Universal education was introduced in the 1870s (Inoue, 1979: 253), but the old form of written Japanese continued to be used. It was not until after World War Two that reforms were instituted. The pronunciation of the *kana* was changed to reflect the speech of Tokyo, which had become the imperial capital after 1868, (though it had been the capital of the powerful shogun, or warrior leader, since the early seventeenth century when it was known as Edo), and the *kanji* were restricted to 1,850 commonly used characters (Shibatani, 1987: 859; Encyclopaedia Britannica, 1985: 754). In 1981 the list of commonly used characters was expanded to 1,945 and this list of *kanji* is known as the 'list of characters for daily use' (Shibatani, 1987: 859).

In Japan today elementary education aims at teaching *hiragana*, *katakana* and the list of 1,945 *kanji* using an 'ideal' form of pronunciation called *hyoozyun-go* 'standard language' which is based on the dialect of Tokyo (Shibatani, 1987: 860). Vance defines this 'standard' form more precisely as the dialect of educated middle class speakers of the 'uptown' or western half of Tokyo proper, and this form represents, he says, 'modern standard Japanese' (Vance, 1987: 1).

In the modern Japanese writing system the 1,945 *kanji* are used for most content words, and the *hiragana* system is used to represent grammatical function words such as particles, noun and verb endings and so on. The *hiragana* system is also used to 'spell out' a *kanji* which is used but is not one of the 'list of characters for daily use', and *katakana* is used to write foreign words or recent loanwords, for scientific words, and to write telegrams and type business memos (Shibatani, 1987: 858; Chaplin & Martin, 1969: 6ff). There are also other more specialised uses of *hiragana* and *katakana* (Chaplin & Martin, 1969: 6ff). There is also a system of romanisation, called romanji, which is occasionally used and is taught in schools (Chaplin and Martin 1969: 14). Japanese is usually written vertically, i.e. from top to bottom and from right to left, but is nowadays sometimes written horizontally from left to right, especially in modern textbooks and some official writings (Chaplin & Martin, 1969: 13).

There are many dialects in Japan, differing from each other to such an extent that some are mutually unintelligible (Shibatani, 1987: 860; Encyclopaedia Britannica, 1985: 750). The dialects are usually divided into two major groups: those of the mainland and those of the Ryukyu Islands in the south. The mainland dialects are then further divided into Eastern, Western and Kyushu groups, and some scholars divide the Western group into two further sub-groups (Encyclopaedia Britannica, 1985: 750).

Until the nineteenth century the standard, or at least the most influential dialect in Japan, was the dialect of Kyoto, the imperial capital (Grootaers, 1982: 328). The dialect of Kyoto is a Western mainland dialect. When the imperial court moved to Tokyo (Edo) in 1868, the merging of the Western dialect of the old standard with the Eastern dialect of the leading social classes of Tokyo led to the formation of the new standard spoken form: an Eastern mainland dialect with influences from the Western (Encyclopaedia Britannica, 1985: 750; Grootaers, 1982: 324).

Although some of the dialects, such as those of the far north-east, are still considered by the Japanese to be 'backward forms of language', there does not appear to be much social stigma attached to dialect use (Grootaers, 1982: 329, 349). In fact, as Grootaers notes, 'the family form of communication is ... still the local dialect, specially in the realm of grammar and phonetics' (1982: 329). The dialects differ in vocabulary, grammar, phonology and tone, i.e. a difference in the pitch with which a word is spoken affects the meaning of that word (Grootaers, 1982: 330ff).

Nevertheless, the spread of the Tokyo based standard is having an effect on the dialects. Thus, nearly everyone in Japan today can speak what is called 'the common language' which is essentially a version of the local dialect modified according to the 'ideal' of the Tokyo standard (Shibatani, 1987: 860). According to Grootaers, a study of a group of Japanese showed that over a period from 1950 to 1972 phonetic and tonal characteristics had moved towards the standard, but grammar and vocabulary had become more dialect-oriented, possibly because of an increasing view of the value of the local environment (1982: 350ff). Consequently, as Grootaers puts it:

> compulsory education and the high literacy rate create a situation in which the Tokyo standard is understood everywhere and encroaches upon the local dialects. But several factors work also in an opposite direction ... . (Grootaers, 1982: 343).

The Tokyo standard is the form of the language used in broadcasting (Shibatani, 1987: 860). It appears that the use of the standard is more prevalent now among the younger generation (Grootaers, 1982: 349; Encyclopaedia Britannica, 1985: 750).

As well as dialectal differences, it is important to note that Japanese also has a complex system of honorifics, or respect forms of language. The use of the respect forms affects grammar and vocabulary (Ide, 1982). This system is difficult for even native Japanese speakers to learn and use properly (Inoue, 1979: 296). According to Ide (1982), women's speech tends to make more use of the respect forms than men's speech. The grammatical and vocabulary forms used in honorific forms depend on various factors. As Ide puts it:

> There are various social and psychological factors involved in the rules of politeness. These factors are numerous and intertwined, but the major ones are (1) social position, (2) power, (3) age, and (4) formality. (Ide, 1982: 366)

For Japanese, therefore, there is a complex writing system which uses Chinese characters, *kanji*, and two syllabaries, *hiragana* and *katakana*, and occasionally uses the Latin alphabet, or *romanji*. The pronunciation of the written language, especially the two *kana systems*, is based on the dialect of Tokyo. The dialect of Tokyo also represents the standard for spoken Japanese. Dialects, some of which are mutually unintelligible, are still used and do not appear to have any stigma attached to them, though most Japanese can use an approximation of the Tokyo standard. Younger speakers appear to be assimilating to the Tokyo standard more than older speakers. The Tokyo standard is used for broadcasting. There is also a system of honorifics or respect language which differs in grammar and vocabulary and can prove difficult for even native speakers to use appropriately.

References

CHAPLIN, H. I. and MARTIN, S. E. 1969, *A Manual of Japanese Writing Book 1*. New Haven: Yale University Press.

CRYSTAL, D. 1987, *The Cambridge Encyclopaedia of Language*. Cambridge: Cambridge University Press.

ENCYCLOPAEDIA BRITANNICA 1985, Japanese language. In: *Macropaedia* Vol. 22, 750–4.

GROOTAERS, W. A. 1982, Dialectology and sociolinguistics: A general survey. *Lingua* 57, 327–55.

HABEIN, Y. S. 1984, *The History of the Japanese Written Language*. Tokyo: Tokyo University Press.

IDE, S. 1982, Japanese sociolinguistics: Politeness and women's language. *Lingua* 57, 357–85.

INOUE, K. 1979, Japanese: A story of language and people. In: T. SHOPEN (ed.) *Languages and their Speakers* (pp. 241–300). Cambridge: MA: Winthrop Publishers Inc.

MILLER, R. A. 1986, *Nihongo: In Defence of Japanese*. London: The Athlone Press.

SHIBATANI, M. 1987, Japanese. In: B. COMRIE (ed.) *The World's Major Languages* (pp. 855–80). London: Croom Helm.

VANCE, T. J. 1987, *An Introduction to Japanese Phonology*. New York: State University of New York Press.

Kannada

Kannada, sometimes called Kanarese, is a member of the Dravidian family of languages. It is spoken by over twenty million people in the state of Karnataka (formerly Mysore) in south-western India (Zograph, 1982: 142). Dravidian may have been the language of the original inhabitants of India, but it is more probable that it was brought to India from the north-west and displaced older linguistic forms (Zograph, 1982: 130). The later arrival of the Aryan languages and culture led to India being divided into an Indo-Aryan speaking north and a Dravidian speaking south.

The ancestor of the Kannada language, called Proto-Kannada, had probably separated from other Dravidian forms by the third century BC. (Zvelebil, 1970: 18). The oldest record of the Kannada language is to be found on an inscription dated to 450 AD. The form of the language used in the inscription is known as 'Old Kannada' (Nayak, 1967: 20–1). The writing of literature in Kannada began in the ninth century (Nayak, 1967: 20; Zvelebil, 1970: 16). From the beginning, the literary language of Kannada has included words borrowed from Sanskrit (Zograph, 1982: 133; Prasad, 1979: 29). Kannada is written using its own script, derived, as are most Indian alphabets, from the Brahmi script (Zograph, 1982: 197).

From the earliest literature till the present day, the form of Kannada used for writing has been different from any of the spoken dialects (Nayak, 1967: 26). Although there were movements in the twelfth and seventeenth centuries to bring the literary language closer to the spoken, there is still a considerable difference between them (Nayak, 1967: 27). As Nayak notes, learning the literary style requires eight to ten years of formal education and virtually means learning a second language (1967: 34).

In early grammars of Kannada, the spoken form of the language was considered 'ungrammatical', 'vulgar' and 'impure' and consequently changes in the spoken language were not incorporated into the literary form (Nayak, 1967: 27ff). At the present time, although there have been some changes, it appears that the literary form is almost the same as when it was first used in the ninth and tenth centuries (Nayak, 1967: 29).

The literary language is used in most writing, including newspapers, though the colloquial style is being used more now for dialogue in novels and also for its novelty value (Nayak, 1967: 32ff). A spoken form of the literary language is used for much public speaking, on radio and in formal situations generally. Thus, as Nayak says:

> In everyday conversation if anybody uses literary style it will be ridiculed as bookish ... . On the other hand, anyone will be a laughing stock if he uses colloquial instead of refined literary style in a public lecture. This observation holds good, even though it is true that the formal language is slowly losing ground in certain formal situations [e.g. political speeches]. (Nayak, 1967: 33)

The differences between the literary and the spoken languages are found in phonology, vocabulary and grammar (Nayak, 1967: 121ff). It would appear that the literary form of Kannada causes problems of comprehension for uneducated speakers, particularly in its vocabulary, and that All India Radio has special broadcasts for villagers in the colloquial style (Nayak, 1967: 120).

Spoken Kannada is usually divided into three main dialectal regions. Nayak says these are Northern, Central and Southern Kannada, and that 'each division within its own area has several subdivisions of considerably significant differences' (1967: 21). Zvelebil, though, says the three major dialect areas are Djarwar, Bangalore and Mangalore (1970: 17). According to Nayak, uneducated speakers from one dialect region have considerable problems understanding speakers from other regions (1967: 24). This suggests that the regional dialects are mutually unintelligible.

As well as regional dialects, Zvelebil notes that there are social dialects corresponding to the three major caste divisions of the society, that is: Brahmin, non-Brahmin and Harijan, 'untouchables' (1970: 16). However, Nayak considers that the association of caste with dialect is over-emphasised and that the important factor in social dialects is not caste but educational background and whether a speaker is from an urban area or a village (1967: 22ff).

According to Nayak educated Brahmins and non-Brahmins speak a standardised form of the colloquial language heavily influenced by the literary form and differing little from area to area, whereas the uneducated speak a regional form which can cause problems of comprehension from region to region (1967: 24). Zvelebil also notes that educated speech is close to the literary form when he says,

> In Kannada, there is a dichotomy between the literary dialects or the so-called educated speech, which is essentially uniform, and colloquial Kannada ... . (Zvelebil, 1970: 16).

Nevertheless, it appears from what Nayak (1967) says, that although the standard spoken form used by educated speakers is close to the literary form, it is still distinct from it. What is probably the case is that there is a continuum of formality which the educated speaker moves along depending on the particular speech situation. In other words, in a formal speech or lecture a form close to the literary form would be used, while in an informal gathering a more 'colloquial' form would be chosen.

For Kannada, therefore, there is a literary language which differs quite considerably from the everyday colloquial forms of Kannada. Kannada, consequently, displays diglossia, i.e. two different forms are used depending on the speech situation. There are regional dialects which may not be mutually intelligible, but educated speakers tend to use a standardised form of the colloquial spoken language which is relatively uniform throughout the Kannada speaking area. The spoken form of the literary language is used in most formal situations, such as public speeches, news broadcasts and so on. It appears that the educated standard spoken colloquial style may approximate to the literary form in more formal situations.

References

NAYAK, H. M. 1967, *Kannada Literary and Colloquial: A Study of Two Styles*. Mysore: Rao and Raqhavan.
PRASAD, N. K. 1979, *The Language Issue in India*. Delhi: Leeladevi Publications.
ZOGRAPH, G. A. 1982, *Languages of South Asia: A Guide*. London: Routledge and Kegan Paul (*Languages of Asia and Africa* Vol. 3).
ZVELEBIL, K. 1970, *Comparative Dravidian Phonology*. The Hague: Mouton.

Khmer

Khmer is a member of the Mon-Khmer family of languages. Khmer is spoken mainly in Cambodia and also in north-eastern Thailand, the Mekong Delta area of Vietnam and parts of Laos. According to Whitaker *et al.* the area has been inhabited by ethnic Khmer since at least the sixth century if not longer (1973: 48).

Approximately 85% of Cambodia's population have Khmer as their mother tongue. The rest of the population is made up of Chinese, Vietnamese, Cham (a Moslem group of Malay origin) and a number of hill tribes who speak related but mutually unintelligible Mon-Khmer languages. The majority of these groups, though, speak Khmer as a second language (Whitaker *et al.*, 1973: 69ff; Steinberg, 1959: 33). (This information is pre-1975. Since that time it appears to be probable that the ravages of the Khmer Rouge regime (1975–early 1979) has, among other things, considerably reduced the number of non-Khmers in the region.)

At the time of the arrival of the French in 1864 most villages had a temple school run by Buddhist monks which taught boys to read and write Khmer. The French gradually introduced secular education, primarily for the élite, but exclusively in French. The temple schools were, however, expanded to complement the French system and these schools taught in Khmer. All secondary and tertiary education, though, was in secular schools and only in French (Whitaker *et al.*, 1973: 110ff).

With the gaining of independence in 1953 primary education was expanded and began to be given in Khmer. In 1955 women were allowed full access to education, previously denied them since many schools were still run by monks and women were forbidden to associate with them. It was only in 1967 that French ceased to be the sole language of education at the secondary level or above and Khmer was scheduled to become the sole language of all education by 1974 (Whitaker *et al.*, 1973: 107, 110ff). However, in 1975 all schools were closed and education virtually ceased (Louie, 1984: 30).

French was also extensively used in Cambodia in government, intellectual and professional circles prior to independence. Since 1953 a determined effort has been made to replace it with Khmer (Steinberg, 1959: 33).

A consequence of the use of French has been that 'borrowings from French have become part of the colloquial language of urban people' (Whitaker *et al.*, 1973: 106). However, French is not the major source of neologisms. The sacred language of the Buddhists, Pali, as well as Sanskrit have been used for centuries, and are still used, for coining new terms. The Thai and Lao languages also make use of Pali and Sanskrit for neologisms and this has led to a substantial number of words used in common, especially in administrative, political, military and literary fields, by these three languages (Whitaker *et al.*, 1973: 106).

Khmer, unlike the Thai, Lao and Vietnamese languages which surround it, is a non-tonal language. That is, variations in pitch do not form part of the basic sound structure of words. Khmer is written in a script derived from a form of Indic script, possibly that of the Coromandel coast of southern India (Huffman, 1970: 4). Evidence of the use of this script, in what is now southern Vietnam, has been dated to the second or third century AD (Whitaker *et al.*, 1973: 106).

There are several dialects of Khmer, though it appears that all are mutually intelligible. Khmer spoken in countries around Cambodia, i.e. Thailand, Laos and Vietnam, also appears to be mutually intelligible with Cambodian Khmer. As Whitaker *et al.* note, 'ethnic Khmer living in Thailand, Vietnam and Laos speak dialects of the Khmer language that are intelligible to Cambodians' (1973: 105). They point out, however, that those ethnic Khmer in Vietnam 'have preserved some unique characteristics, a regional accent, and a sense of separate group identity' (1973: 79).

Steinberg considers that:

Cambodians do not pay particular attention to dialects in their language. There are, however, as in all languages, some dialect regions that are more distinct than others; the northwest provinces of Cambodia, for example, have easily identified dialects. (Steinberg, 1959: 36)

However, it appears that there is a standard form of Khmer. According to Huffman:

[Standard Khmer] is taught in the schools and spoken by educated Cambodians. Although some colloquial dialects, notably that of Phnom Penh and the immediately surrounding area, differ considerably from the standard at the phonological level, standard Cambodian is virtually identical with the dialect spoken by the majority of the people in the central provinces, and is understood throughout the country. (Huffman, 1970: 6)

Noss, in a discussion of two Khmer dialects states that:

[Standard Khmer] is spoken by educated people throughout the country, and is the primary vehicle of mass communication — e.g. radio and public speaking. While the regional speech of the capital is coming to be more and more confined to the uneducated, there are still many people who can and do handle both standard and Phnom Penh in daily life .... In simplest terms, standard has an [r] sound and Phnom Penh does not … .So great is the prestige of standard, and hence its distinguishing sound, that the writer has yet to meet a native speaker of Cambodian, of whatever regional or class origin, who could not produce some sort of [r] (phonetically speaking) when he thought the situation called for it. (Noss, 1966: 89)

However, pronunciation or accent may be less important than style and vocabulary. It appears that educated speech is relatively homogeneous in terms of style and vocabulary and is prestigious, even though there may be variation in accent. The Khmer dialect spoken in Thailand, however, is generally not considered to be standard. This may also be the case with the Khmer dialects spoken in Laos and Vietnam (Vickery, 1988).

It would seem, therefore, that standard Khmer equates with educated Khmer from Cambodia. According to Dr Vickery, educated Khmer speakers are those who have completed high school or above (Vickery, 1988). Although there are different accents in Cambodia, these appear to be less important in terms of prestige than the educated/uneducated differences.

A further point which is perhaps worth noting is that in Khmer there are special speech styles which are used to show status relationships (Steinberg, 1959: 56; Louie, 1984: 45). As Louie puts it, 'in Khmer, the language used … is influenced strongly by the relative status of the two people involved in a discussion' (1984: 45). For example, the English word 'eat' can be expressed in at least eight ways in Khmer depending on who a speaker is addressing; e.g. with younger relatives and friends the word *si* is used; a more educated term used with people of the same status is *nyam*; when talking about older people the word *pisar* is used; the word *saoy* is used when talking about royalty (Louie, 1984: 45–6).

It should also be noted that since the Khmer Rouge regime the situation in Cambodia is likely to have changed radically. The suppression and, it appears, attempted extermination of all educated Khmer, as well as the massive population movements, may well have created a linguistic situation different to that reported above. Unfortunately, the present linguistic situation in Cambodia is not known. It is presumed, however, that many emigré Khmer speakers will be aware of the educated speech style and that it will still be considered prestigious.

References

HUFFMAN, F. E. 1970, *Cambodian System of Writing and Beginning Reader*. New Haven: Yale University Press.
LOUIE, G. 1984, *Language and Culture: Kampuchea*. Sydney: Commonwealth Department of Immigration and Ethnic Affairs (Produced for the Adult Migrant Education Program)

Noss, R. B. 1966, The treatment of */r/ in two modern Khmer dialects. In: N. H. Zide (ed.) *Studies in Comparative Austroasiatic Linguistics*. The Hague: Mouton (*Indo-Iranian Monographs* Vol. V)

Steinberg, D. J. 1959, *Cambodia: Its People, Its Society, Its Culture*. New Haven: HRAF Press.

Vickery, M. 1988, Asian Studies, University of Adelaide, personal communication.

Whitaker, D. P. *et al.* 1973, *Area Handbook for the Khmer Republic (Cambodia)*. Washington, D.C.: US Government Printing Office.

Korean

There are two major theories on the origins of the Korean people and their language. One theory states that they came from the north and that the language is part of the Altaic family of languages. The other theory posits that they came from the south and that the language is related to the Austronesian languages (Kim N-K., 1987: 881ff). The Northern theory seems to be the one most favoured by linguists at present (Kim N-K., 1987: 882; Encyclopaedia Britannica, 1985: 748), though Crystal notes that while there are evident similarities between the Korean language and the Altaic family, it 'is not clear whether these can best be explained by a hypothesis of common descent or one of influence through contact' (1987: 306).

Around the fourth century AD the small tribal states which had characterised the Korean peninsula up till that time were vanquished as three kingdoms with strong central governments appeared (Kim N-K., 1987: 883). These three kingdoms were Kokuryo in the north, Paekche in the southwest, and Silla in the southeast (Kim N-K., 1987: 883). It is believed that Silla and Paekche spoke dialects of the Han language, and Kokuryo spoke a different, though related, language known as the Puyo language (Encyclopaedia Britannica, 1985: 748). Kim N-K., in fact, considers both Han and Puyo to be dialects of the ancient Korean language (1987: 882).

In the seventh century the Silla kingdom conquered and annexed the other two kingdoms. The dialect of the Han language spoken by the people of Silla became, in consequence, the dominant, and eventually the sole language of the unified Korean peninsula and the direct precursor of the modern Korean language (Kim N-K., 1987: 883; Encyclopaedia Britannica, 1985: 748).

The Korean language has been heavily influenced by Chinese. Pihl notes that Chinese characters may first have been used in Korea around 100 BC and that by the fourth or fifth century AD they were probably extensively used (1983: 112). Literate Koreans at this time, therefore, learned both Chinese characters and the Chinese language. Korean scholars, though, sought a way of rendering the Korean language using Chinese characters (Lee, 1983: 72). A system was devised, known as *Idu*, whereby some Chinese characters were used only for their sound while others were used only for their meaning, and this system 'was both written and read in Korean grammatical order and would have made little sense to a Chinese reader' (Pihl, 1983: 113). However, according to Pihl,

Idu was 'inefficient and inconsistent', and it seems that classical Chinese continued to be used to some extent (1983: 113).

In the fifteenth century a totally new alphabet was invented for Korean by King Sejong (Lee, 1983; Kim J-P., 1983; Kim N-K., 1987: 884). This alphabet, known as Han'gul, was proclaimed in 1446 (Kim J-P., 1983: 80). The symbols of Han'gul are based on eight shapes: the five basic shapes for consonants are representative of the place of articulation of the sounds, e.g. dental 'ʌ', bilabial (two lips) ' □ ' and the three basic vowel shapes represent the symbols for 'Heaven' i.e. a round dot, 'Earth', i.e. a horizontal line, and 'Man', i.e. a vertical line. From these eight basic shapes twenty-eight symbols were made (Kim J-P., 1983: 81ff). The Korean alphabet can be written in several ways. As Yi puts it:

> The symbols can be written vertically or horizontally and left to right or right to left [though this way is no longer used] at will. Symbols for initial, medial and final sounds of each syllable can be combined into one letter, so as to resemble and harmonise with Chinese characters. It is also possible to separate the symbols so that they can be printed like the Roman alphabet. (Yi, 1983: 51)

However, as Kim N-K. points out:

> Even after the Korean script was invented, Chinese characters were continuously used as the main means of writing until the twentieth century. In traditional Korean society, the learning and study of Chinese characters and classical Chinese were entirely monopolised by a small class of élite aristocrats. (Kim N-K., 1987: 884)

The use of Chinese and Chinese characters in Korea has led to the borrowing of a massive number of Chinese words into Korean. According to Kim H-G, in a Korean dictionary 52% of the words are Chinese, while only 45% are native Korean words, and the other 3% is made up of foreign words other than Chinese (1983: 125). In many cases, the Chinese loanwords had the same, or a similar, meaning to a native Korean word. The Chinese words tended to dominate with the result that either the native word disappeared or it was seen as having a 'less respectful' meaning (note that this is important in Korean which has a highly developed system of honorifics and respect forms) (Kim H-G., 1983: 126; Kim N-K., 1987: 884).

At the end of the nineteenth century a movement began to restore native culture by stimulating interest in the Korean language. At the beginning of the twentieth century the government proclaimed that the official government documents would be written both in Korean script and in Chinese characters (Kim N-K., 1987: 884).

The Korean writing system was modernised in the early part of this century when efforts were made to standardise the spoken and written forms of the language (Kim Y-G., 1983; Encyclopaedia Britannica, 1985: 748). The spelling system in use today was published in 1933 (Kim Y-G., 1983: 107). But this system did not become official till 1945 due to the fact that in 1933 the Japanese banned the use of *Han'gul* and the use of spoken Korean was banned in 1938 (Kim J-P., 1983: 97–8).

In present day South Korea both *Han'gul* and Chinese characters are used. The Chinese characters are incorporated in what is known as 'mixed-script' where both Korean letters and Chinese characters are used side-by-side in the same piece of text. *Han'gul* by itself is also used (Encyclopaedia Britannica, 1985: 748). According to Kim N-K., students in secondary schools in South Korea must learn 1,800 basic Chinese characters (1987: 885).

In North Korea only *Han'gul* is used, and no instruction in Chinese characters is given. *Han'gul*, in North Korea, is known as *Choson muntcha* (Kim N-K., 1987: 885; Encyclopaedia Britannica, 1985: 748).

Since the original unification of the Korean peninsula under the kingdom of Silla, and through the succeeding dynasties of Koryo (936–1392) and Choson, or Yi, (1392–1910), it seems that the language spoken in the capital city has been the standard dialect (Kim N-K., 1987: 883). Thus, ever since the Yi dynasty established its capital at Seoul at the end of the fourteenth century, this dialect has been the standard. In the twentieth century, though, with the division of Korea, the standard for North Korea is the dialect of its capital, Pyongyang, while the dialect of Seoul remains the standard for South Korea (Kim N-K., 1987: 883).

The governments of both North and South Korea have 'established prescriptive criteria for its own standard dialect and made separate policies on language' (Kim N-K., 1987: 883). In the North, the government has been actively involved in the 'purification' of Korean. That is, they encourage the use of native Korean words in everyday life by removing foreign, especially Chinese, words from the language. While there is a movement in South Korea which is also attempting to 'purify' the language, the government has never officially participated in this attempt (Kim N-K., 1987: 885).

There are several dialects in Korea where 'each region has its own characteristic dialects' (Kim N-K., 1987: 883). These dialects can be grouped into six major divisions, and although there are differences there does not appear to be any problems of comprehension between them. The major differences are in intonation, vocabulary and in some grammatical endings (Encyclopaedia Britannica, 1985: 748).

It is important to note that in Korean there are several levels of language which reflect the social position, or relative status, of the speaker and the person spoken to (Kim C-U., 1983: 35). These levels of language can differ quite considerably in both vocabulary and grammar (Kim N-K., 1987: 890ff). This system of honorifics and respect is important in Korea, but is extremely complex, and difficult even for native speakers. As Kim C-U. notes, 'I am frequently surprised by the innocent rudeness of the language that some of my students use ...' (1983: 34).

Korean, therefore, has several dialects, but the standard is considered to be that of the capital city. In South Korea it is the dialect of Seoul and in North Korea that of Pyongyang. Chinese has had a considerable influence on Korean, but North Korea now only uses *Han'gul* and is attempting to reduce the number of Chinese words, while in South Korea both Chinese characters and *Han'gul* are used and there is less effort being made to 'purify' the language.

References

CRYSTAL, D. 1987, *The Cambridge Encyclopaedia of Language*. Cambridge: Cambridge University Press.
ENCYCLOPAEDIA BRITANNICA 1985, Korean language. In: *Macropaedia* Vol. 22, pp. 748–50.
KIM, C-U. 1983, The making of the Korean language. In: *The Korean Language* pp. 13–42. Oregon: Pace International Research Inc. (edited by the Korean National Commission of UNESCO).
KIM, H-G. 1983, Chinese characters and the Korean language. In: *The Korean Language* pp. 121–7. Oregon: Pace International Research Inc. (edited by the Korean National Commission for UNESCO).
KIM, J-P. 1983, The letterforms of Han'gul. In: *The Korean Language* pp. 80–102. Oregon: Pace International Research Inc.
KIM, N-K. 1987, Korean. In: B. COMRIE (ed.) *The World's Major Languages* pp. 881–98. London: Croom Helm.
KIM, Y-G. 1983, Chu Si-gyong and modernization of Han'gul. In: *The Korean Language* pp. 103–8. Oregon: Pace International Research Inc.
LEE, K-M. 1983, Foundations of Hunmin Chongum. In: *The Korean Language* pp. 71–9. Oregon: Pace International Research Inc.
PIHL, M. R. Jr 1983, The alphabet of East Asia. In: *The Korean Language* pp. 109–20. Oregon: Pace International Research Inc.
YI, S-O. 1983, The theory of Altaic languages and Korean. In: *The Korean Language* pp. 43–54. Oregon: Pace International Research Inc.

Kurdish

Kurdish is a member of the Iranian branch of Indo-European languages (Ghareeb, 1981: 3). Estimates of the number of speakers of Kurdish vary between 7 million and 18 million (Ghareeb, 1981: 3; Blau, 1980: 13). Despite such a large number of speakers, very little information is available on the Kurdish language.

The area in which Kurdish is spoken, sometimes known as Kurdistan, is divided between Turkey, Iraq, and Iran, with small areas also inside the USSR and Syria (O'Ballance, 1973: 18; Ghareeb, 1981: 3). But the Kurds have not, in historical times, achieved nation-state status (Encyclopaedia Britannica, 1985: 40). In some of these areas, especially Turkey, Kurdish is suppressed, while in Iraq the Kurds have achieved a limited autonomy and Kurdish is taught in primary and, in some areas, secondary schools (Ghareeb, 1981: 7ff; Blau, 1980: 14).

There are two major dialects in Kurdish. In the northern areas, that is Turkey, Syria, the north of Iraq, and parts of Iran, the Kurmandji, or Kermanyi, dialect is spoken; in the southern areas, i.e. most of the Iranian and Iraqi Kurdish regions, the Sorani, or, as it is sometimes called, the Kurdi, dialect is spoken (Blau, 1980: 14; Encyclopaedia Britannica, 1985: 40).

According to Blau, Kurdish can be written in three alphabets: in Iraq and Iran the Arabic alphabet is used; in Turkey the Latin alphabet is used; and in the USSR the Cyrillic alphabet (1980: 13).

The literary form of Kurdish is the southern, Sorani, or Kurdi, dialect and this is also the form officially recognised and taught in schools in Iraq (Blau, 1980: 14; Encyclopaedia Britannica, 1985: 40). However, Blau notes that prior to 1973 the Kurmandji dialect was used, at least in Europe, for Kurdish publications (1980: 15). The form of the Arabic alphabet used for literary Kurdish and for teaching was established in the 1920s, though certain modifications have been carried out by the Iraqi Academy of Science (Blau, 1980: 14).

References

BLAU, J. 1980, *Manuel de Kurde (Dialecte Sorani)*. Paris: C. Klincksieck.
GHAREEB, E. 1981, *The Kurdish Question in Iraq*. Syracuse: Syracuse University Press.

ENCYCLOPAEDIA BRITANNICA 1985, 'Kurd' and 'Kurdish Language'. In: *Micropaedia, Ready Reference* Vol. 7 p. 40.

O'BALLANCE, E. 1973, *The Kurdish Revolt: 1961–1970*. London: Faber and Faber.

Lao

Lao, or Laotian as it is sometimes called, is a member of the Thai group of languages (often spelt Tai to distinguish the group from the official national language of Thailand). The Tai group of languages is generally believed to have originated in what is now southern China (Matisoff 1985: 21). It is possible that the use of 'Lao' or 'Laotian' as the language name may have socio-political overtones. The use of 'Laotian' may be reminiscent of colonialism since this name was used primarily by the French during their rule of Laos.

Lao is the language of the Lao people and it is spoken principally in Laos and Thailand. According to Yates and Sa, in the 1960s there were some three million speakers of Lao in Laos and about ten million in Thailand (1970: xvi). Condominas, however, puts a much lower figure on the population. He says there are less than a million Lao in Laos and about five million in Thailand (1970: 10).

Within Laos itself the Lao constitute less than half the population, although they make up the largest single ethnic group (Morechand, 1970: 31). The rest of the population is composed of a variety of ethnic groups, culturally and linguistically distinct from the Lao. Some of these groups speak related but mutually unintelligible Tai languages, while others speak unrelated languages such as Meo, Mon-Khmer and various Sino-Tibetan languages (LeBar & Suddard, 1960: 35ff; Morechand, 1970: 29ff).

The Lao, or rather a small minority of the Lao, however, formed the political and social élite of Laos (Hawkins, 1970: 5). In consequence, Lao was the language of government and administration. But, as Hawkins points out, the control of the Lao élite did not extend far beyond the major cities and most Laotians (of whatever ethnic group) owed allegiance only to their village (1970: 5).

Towards the end of French colonial rule in the mid 1940s the language of the cities was mainly French and Vietnamese and there were no newspapers whatsoever in Lao (McCoy, 1970: 84-85). Also, the Lao language hardly existed in schools or in books during the French period (Phimphachanh, 1970: 448).

Thus, although Lao was the language of the élite in Laos, it would be difficult to say that it was the national language. However, since the end of the war in Laos in the mid 1970s the government has apparently been attempting to introduce compulsory primary education in Lao throughout the country (Diller, 1988).

In Thailand the Lao do not form the political or social élite. The official national language is Thai, and Lao is merely one of a number of languages spoken by the diverse population of that country (Brudhiprabha, 1979: 296). The Lao dialects spoken in Thailand are also known as 'Northeastern Thai' (Strecker, 1987: 749).

Lao, like all the Tai languages, is a tonal language. In other words, the tone, e.g. high, mid, low, rising, falling and so on, with which a word is spoken is as important as the sounds of the word in indicating the meaning. For example, in Thai the word *naam* (water) must be pronounced with a low tone and the word *ma* (mother) with a falling tone (Brudhiprabha, 1979: 299). Lao uses an alphabet derived from Indian alphabets and similar to that used in Thailand (Strecker, 1987: 755).

According to Brown (1962) there are three major dialect groups of Lao. These are: the Luang Prabang group; the Vientiane group; and the Yo group. Brown distinguishes 28 different dialects within these three groups (1962: 14ff), though this is not necessarily an exhaustive list (1962: 12).

It appears that one of the main ways in which dialects differ from one another is in the tonal system. However, the dialect situation in Laos has been confused by the major population movements caused by the recent wars in the area. As a consequence, a great variety of local variation of tone is acceptable and there is no definite expectation on the part of listeners as to what tone will be used (Gedney, 1967: 791).

As far as a standard pronunciation is concerned, Gedney notes that 'no single dialect has the prestige of a national standard, and the dialects of the two capitals Vientiane and Luang Prabang differ markedly, especially in tones' (1967: 791). Also, for a considerable period the King resided in Luang Prabang but the main administration and government was centred on Vientiane. Consequently, speakers of the urban educated variety of each of these dialects felt that theirs was the 'standard' form (Diller, 1988).

A further complication is the influence of Thai. According to Gedney:

As regards social level, a common experience among people who know Thai is to find that the upper class educated Lao used, for example, in radio broadcasts, sounds like Thai with a slight accent, the vocabulary and syntax being virtually identical with those of standard Thai, whereas the Lao that one hears in the street and in the market and among friends is so different as to be incomprehensible. Almost everyone, at least in the cities, understands Thai, as a result of radio and movies and frequent contact, so that speakers of Thai usually find themselves easily understood but unable to understand what they hear. (Gedney, 1967: 791)

This situation appears to be similar today in that the urban educated speech sounds like Thai and uses a fairly large amount of Thai vocabulary, especially in bureaucratic and technical language, but the tones are those of Lao and not Thai (Diller, 1988). Lower class and rural speech, on the other hand, sounds very different from Thai and uses far fewer items of Thai vocabulary. The rural speech is, it seems, often considered to be impolite, even rude, and is generally negatively viewed by the urban élite (Diller, 1988).

References

BROWN, J. M. 1962, From ancient to modern Thai dialects: A theory. PhD Thesis, Cornell University.

BRUDHIPRABHA, P. 1979, Languages of Thailand. In: T. A. LLAMZON (ed.) *Papers on Southeast Asian Languages* (pp. 295–307). Singapore: Singapore University Press (SEAMEO Regional Language Centre Anthology Series 5).

CONDOMINAS, G. 1970, The Lao. In: N. S. ADAMS and A. W. McCOY (eds) *Laos: War and Revolution*. New York: Harper and Row.

DILLER, A. 1988, Southeast Asia Centre, Australian National University, personal communication.

GEDNEY, W. J. 1967, Thailand and Laos. In: T. A. SEBEOK (ed.) *Current Trends in Linguistics* Vol. II (pp. 782–814). The Hague: Mouton.

HAWKINS, R. S. D. 1970, Contours, cultures, and conflict. In: N. S. ADAMS and A. W. McCOY (eds) *Laos War and Revolution* (pp. 3–8). New York: Harper and Row.

LEBAR, F. M. and SUDDARD A. (eds) 1960, *Laos: Its People, Its Society, Its Culture*. New Haven: HRAF Press.

MATISOFF, J. A. 1985, New directions in East and Southeast Asian linguistics. In: G. THURGOOD, J. A. MATISOFF and D. BRADLEY (eds) *Linguistics of the Sino-Tibetan Area: The State of the Art* (pp. 21–35). Canberra: Australian National University (Pacific Linguistics Series C. No 87).

McCOY, A. W. 1970, French colonialism in Laos, 1893–1945. In: N. S. ADAMS and A. W. McCOY (eds) *Laos: War and Revolution* (pp. 67–99). New York: Harper and Row.

MORECHAND, G. 1970, The many languages and cultures of Laos. In: N. S. ADAMS and A. W. McCOY (eds) *Laos: War and Revolution* (pp. 29–34). New York: Harper and Row.

PHIMPHACHANH, P. 1970, The Pathet Lao's revolutionary program: Noam Chomsky interviews Phao Phimphachanh. In: N. S. ADAMS and A. W. McCOY (eds) *Laos: War and Revolution* (pp. 444–50). New York: Harper and Row.

STRECKER, D. 1987, Tai languages. In: B. COMRIE (ed.) *The World's Major Languages* (pp. 747–56). London: Croom Helm.

YATES, W. G. and SA S. 1970, *Lao: Basic Course* Vol. 1. Washington, D.C.: Foreign Service Inc.

Latvian

Latvian is a Baltic language, a member of the Indo-European family. According to Comrie, there is some debate as to whether the Baltic languages, divided into East Baltic (i.e. Latvian and Lithuanian), and West Baltic (i.e. Old Prussian-now extinct), represent a separate branch of Indo-European, or whether they should be classed together with the Slavonic languages in a single, Balto-Slavonic, branch (1981: 143–4).

East Baltic probably began to split into Latvian and Lithuanian in about the ninth century AD, and by the thirteenth century 'we already find all the phonetic changes which separate Latvian from Lithuanian and which are characteristic of Latvian today' (Rūķe-Dravina, 1977: 17).

By the sixteenth century a literary language, based on the Central Dialects, was in use in Latvia (Rūķe-Dravina 1977: 20ff). It appears, though, that the majority of texts produced were religious works read by a, mostly foreign, religious and feudal élite (Rūķe-Dravina, 1977: 29).

Up until relatively recently Latvian, as a native language, was confined primarily to the peasant class. The landowning feudal élite, the Hanseatic traders and many clergymen spoke German, and Latvia was ruled, for much of its history, by foreign powers, including Poland, and, from the early eighteenth century, Russia (Bilmanis, 1970).

As a consequence, as Bilmanis puts it:

Long relegated to the unofficial vernacular during successive foreign dominations, [Latvian's] formal preservation, from the seventeenth to the beginning of the nineteenth century, lay in the hands of German Lutheran pastors who compiled dictionaries and handbooks for their own use in dealing with their Latvian flocks. The purification of the language, inevitably distorted by this German interpretation, began in the middle of the nineteenth century. (Bilmanis, 1970: 17)

Comrie appears to agree with Bilmanis when he says that Latvian developed as a written language very recently, 'not until the nineteenth century' (1981: 147). However, Rūķe-Dravina considers that the Latvian literary language began to develop in the sixteenth century and that the translation of the Bible in the late seventeenth was 'central to the development of the written language in the 18th and early 19th centuries' (1977: 29–30). This author does note, though, that with the 'National Awakening' movement in the middle of the nineteenth century there were attempts to 'purify, enrich and develop Lativan' and that 'since this period, the development of the Latvian language towards a standardised Modern Standard Latvian has proceeded at a rapid pace' (Rūķe-Dravina, 1977: 30).

Latvian has been written in three scripts. During the centuries of dominance by German landowners the Gothic script, i.e. the script used for German till the 1930s, was the most commonly used one. Under the Russians the Cyrillic script was introduced. Between 1865 and 1904, in fact, the use of any script other than the Cyrillic was forbidden in Latvia. The third script, and the one now used, is the Roman. Since 1921 several orthographic changes have been instituted, but it seems that since 1957 the orthographic system using the Latin alphabet has stabilised (Rūķe-Dravina, 1977: 46ff).

Latvian reached full development as a written literary language during the inter-War period in the twentieth century when Latvia was independent and Latvian became the official language (Comrie, 1981: 147). The standardised literary language is also used as the standard spoken form of the language (Rūķe-Dravina, 1977: 9).

In recent time there has been a tendency towards purism in the Latvian standardisation process. German and Slavic elements were discarded wherever possible and neologisms formed from the Latvian dialects, especially from within the borders of the Central dialects area. Foreign terms, though, are still fairly extensively used in the Latvian literary language (Rūķe-Dravina, 1977: 75ff). Since 1959 the standardisation and normalisation of Latvian has been under the control of the Institute of Latvian Language and Literature at the Latvian Academy of Sciences (Rūķe-Dravina, 1977: 71).

Latvian is a tonal language; that is, a difference in the tone, e.g. level, falling, may make a difference to the lexical meaning, for example *liêls* pronounced with what is called 'broken tone' means 'shin, calf of the leg' whereas *liēls* pronounced with a 'level tone' means 'big' (Endzelins, 1971: 26–7). The tones, however, differ from dialect to dialect (Rūķe-Dravina, 1977: 110).

The standard form of Latvian is based on the Central dialects which include the dialect of Riga, the capital (Comrie, 1981: 147). However, it appears that tonal differences are apparent when speakers from other dialect regions are using the standard (Rūķe-Dravina, 1977: 110). Also, the standard has been influenced by other dialects particularly in the area of vocabulary (Rūķe-Dravina, 1977: 111).

Latvian is usually divided into two major dialect areas, High Latvian, in the east, and Low Latvian. Low Latvian is, in turn, divided into the Tamian dialects and the Central dialects (Endzelins, 1971: 21; Rūķe-Dravina, 1977:

20–1). Until the beginning of this century the differences between the more remote dialects was so great that there were problems of comprehension (Rūķe-Dravina, 1977: 20).

In recent times, though, the influence of radio and television, as well as education has tended to level out dialectal differences. But, as Rūķe-Dravina puts it:

> Marked dialect differences are, however, still evident despite the strong general tendency towards centralisation in the spoken language. This is especially true of phonetic differences not reflected in the orthography but noticeable when reading a literary text … . (Rūķe-Dravina, 1977: 114)

For Latvian, therefore, there is a standard based on the Central dialects which is used as the literary and standard spoken form. There are numerous dialects which exhibit marked variation, though the influence of education and the mass media are tending to level out differences. The standard spoken form, it seems, also exhibits differences from region to region particularly in the tones which are used, but no information was available as to whether one region's pronunciation would be considered more prestigious than any other.

It is perhaps worth noting that one of the High Latvian dialects, Latgal, 'has been used considerably as a written language, but its use is discouraged in Soviet Latvia, where only the one standard written language is used' (Comrie, 1981: 147). Latvia became a Soviet Republic after the Second World War. But Comrie gives no indication as to whether the Latgal written form is also used as a standard for spoken usage, nor was any information available on whether this form is used by emigre Latvians. It is also worth noting that Latvians are only in a slight majority in Latvia (56.8%) and that there are actually more Russians than Latvians in the population of Riga (Comrie, 1981: 148). This may have implications for the influence of Russian on the Latvian language.

References

BILMANIS, A. 1970, *A History of Latvia*. Westport, Connecticut: Greenwood Press.

COMRIE, B. 1981, *The Languages of the Soviet Union*. Cambridge: Cambridge University Press.

ENDZELINS, T. 1971, *Comparative Phonology and Morphology of the Baltic Languages*. The Hague: Mouton.

RŪĶE-DRAVINA, V. 1977, *The Standardization Process in Latvian: 16th Century to the Present*. Stockholm: Almgvist and Wiksell International (*Stockholm Slavic Studies* 11).

Lithuanian

Lithuanian is an East Baltic language, a sub-branch of the Baltic branch of the Indo-European family of languages (Comrie, 1981: 144). There is some question among scholars as to whether the Baltic languages should be considered to be a separate branch of the Indo-European family, or if they should rather be represented as a sub-branch of a single Balto-Slavonic branch (Comrie 1981: 143). Lithuanian is the official language of the Lithuanian SSR, a part of the Soviet Union.

The Balts probably moved to the area they now inhabit around 2000 BC (Puzinas, 1969: 26; Encyclopaedia Britannica, 1985: 690). At this time the Balts spoke one language, which scholars call Proto-Baltic (Puzinas, 1969: 19). Although linguists believe that Proto-Baltic began to split up into different dialects around 1000 BC, it is not till about 700 AD that Lithuanian is considered to have separated from other East Baltic forms as a language in its own right (Puzinas, 1969: 20; Encyclopaedia Britannica, 1985b: 691).

In the thirteenth century the Grand Duchy of Lithuania was formed which, by the fourteenth century, stretched from the Baltic Sea in the north to the Black Sea in the south and included areas which are today parts of Russia, Byelorussia and Ukraine (Dembrowski, 1982: 14ff). At this time the official language of the Grand Duchy was a Slavonic language based primarily on Byelorussian (Encyclopaedia Britannica, 1985: 691; Jakstas, 1969: 51, 84).

However, successive unions with Poland, culminating in the Union of Lublin in 1569, led to the use of Latin, through the influence of the Roman Catholic Church, and the increasing Polonisation in language and culture of the Lithuanian élite (Dembrowski, 1982: 198–9; Senn, 1959: 4). Thus, when the Protestant reformation came to Lithuania the Bible was translated only into Polish and Byelorussian (Jakstas, 1969: 76, 85).

The influence of Poland and Polish continued to increase to the point that in 1697 Polish was made the official language of the Grand Duchy of Lithuania (Senn, 1959: 17), and Lithuanian land holders came to see themselves as 'Lithuanian by birth, Polish by nationality' (Dembrowski, 1982: 199). Senn notes that as late as the end of the nineteenth century and the beginning of the twentieth century many Lithanians still considered themselves to be Polish in language and culture (1959: 7–8).

Nevertheless, the lower classes of Lithuanian society were relatively unaffected by Polonisation and remained Lithuanian speaking (Dembrowski, 1982: 199). Also, although much of the literature produced during the Reformation was in Polish or Byelorussian, this period also saw the publication of the first works written in Lithuanian, albeit very few (Jakštas, 1969: 77).

With the Counter-Reformation, the Jesuits began to make greater use of Lithuanian, both in sermons and in the production of religious works (Jakštas, 1969: 87–8). The Jesuits also produced several grammars and dictionaries for Lithuanian (Jakštas, 1969: 88). Literature in Lithuanian, therefore, began in the sixteenth to seventeenth centuries.

It would appear, though, that more than one form of written Lithuanian was developed in the seventeenth century. Comrie says that the earliest writings in Lithuanian were in Low Lithuanian, i.e. the dialects of the Lowlands (1981: 147), and the Encyclopaedia Britannica notes that a fairly uniform written Lithuanian language was developed in the seventeenth century based on the 'West High Lithuanian dialects', i.e. the dialect of the western highlands (Encyclopaedia Britannica, 1985b: 691). It seems that it was the practice to draw on various Lithuanian dialects in creating written Lithuanian (Encyclopaedia Britannica, 1985: 691).

By the nineteenth century three literary dialects of Lithuanian were in use (Encyclopaedia Britannica, 1985a: 401). During the first half of the nineteenth century, though, a movement arose to create a single, unified standard literary language (Encyclopaedia Britannica, 1985: 401). This movement led to the creation of modern literary Lithuanian which is based on the southern dialects of the western High Lithuanian dialect region (Encyclopaedia Britannica, 1985b: 691; Endzelins, 1971: 21). Like the other Lithuanian literary forms, the modern literary language uses the Latin alphabet.

However, from the middle of the nineteenth century the Russians, who had taken control of Lithuania after the partition of Poland and Lithuania in the late eighteenth century, tried to Russify Lithuania (Jakštas, 1969: 122ff). The Russian authorities banned the use of the Latin alphabet and attempted to force the Lithuanians to use the Cyrillic alphabet. They also replaced Polish with Russian in schools and administration (Jakštas, 1969: 130).

During this period, though, literature in Lithuanian continued to be published abroad and books were smuggled into Lithuania by the tens of thousands (Jakštas, 1969: 132ff). Much of this literature sought to rally Lithuanians against Russian political control and Polish cultural dominance (Encyclopaedia Britannica, 1985a: 401). In 1904 the prohibition against Lithuanian written in the Latin alphabet was lifted, and in 1905 Lithuanian was allowed in schools — at least in the study of religion (Jakštas, 1969: 135–6).

In 1918 Lithuania became an independent country and Lithuanian its official language (Gerutis, 1969: 145ff). In the 1920s a terminology commission was set up to 'form and standardise terminologies for the state administration and various scientific fields' (Gerutis, 1969: 196). The influence of the standard literary language developed in the nineteenth century led to the 'mixing and levelling of the Lithuanian dialects' from this time (Encyclopaedia Britannica, 1985b: 691). The creation of the Lithuanian SSR after the Soviet take-over of Lithuania in the 1940s has resulted in an intensification of the levelling of dialects (Encyclopaedia Britannica, 1985b: 691).

Lithuanian is divided into several dialect areas. The basic division is between the Low, or lowland, dialect group, sometimes called Samogitian, and the High, or highland, dialect group (Comrie, 1981: 147; Endzelins, 1971: 21). The High dialect group is further divided into western, central and eastern dialects (Endzelins, 1971: 21). The dialects differ quite considerably from one another though these differences do not appear to cause problems of comprehension. The diffusion via education and the media of the standard literary form of the language, which is based on the western High Lithuanian dialects, has led to a levelling of the other spoken dialects, and the spoken version of literary Lithuanian is now probably seen as the standard form.

For Lithuanian, therefore, a standard form was developed in the nineteenth century based on the western High Lithuanian dialects. This form is probably also now the spoken standard due to its diffusion through education and the media. There are several spoken dialects of Lithuanian which differ quite markedly from each other, but do not appear to cause problems of comprehension. These dialects are being levelled by the influence of the standard.

References

COMRIE, B. 1981, *The Languages of the Soviet Union*. Cambridge: Cambridge University Press.

ENCYCLOPAEDIA BRITANNICA 1985a, Lithuanian language and literature. In: *Micropaedia* Vol. 7, p. 401.

ENCYCLOPAEDIA BRITANNICA 1985b, Baltic languages. In: *Macropaedia* Vol. 22, pp. 690–93.

ENDZELINS, J. 1971, *Comparative Phonology and Morphology of the Baltic Languages*. The Hague: Mouton (translated by W. R. Schmalstieg and B. Jegers).

DEMBROWSKI, H. E. 1982, *The Union of Lublin: Polish Federalism in the Golden Age*. New York: Columbia University Press (East European Monographs, No. CXVI).

GERUTIS, A. 1969, Independent Lithuania. In: A. GERUTIS (ed.) *Lithuania: 700 Years* (pp.145-256). New York: Manylands Books.

JAKŠTAS, J. 1969. Lithuania to World War 1. In: A. GERUTIS (ed.) *Lithuania: 700 Years* (pp. 43–144). New York: Manylands Books.

PUZINAS, J. 1969, The origins of the Lithuanian nation. In: A. GERUTIS (ed.) *Lithuania: 700 Years* (pp. 1–42). New York: Manylands Books.

SENN, A. E. 1959, *The Emergence of Modern Lithuania*. New York: Columbia University Press.

Macedonian

Macedonian is a South Slavonic language which was brought to the Balkan region by Slav settlers sometime in the sixth or seventh centuries. Like other South Slavonic languages such as Serbian and Bulgarian it is written in the Cyrillic alphabet.

It should be noted at the outset that in purely linguistic terms Macedonian is very closely related to Serbian and Bulgarian (Lunt, 1952: 6). The situation appears to be that there is a continuum of dialects which shade into one another so that at the extreme ends, i.e. south-eastern Bulgaria and north-western Serbia there may be problems of comprehension, but at any two proximate points there will be complete mutual intelligibility. As Darby puts it 'the Macedo-Slavs pass by scarcely perceptible grades from the Bulgars of eastern Macedonia to the Serbs north of Skoplje' (1966: 136). And Friedman says:

> the transitions ... from Serbo-Croatian to Macedonian and to Bulgarian, and from Macedonian to Bulgarian are so gradual that no linguistic criterion such as mutual intelligibility can serve as the defining concept of language. The decision as to whether a given transitional Slavic dialect belongs to one or another language is not a linguistic one but a sociopolitical one. (Friedman, 1985: 36)

However, the gradual shading of one dialect into another across political frontiers is not unique to the Balkans. It occurs in many languages, for example Dutch and German shade into one another in the border regions. In the Balkan region, though, mutual intelligibility is perhaps more dependent on lexical items than grammar.

Macedonian, or at least the dialect spoken around Salonika, was the basis of the first Slavonic literary language. This language, Old Church Slavonic, was developed for religious works (Comrie, 1979: 129), but was also used for secular writing.

After the development of Old Church Slavonic a separate literary form of Macedonian did not appear until the nineteenth century and was not officially recognised and codified until the mid-twentieth century (Friedman, 1985: 34). As De Bray puts it, by an irony of history the people whose ancestors gave to the Slavs their first literary language, were the last to have their modern language recognised as a separate Slavonic language, distinct from the neighbouring Serbian and Bulgarian. (De Bray, 1951: 243)

Throughout their history the Macedonians have almost never been in control of an independent state. Macedonia has, at various times, been ruled by the Byzantines, the Bulgarians, the Serbs and the Ottoman Turks (Darby, 1966: 138ff). During most of the period of Turkish rule Greek was very influential in Macedonian life. Friedman says of Macedonia and Bulgaria at the end of the eighteenth century:

At this time, the principal determining factor in ethnic identification was religion, and the majority of Slavs in Bulgaria and Macedonia were Orthodox Christians. As the Orthodox Church in European Turkey was controlled by the Greek patriarchate of Constantinople, which by 1767 had succeeded in eliminating the last vestiges of the independent Slavic churches in its jurisdiction, these Orthodox Slavs were considered *Greek*. The Greek Church actively sought to extend this definition to all spheres of cultural life, i.e. it sought to Hellenise those people under its jurisdiction. Thus, for example, while the few literate Orthodox Slavs of this period had essentially two literary languages at their disposal — dialectally influenced recessions of Church Slavonic and Greek — the Greek Church vigorously discouraged the use of the former and wished to replace it completely with the latter. (Friedman, 1985: 33)

In the early decades of the nineteenth century there was a reawakening of nationalism among the Southern Slavs. This led to a literary and educational revival of Macedonian and Bulgarian (Darby, 1966: 142; Friedman, 1985: 33). However, as Friedman points out:

All the writers of this early period who were attempting to combat Hellenisation and archaisation [i.e. the use of Old Church Slavonic] and to raise vernacular Slavic to literary status called their language *Bulgarian*. The distinction between *Macedonian* and *Bulgarian* is essentially immaterial for this time as the proponents of a literary language based on colloquial Slavic all wrote in their local dialects. In their struggle with Hellenisation and archaisation, these writers did not concern themselves with the choice of a particular dialectal base. (Friedman, 1985: 33, his emphasis)

In the 1840s, however, two major centres of literary activity grew up. One in Macedonia and the other in Bulgaria. According to Friedman, the Macedonians envisioned a literary language incorporating both Macedonian and Bulgarian elements whereas the Bulgarians wanted a literary language incorporating solely Bulgarian elements (1985: 33).

In 1872 Bulgaria was granted ecclesiastical autonomy. The authority of the Bulgarian exarchate extended also over parts of Macedonia. Consequently the Bulgarian form of the literary language tended to dominate and the form with Macedonian elements was suppressed (Darby, 1966: 144; Lunt, 1952: 4).

Thus, Bulgarian and Greek vied with each other as the language of literature and education in Macedonia in the latter part of the nineteenth century. However, these were not the only two languages attempting to gain influence. Serbian was also being pushed by the Serbian government, as was Romanian in support of the Vlachs (Romanians) who lived in the region. According to Darby, at the turn of the century there were upwards of 800 schools teaching in Bulgarian, about 180 schools teaching in Serbian and over 900 teaching in Greek (1966: 146).

After the Balkan wars of 1912 and 1913 Macedonia was divided into three parts. Bulgaria got the area known as Pirin Macedonia, Greece the area known as Aegean Macedonia, and Serbia got Vardar Macedonia (Lunt, 1952: 4; Karoski, 1983: 22).

Many Anatolian Greeks were settled in Aegean Macedonia and many Macedonians moved out of the area. Karoski says that an estimated 80% of Macedonian arrivals in Australia up to 1940 were from Aegean Macedonia (1983: 26). And Lunt notes that 'those Macedonians who did not emigrate were subjected to intensive Hellenisation' (1952: 4). A Greek professor, in fact, states that Aegean Macedonia 'is inhabited solely by Greeks. It has resisted Slavic penetration' (Andriotis, 1966: 56).

In Pirin Macedonia 'the Bulgarians continue to maintain that Macedonian is a Bulgarian dialect, or "regional variant" ...' (Friedman 1985: 48). As a consequence, literary Bulgarian is the standard form of the language for the Pirin Macedonians in Bulgaria. This applies as well to those Aegean Macedonians who migrated to Bulgaria earlier this century (Friedman, 1985: 34, 49).

According to Friedman, up until 1944 Vardar Macedonia was treated as being a part of Serbia and Macedonian was treated as a dialect of Serbian. Literary Serbian was the language used in schools, the press, and all facets of public life between the two World Wars (1985: 34). However, there were some authors who were writing in Macedonian at this time, even though this form was considered as a dialectal, folkloristic genre (Lunt, 1952: 5; Friedman, 1985: 34–5).

In 1944 Vardar Macedonia was proclaimed as a republic of Yugoslavia, and the official language was declared to be Macedonian (Lunt, 1952: 5). The dialect chosen as the basis of the official language was that of the central region of Vardar Macedonia. De Bray considers that this dialect had been used by some of Macedonia's best-known poets and their writing influenced the choice of this dialect (1951: 246). But Palmer and King believe that more important reasons for the choice were that the central dialect was the most unlike both Serbian and Bulgarian, and that this region was the most populous area in Vardar Macedonia (1971: 155). However, as Lunt notes 'Macedonian, like most literary languages, contains elements from several regional dialects, and is not identical with any single dialect' (1952: vii). The Cyrillic alphabet, as used for Serbian but with minor modifications, was chosen for the orthography (De Bray, 1951: 24f).

Since the 1940s 'the standardisation of the new literary language has been a continuing process' (Palmer & King, 1971: 157). Grammars and dictionaries have been published and the language is in constant use in schools, the press, radio, books and so on. An effort has been made to enrich the language with neologisms taken from or based on Macedonian dialects, while purging the new language, as far as possible, of terms borrowed from other languages such as Serbian, Bulgarian and Russian (Palmer & King, 1971: 157; Friedman, 1985: 46).

However, the influence of Serbian, and, perhaps, Croatian is still felt since many textbooks are written in Serbian or Croatian and many television and radio programmes as well as films are produced in Serbia (Friedman, 1985: 48).

According to Videoski there are three institutions responsible for the new Macedonian literary language. These are: the Department of Yugoslav Languages; the Institute for the Macedonian Language; and the Macedonian Academy of Arts and Sciences (1971: 212–3).

Although the literary language has by now been more or less fully standardised, and at least one generation has been educated exclusively in the new language, dialectal variation is still common. Friedman notes that dialectal forms are still used, by some speakers, at home and at work and sometimes on radio and TV, though professional news readers tend to use the standard form exclusively (1985: 47).

Thus, in what was Vardar Macedonia but is now a republic within Yugoslavia, a new standard literary language has been developed. This language is now the official language of the republic of Macedonia and is used in education, the media, books and so on, though dialectal forms have by no means died out. In Pirin Macedonia, now part of Bulgaria, dialects spoken by Macedonians are considered to be Bulgarian dialects and publications in the Macedonian literary language are generally not permitted (Friedman, 1985: 49). In Aegean Macedonia, now part of Greece, 'Macedonian is not permitted in the press, in schools, or in any phase of public life' (Friedman, 1985: 50).

De Bray divides the spoken dialects of Macedonian into six major groups, of which three are in the Socialist Republic of Macedonia, two in Aegean

Macedonia, and one in both the Socialist Republic of Macedonia and Pirin Macedonia (1952: 254–6). Friedman, basing his work on the Macedonian linguist Videoski, says there are three major groups; northern, eastern and western which can be further broken down into eleven minor groups (1985: 36). As noted earlier, though, these dialects shade gradually into Serbian in the north and Bulgarian in the east. Also, it is perhaps worth noting that the dialect on which literary Macedonian is based is considered to be a member of the western group spoken around Prilep, Titov Veles, Bitola and Kicevo (Friedman, 1985: 36; De Bray, 1952: 254–5).

It is unclear to what extent, or in what situations, speakers use their local dialect or the new 'standard' form. Within Macedonia it is, however, probable that the new standard language will be the prestigious code, though no information was available on whether regional dialects were now considered stigmatised or merely inappropriate in certain situations. Because of the recent development and introduction of the new standard form it is possible that migrants from Macedonia may not be altogether clear as to what constitutes standard Macedonian.

In Australia, according to a report commissioned by the Australian Department of Immigration and Ethnic Affairs, it appears that regional dialects are considered to be acceptable. The report says:

> There was some disagreement [among Macedonian informants] about which form of Macedonian should be taught and, in particular, whether there was a standard Macedonian language or not. Some said standard Macedonian was spoken in Macedonia but not here. Others said standard Macedonian was the language formalised in grammar tests. Dialect was not regarded as a problem, as it was claimed that all forms of Macedonian were mutually comprehensible. But it was also somewhat contradictorily claimed that books are written in standard Macedonian, yet only the educated could use and understand this language adequately. (Kalantzis *et al.*, 1986: 378)

The report also cites a letter written on behalf of the Macedonian Welfare Association which states:

> We are of the opinion that you of the Centre for Multicultural Studies may be at this stage confused as to whether or not there is in fact a 'standard' Macedonian Language ... . Let us assure you that the language we all speak, whether it be colloquial or literal, is 'standard' Macedonian. (quoted in Kalantzis *et al.*, 1986: 378)

It would appear, therefore, that dialects are in no way stigmatised in Australia since all forms of Macedonian are considered 'standard'. However, there also appears to be a perception of differences between a 'standard' form and regional dialects. This paradox is a fairly common one in sociolinguistics and reflects the problems of languages which have had a standardised literary language for only a relatively short time.

The situation among migrants from Macedonia is compounded, though, by the fact that some of them may have migrated before the new literary language was fully implemented. Also some migrants may have come from Aegean or Pirin Macedonia where the literary form of Macedonian has not been implemented at all. A further problem is political, where migrants may be opposed to the political situation in the Socialist Republic of Macedonia and hence reject the literary language as a manifestation of that government.

For example, according to a member of the Slavic Studies department at Macquarie University, of the publications available in Australia for Macedonians, one tends to use Bulgarian orthography and another uses non-standard Macedonian as much, if not more, than standard Macedonian.

On the other hand, of those Macedonians who are aware of the standard form, at least some, if not most, are likely to consider it to be prestigious. It is probable that these speakers would desire the standard on radio and other areas of the media. Unfortunately, it is impossible to say what percentage of the Macedonian migrant population are aware of the standard or, if aware, accept its use.

As a consequence, for Macedonian, even though there is a standard form of the language which would normally be considered prestigious, its use may cause problems of comprehension (perhaps more due to lexical items than grammar) for some sections of the migrant population, or it may arouse political debate as to its appropriateness. However, using any other dialect would be likely to cause as many, if not more, problems of comprehension and would probably be looked down on by those members of the community who expect to hear the standard form in the media.

References

ANDRIOTIS, N. P. 1966, *The Federative Republic of Skopje and its Language*. Athens.
COMRIE, B. 1979, Russian. In: T. SHOPEN (ed.) *Languages and their Status* (pp. 91–151). Cambridge, MA: Winthrop Publishers Inc.
DARBY, H. C. 1966, Macedonia. In: S. CLISSOLD (ed.) *A Short History of Yugoslavia: From Early Times to 1966* (pp. 135–53). Cambridge: Cambridge University Press.
DE BRAY, R. G. A 1951, *Guide to the Slavonic Languages*. London: J. M. Dent and Sons.
FRIEDMAN, V. A. 1985, The sociolinguistics of literary Macedonian. *International Journal of the Sociology of Language* 52, 31–57.
KALANTZIS, M., SLADE D. and COPE B. 1986, *The Language Question: The Maintenance of Languages Other Than English*. Canberra: Australian Government Publishing Service (Report for the Department of Immigration and Ethnic Affairs).
KAROSKI, S. 1983, *Macedonians in Sydney: The Macedonian Community Profile*. Sydney: Ethnic Affairs Commission of NSW.

LUNT, H. G. 1952, *A Grammar of the Macedonian Literary Language*. Skopje.
PALMER, S. E. and KING, 1971, *Yugoslav Communism and the Macedonian Question*. Hamden, Connecticut: Archon Books.
VIDEOSKI, B. 1971, The Macedonian language and its affirmation in the world of Slavonic studies. *Macedonian Review* 1 (2–3), 211–6.

Maltese

The language spoken in Malta can be traced back only as far as the Arab conquest of the island in 870 AD. The language spoken prior to the Arab conquest has disappeared, though Nelson asserts that civilisation on the island can be dated to at least 3800 BC and that the Phoenecians, Carthaginians, Romans and Byzantines all had settlements on the island (Nelson, 1978: 14). Aquilina believes the language spoken by the Maltese prior to the Arab invasion was probably Punic. He says,

> Punic, an offshoot of Phoenecian was phonetically and lexically so akin to Arabic that the new overlords must have found little difficulty in overpowering the language of the not very numerous natives. (Aquilina, 1961: 121)

The Arabic conquest, therefore, laid the foundations of the Maltese language as it is known today. Aquilina says that

> Maltese is morphologically Arabic with a close kinship to the North African dialects, and specifically a closer kinship to Tunisian, with sporadic evidences of Moorish influences from Spain. (Aquilina, 1976: 9)

Beeston puts it more strongly when he says, 'Maltese is unquestionably an Arabic vernacular' (1970: 12).

It is worth noting that while the Arabs succeeded in imposing their language on the Maltese, they did not succeed in imposing their religion. Christianity on Malta dates back probably to around 60 AD when St. Paul was shipwrecked on the island and in 1049 AD the majority of Maltese were still Christian (Owen, 1969: 26–8). Aquilina notes that there is no evidence of Islamic words in Maltese though there are words which Maltese shares with the Christian Arabs of Syria (1961: 46). He also notes, however, that

> the Maltese are the only Christian people with an entirely Western Civilisation who are members of the Catholic Church and address God as Alla, a word which belongs tc ie world of Semitic worship. (Aquilina, 1976: 3).

Arabic, however, is not the only language which has contributed to modern Maltese. In 1090 AD the Normans arrived from Sicily and took the island from the Arabs. They brought Sicilian, a Romance language, with them. The introduction of Sicilian by the ruling élite, though, did not affect the structure, or morphology, of Maltese. What it did affect was the vocabulary and the phonology, or sounds. As Aquilina puts it:

... as the new masters of the Maltese Archipelago they began to exercise considerable phonetic and lexical influences on the language of the natives. But while the Arabs had practically imposed their language on the people, the Normans affected the morphology and syntax of Maltese very superficially. When the Normans conquered the island, they found a Semitic language which had already become an integral part of the speech-habits of the people. (Aquilina, 1961: 58)

Many new words, originally of Sicilian and later of Southern Italian origin, therefore, began to enter the basically Arabic structure of Maltese. The borrowing from these Romance languages continued through successive European rulers of Malta who usually maintained Sicilians and Italians in positions of authority (Aquilina, 1961: 58). During the rule of the Knights of the Order of St John of Jerusalem (1530–1798) the number of words of Romance origin entering Maltese was probably greater than at any other time since they, unlike most rulers, actually lived on the island. They also maintained Sicilians and Italians in positions of authority in both religious and secular areas (Aquilina, 1961: 58).

The consequence of this borrowing is that in Maltese today there are more words of Romance origin than of Arabic origin (Aquilina, 1976: 4). Also, the phonology has been altered by the influence of the European élite and although it is still basically Arabic there are now distinct differences (Aquilina, 1961: 122). Thus, for Maltese today, Arabic is not easily intelligible, apart from simple phrases, even when the words used still survive in the Maltese language (Aquilina, 1961: 122).

In fact, as Aquilina puts it,

linguistically, Maltese is a unique cross-breed of East and West, with the individuality of a separate language, compounded of Semitic and Romance elements, but still essentially a Semitic tongue ... . (Aquilina, 1959: 351).

The Maltese language, however, was for a considerable period of time used only as a vernacular and not as the language of the church or the state. The language of the élite and consequently the prestige language was Italian (Aquilina, 1961: 59; Owen, 1969: 52). The arrival of the British in 1800 brought English to Malta and English and Italian were the official languages of Malta till 1934. It was only in 1934 that Maltese replaced Italian as an official language with English (Aquilina, 1961: 102). Though Owen notes that at this time English was the language of administration and Maltese the language of the courts (1969: 70).

As well as not being an official or prestigious language, Maltese had no official written form of any consequence till this century. Owen notes that as Maltese had no written format, Italian had gradually become the indigenous written language and, consequently, the spoken language of the literate sections of the community. (Owen, 1969: 52)

Aquilina notes that most writing was in Italian (1961: 63) and he says:

The standard orthography of Maltese, known as *Tal-Ghagda*, was officially recognised by the government in 1934. There had been other short-lived, officially recognised, systems of spelling before, but for one reason or another they did not strike root, and were disused after a short trial. (Aquilina, 1961: 75)

At the present time English and Maltese appear to co-exist on Malta. According to Owen, in the early sixties half of the daily newspapers were in English and half in Maltese and there were two radio stations, one English and one Maltese (1961: 122). And, according to Nelson, English programs are still regularly broadcast on radio (1978: 30).

Aquilina notes that there are many dialects of Maltese. He says,

though Maltese is spoken by a population of little more than 300,000 inhabitants in an area of 122 square miles, the number of phonetic dialectal variations, none unintelligible elsewhere in the same area, is considerable … . (Aquilina, 1959: 1)

Though there is no recognised standard pronunciation (Aquilina, 1959: 1) the dialect used in the capital, Valletta, and that used by educated speakers are generally considered to be prestigious (Aquilina, 1959: 1; 1976: 47).

The introduction of Maltese into the schools, which only occurred in 1941, and the spreading of radio and television is tending to level out dialectal differences. As Aquilina puts it, 'even if the dialectal differences will not be wiped out completely, they are bound to suffer serious damage' (1976: 47).

References

AQUILINA, J. 1959, *The Structure of Maltese: A Study in Mixed Grammar and Vocabulary*. Malta: The Royal University of Malta.
AQUILINA, J. 1961, *Papers in Maltese Linguistics*. Malta: The Royal University of Malta.
AQUILINA, J. 1976, *Maltese Linguistic Surveys*. Malta: The Royal University of Malta.
BEESTON, A. F. L. 1970, *The Arabic Language Today*. London: Hutchinson.
NELSON, N. 1978, *Malta*. London: B. T. Batsford.
OWEN, C. 1969, *The Maltese Islands*. Newton Abbot: David and Charles.

Mandarin

Mandarin is usually considered to be a dialect of Chinese, and Chinese to be an independent branch of the Sino-Tibetan family of languages (Li & Thomspon, 1979: 295–6). Chang and Chang place the origin of Chinese in the Yellow River basin sometime between 3000 and 2500 BC (1980: 182), though Forrest considers that the history of Chinese

> extends into the past indefinitely, to a date which we cannot even conjecture, when Chinese and Tibetan formed one common language as yet undifferentiated. (Forrest, 1965: 112)

The name 'Mandarin' is actually an English translation of *Guanhua* 'officials' language' or 'officials' speech'. That is, Mandarin means the speech form used by officials, the Mandarins (Li & Thompson, 1979: 296; Hsu, 1979: 120).

However, the name 'Mandarin' is in general use in the West for the major dialect group in China. Mandarin is spoken by perhaps as many as 700 million Chinese (DeFrancis, 1984: 54). It is spoken as a native language throughout most of China except the central and southern coastal provinces. It is also spoken in Taiwan and by large Chinese communities in Singapore and Malaysia as well as in other Chinese communities throughout the world. In Taiwan and Singapore, though, Mandarin is not the mother tongue dialect of most of the population but is learnt as a second dialect.

The history of spoken Chinese is usually divided into five periods: Proto-Chinese, Archaic, Ancient, Middle, and Modern Chinese (Forrest, 1965: 48). Forrest dates the rise of the modern dialects to about 1500 AD (1965: 209).

The history of the written language goes back to at least 1500 BC as is evidenced by the characters found on bones used for divination known as 'oracle bones'. These characters are, however, already so sophisticated that, as Chang and Chang note, writing probably began at least a thousand years earlier (1980: 50ff).

The Chinese writing system is not alphabetic. Instead of letters, a system of characters is used to represent words. The characters began as pictographs but soon evolved beyond this stage, and complex characters using semantic elements and semantic plus phonetic elements became the more usual forms (DeFrancis, 1984: 74ff).

The characters were first codified and standardised in about 200 BC (Forrest, 1965: 48; Chang & Chang, 1980: 61). And by about 200 AD, in the Han dynasty, the system of characters still in use today had taken shape (DeFrancis, 1984: 83). According to DeFrancis, in the second century AD about 82% of Chinese characters were formed using the semantic–phonetic principle, and in the eighteenth century about 97% used this principle (1984: 84). Chinese is written vertically and from right to left (Hsu, 1979: 123).

Since the Communist takeover of mainland China certain changes to the writing system have been introduced. A simplification of some of the characters has been undertaken; by 1964 some 2,000 had been simplified, and this process is still continuing (Li & Thompson, 1979: 329). The simplified characters are not, however, used in Taiwan. As well, a phonetic system for writing Mandarin using the Roman alphabet was officially introduced in 1958 (Seybolt & Chiang, 1979: 25). This system, known as Pinyin, is used in schools to teach the pronunciation of characters (Chang & Chang, 1980: 72), and, since 1979, has replaced all other 'Romanisations', such as the Wade–Giles system, which were in use; thus 'Peking' in one of the old systems of Romanisation has become 'Beijing' and 'Mao Tse-tung' has become 'Mao Zedong' (Chang & Chang, 1980: 33).

It is important to note that written Chinese, in both characters and Romanised Pinyin, is based on the structure and vocabulary of Mandarin (Li & Thompson, 1987: 811). Speakers of all other dialects, though, use the same characters since there is only one written language. As Li & Thompson say:

Since the initial appearance of the Chinese written system more than 4,000 years ago, the Chinese people have had only one written language. Thus, no matter how different the dialects are, literate Chinese people from different parts of the country have always been able to communicate with each other through writing, and they all have access to the same body of literature. (Li & Thompson, 1979: 326)

Literature in Chinese has a long history, but, as is often the case, the literary form of the language became divorced from the spoken language. As Chang & Chang put it:

Like other tongues, the Chinese spoken language has also altered over the centuries. Yet while the speech of all classes of Chinese mutated as years passed, the written language used by scholars and bureaucrats diverged more and more from the spoken language, and developed at last into a unique literary style that came to be known as *wenyan*, or 'literary speech'. (Chang & Chang, 1980: 63)

In the early twentieth century a movement began to reform the literary language and bring it closer to the spoken language. This movement was helped by the end of imperial rule in 1911, but only really became effective after demonstrations in 1919. The new literary form encouraged people to write as they spoke and this form is known as *bai hua* 'plain language' (Chang & Chang, 1980: 68–9). It would appear that *bai hua* has now taken over from *wenyan* as the literary form of the language in mainland China, though *wenyan* is still in use to some extent. Chang & Chang note that:

> Enclaves of scholars and poets in Taiwan and other overseas Chinese communities still read and write in the old way. Middle school students in the People's Republic are taught to read *wenyan* through textbooks of selected readings, but are not asked to compose or to read the original classics in their entirety; for reasons that are as much political as educational. (Chang & Chang, 1980: 74–5)

Spoken Mandarin is not uniform throughout China. Most scholars divide the Mandarin speaking area into a number of sub-dialects. There does not seem, though, to be agreement as to how many sub-dialects are manifest. Li & Thompson divide Mandarin into five sub-dialects (1979: 297), whereas Chao divides it into only three (1976: 22–3). However, the sub-dialects do not appear to differ greatly from each other, as DeFrancis notes:

> Within the [Mandarin] speech community there are some relatively minor differences … which like those in the English-speaking community are not great enough to cause any serious problems of comprehension. Nevertheless, they are not insignificant. (DeFrancis, 1984: 59)

During imperial times when Beijing was the political and cultural centre of China, the Beijing dialect acted as the basis for the *Guanhua* 'officials' speech' which was the language spoken by all officials and educated people from all over China (Hsu 1979: 119). The Beijing dialect, consequently, acted as a kind of standard, at least for government officials and educated speakers, since, as Seybolt & Chiang say,

> in dynastic times there was no attempt to spread the use of Mandarin throughout the empire. It was simply a medium for official communication. (Seybolt & Chiang, 1979: 25)

When the Republican regime took over China in 1911 they made efforts to introduce a spoken norm based on the everyday speech of an educated native speaker of the Beijing dialect and known as *Guoyu* 'national language' (Hsu, 1979: 119).

The takeover of mainland China by the Communists and the formation of The People's Republic led to the migration of many Republican nationalists to Taiwan. The Republicans imposed their form of Mandarin, *Guoyu*, on the indigenous population who were mostly speakers of Fukienese, a different, mutually unintelligible, dialect of Chinese (DeFrancis, 1984: 59). Fukienese had some influence on *Guoyu*, however, so that although officially the Beijing dialect represents the norm in Taiwan 'there exists everywhere a gap between language norm and language performance' (Hsu, 1979: 124).

In the People's Republic of China a form of Mandarin known as *Putonghua* 'common language' was officially introduced as the standard form in 1955. *Putonghua* is officially defined as

> the Common Speech or Language of the Han people, which adopts the Peking [sic] sound system as its standard of pronunciation, the northern Chinese dialects as its lexical and grammatical bases, and the exemplary works of modern colloquial (*Baihua*) literature as its grammatical model. (Hsu, 1979: 120)

Putonghua is nowadays often referred to as Modern Standard Chinese (Light, 1980: 261).

It appears that *Guoyu* and *Putonghua* are relatively closely related, though there are differences. Both forms are based on the Beijing dialect, but *Guoyu* is based on the dialect as it was spoken prior to 1949 and *Putonghua* is based on the dialect as it is spoken today (Hsu, 1979: 121). As well, the Communist regime has introduced many new vocabulary items into *Putonghua* to replace older words, still found in *Guoyu*, which were considered elitist or derogatory (Li & Thompson, 1979: 327). The influence of the local Fukienese dialect on *Guoyu* has also caused divergence, as noted above. And, as Lock notes

> *Guoyu* also differs from *Putonghua* in not explicitly allowing lexical items from other dialects, from classical literature or borrowings from other languages. (Lock, 1988)

It is perhaps worth noting that in Taiwan the name '*Putonghua*' may be used to denote

> different versions of *Guoyu* spoken by various Chinese dialect speakers with varying degrees of imperfection, the inferior varieties of which amount to some sort of 'pidgin Mandarin'. (Hsu, 1979: 120)

According to Hsu, Radio Peking is considered to be authoritative as far as the pronunciation, terminology and usage of the spoken norm of *Putonghua* is concerned (1979: 128). However, it seems that little prestige or stigma attaches to the actual pronunciation of *Putonghua*. As Li & Thompson put it:

> There is no stigma attached to regional accents in *Putonghua* or to local accents in other dialects. There is a significant absence of social distinction on the basis of accent of speech. For example, several of the national leaders, like the late Zhou En-lai, the late Mao Ze-dong, and Deng Xiao-ping have noticeable regional accents in their *Putonghua*. (Li & Thompson, 1979: 327)

This lack of status or stigma attached to accent is also noted by Lehmann who remarks that

> there seems to be no pressure on speakers to emulate the patterns of intel-
> lectuals or officials ... it is clear that the official status of Peking [sic] pro-
> nunciation is competing with other sources of status. (Lehmann, 1975: 37)

It should be noted, though, that accent in speaking *Putonghua* does not refer only to native Mandarin speakers. In 1955 the Communist regime institut-ed a programme to teach *Putonghua* throughout China, and in 1956 all schools began to use it as the basic instructional medium (Seybolt & Chiang, 1979: 25). Consequently, speakers of other dialects such as Cantonese, Hakka, Fukienese and so on have had to learn *Putonghua*, but there is apparently no stigma attached to *Putonghua* spoken with an accent, nor is there an attempt to eradi-cate other dialects. Rather, speakers are becoming bilingual (Li & Thompson, 1979: 326). As Lehmann points out:

> Leading members of revolutionary committees tell us that they really spoke
> dialect rather than *Putonghua*, referring to the heavy local influence on
> their *Putonghua*. These statements are made without shame or embarrass-
> ment, and the sparkle of local pride below the surface is not hard to detect.
> (Li & Thompson, 1975: 37)

In Singapore a campaign has been underway since 1979 to induce the Chinese population to 'speak more Mandarin' although only 10.3% of the Chinese in Singapore used Mandarin as the main household language in 1980 (Kuo, 1984: 57). The form of Mandarin being promoted in Singapore is essen-tially the same as standard *Putonghua*, but with some lexical differences (Lock, forthcoming). However, a form of Mandarin, known as *Huayu* 'Chinese lan-guage', has been in use in Singapore as the medium of instruction in all Chinese schools for some time, and this form has been heavily influenced by the other Chinese dialects spoken by the majority of Chinese (Hsu, 1979: 129).

Consequently, the imposition of standard *Putonghua*, even though it is now required as the pronunciation of broadcasters, may prove difficult. As Lock (forthcoming) shows in his study of Singaporeans,

> the majority of the sample (77%) explicitly reject the idea that they should
> model their speech on an exonormic standard [i.e. *Putonghua*] and several
> make it clear that they recognise contending norms and/or that norms have
> changed but that they are not prepared to alter their own speech patterns in
> favour of the prescribed standard norm. (Lock, forthcoming)

For Mandarin, therefore, there are at least three forms. *Putonghua* in main-land China which has an official standard form and is being taught to all Chinese no matter what their mother tongue dialect may be, but in which there is no apparant stigma attached to variations in pronunciation, though the form used on

Beijing radio is usually considered to be standard. *Guoyu* is used in Taiwan, and, although similar to *Putonghua*, differs in pronunciation and vocabulary. And in Singapore *Putonghua* is being promoted in the 'speak more Mandarin' campaign but it seems that some people, at least those who are already able to speak Mandarin, may prefer to retain their own form, *Huayu*, though broadcasting is now conducted in as close an approximation to standard *Putonghua* as possible.

As well as these regional differences, there are also socially and educationally conditioned variants, which Lehmann calls 'a series of formal and informal dimensions' (1975: 11). The differences in these forms is primarily in vocabulary and

> range from forms used only by uneducated speakers up to the rather strange local variants of language forms associated with units in the traditional written style and usually used only in the sophisticated milieu of literary discussions among intellectuals. (Kratochvil, 1968: 18).

References

CHANG, R. and CHANG M. S. 1980, *Speaking of Chinese*. New York: Andre Deutsch.

CHAO, Y. R. 1976, *Aspects of Chinese Socio-linguistics: Essays by Y. R. Chao*. Selected by A. S. Dil, Stanford: Stanford University Press.

DEFRANCIS, J. 1984, *The Chinese Language: Fact and Fantasy*. Honolulu: University of Hawaii Press.

FORREST, R. A. D. 1965, *The Chinese Language*. London: Faber and Faber.

HSU, R. S. W. 1979, What is standard Chinese? In: R. LORD (ed.) *Hong Kong Language Papers* (pp. 115–41). Hong Kong: Hong Kong University Press.

KRATOCHVIL, P. 1968, *The Chinese Language Today: Features of an Emerging Standard*. London: Hutchinson University Library.

KUO, E. C. Y. 1984, Television and language planning in Singapore. *International Journal of the Sociology of Language* 48, 49–64.

LEHMANN, W. P. (ed.) 1975, *Language and Linguistics in the People's Republic of China*. Austin: University of Texas Press.

LI, C. N. and THOMPSON S. A. 1979, Chinese: dialect variations and language reform. In T. SHOPEN (ed.) *Languages and Their Status* (pp. 295–335). Cambridge, MA: Winthrop Publishers.

LI, C. N. and THOMPSON S. A. 1987, Chinese. In: B. COMRIE (ed.) *The World's Major Languages* (pp. 811–33). London: Croom Helm.

LIGHT, T. 1980, Bilingualism and standard language in the People's Republic of China. *Georgetown University Roundtable on Language and Linguistics*, pp. 259–79.

LOCK, G. 1988, Standards, norms and variation in Singapore Mandarin. Phd Dissertation, Department of Linguistics, University of Sydney.

SEYBOLT, P. J. and CHIANG G. K. K. 1979, Introduction. *Language Reform in China*. New York: M. E. Sharpe.

Norwegian

Norwegian is a Scandinavian language, part of the Germanic branch of the Indo-European family (Haugen, 1976: 89ff). A characteristically Scandinavian form probably emerged in about the sixth century AD, and in the tenth or eleventh century this form, known as Common Scandinavian began to split into Old West Scandinavian and Old East Scandinavian (Haugen, 1976: 91; 1982: 5). Norwegian is descended from Old West Scandinavian (Vikør, 1975: 35). And, according to Kristensen & Thelander,

> by 1350 the main characteristics of the various dialects [i.e. what we now know as Danish, Swedish, Norwegian etc.] had already emerged, and towards the end of the middle ages, around 1500, the linguistic diversification of Scandinavia [i.e. the evolution of regional dialectal varieties] was reaching its peak. (Kristensen & Thelander, 1984: 223)

The first writing system used in Scandinavia was an alphabetic system known as the Runes, or the *futhark* (Haugen, 1982: 4–5). When Christianity was brought to Scandinavia in the tenth century the Latin alphabet was also introduced (Haugen, 1976: 180ff). For most of the Middle Ages, though, the Latin alphabet was confined mainly to a small educated élite from the church and the court, whereas the Runes were 'generally known and read by every sector of the population, high and low' (Haugen, 1976: 191).

Nevertheless, in Norway a fairly extensive body of literature was produced using the Latin alphabet. The form of language used for these early writings was generally based on the dialect of the region where they were produced, particularly the dialects of Trondheim, Bergen and Oslo (Vikør, 1975: 36). Although, as Vikør notes, a sort of standardisation and codification of the literary language developed in the twelfth and thirteenth centuries, 'standardisation was in the whole period very lax' (1975: 36).

In the fourteenth century Norway was brought into a union with Denmark and Danish administrators gradually introduced Danish as the written language in Norway (Vikør, 1975: 37). The use of Norwegian as a written language declined steadily. In the mid-sixteenth century, with the introduction of the Reformation, the Bible was translated into Danish, but not into Norwegian, even though the Bible translation was used in the Lutheran Church in Norway (Vikør, 1975: 37; Haugen, 1976: 247). After the Reformation, virtually everything which was written in Norway was written in Danish (Haugen, 1982: 13).

The Norwegian population, however, continued to speak Norwegian. The spoken language, though, had evolved to such an extent that the old Norwegian literary language 'was almost incomprehensible to the Norwegians of the sixteenth century' (Abrahamsen, 1965: 126).

One reason for the change in the Norwegian spoken dialects was probably the influence of Low German spoken by traders of the Hanseatic League who dominated trade in Scandinavia for several centuries (Haugen, 1982: 14). According to Haugen, the influence of Low German on Norwegian, as well as other Scandinavian languages, can be found in the vocabulary, syntax and grammar of the language (1982: 14).

By the end of the sixteenth century, then, all writing in Norway was in Danish; the old Norwegian literary language was virtually incomprehensible to Norwegian speakers due to the evolution of the spoken dialects; but the vast majority of Norwegians still spoke Norwegian. Vikør, in fact, considers that it was by about this time that Norwegian dialects had acquired the general features which they still have today (1975: 37).

During the seventeenth and eighteenth centuries the ruling classes and the bureaucratic élite began to speak Danish but with a Norwegian pronunciation, and incorporating a few Norwegian words (Vikør, 1975: 38). According to Abrahamsen, this form of speech arose in the south-east of Norway and was differentiated such that: sermons and public speeches were in pure Danish with a Norwegian pronunciation; the bourgeoisie used a mixed Danish and Norwegian grammar with more Norwegian vocabulary; and everyone knew and used the local dialect at least sometimes (1965: 126; also Marm & Sommerfelt, 1967: x).

The union with Denmark ended in the early nineteenth century, and, although a new union with Sweden was established which lasted till 1905, Norway gained internal independence (Haugen, n.d.: 7). This internal independence, and the rise of Norwegian nationalism which followed it, brought about major changes in the linguistic situation (Vikør, 1975: 38).

The Norwegian Constitution, written just after the disolution of the union with Denmark, stated that the business of the state should be conducted 'in Norwegian' (Haugen, 1966: 29). Initially, though, the influence of Danish increased, especially because of improved education which used Danish grammars (Marm & Sommerfelt, 1967: x).

The speech of the upper classes and the bourgeoisie, i.e. the mixed form of Danish and Norwegian grammar with a Norwegian pronunciation soon became the prestigious spoken form (Haugen, 1976: 407–8). This form is sometimes referred to as Dano-Norwegian, though use of this term is felt to be pejorative by its users who prefer the name *Riksmål* 'language of the realm' (Haugen, 1982: 16). The written form was still almost pure Danish (Haugen, 1976: 408).

During the nineteenth century there was considerable agitation for the written language to be 'Norwegianised' by incorporating more Norwegian vocabulary into it, removing some specifically Danish features, and generally bringing it closer to the speech of the leading classes (Haugen, 1976: 408; Marm & Sommerfelt, 1967: x).

During the nineteenth century too, a movement arose to establish a Norwegian written language based on the Norwegian dialects. The most important figure in this movement for a new Norwegian written language was Ivar Aasen. Aasen studied the old Norwegian dialects and from these he developed a norm for a written language based not on any one dialect but on a synthesis of all of them, though with the conservative Western dialects as the major influence (Haugen, 1982: 16; Vikør, 1975: 40ff; Marm & Sommerfelt, 1967: xi).

The written form of the language developed by Aasen was officially adopted by the Norwegian parliament in 1885 when it was accorded equal status with the usual written form, or *Riksmål* (Haugen, n.d.: 8). This new form was given the name *Landsmål* 'language of the land' by Aasen (Haugen, n.d.: 8).

The introduction of *Landsmål* set the stage for cultural and linguistic conflict between supporters of the two written forms. This conflict does not appear to have been resolved as yet (Haugen, 1967; Vikør, 1975).

In the twentieth century several language reforms have been carried out in Norway. The most important of these were in 1907, 1917 and 1938 (Haugen, n.d.: 9). The object of these reforms was, it appears, twofold; firstly to 'Norwegianise' the spelling of *Riksmål*; and secondly to attempt to bring *Riksmål* and *Landsmål* closer together by introducing some *Landsmål* spellings into *Riksmål* and vice-versa (Marm & Sommerfelt, 1967: xii; Vikør, 1975: 57ff). In the 1920s the names of the two written forms were officially changed: *Landsmål* became known as *Nynorsk* 'New Norwegian' and *Riksmål* as *Bokmål*, 'Book Language' (Haugen, 1982: 16).

At the present time the 'Norwegian Language Council', a kind of language academy, debates problems and makes proposals for changes in the language (Haugen, n.d.: 9).

In Norway, therefore, there are two officially recognised written forms of the language. One, *Bokmål*, is based on Danish though it has been 'Norwegianised' by several language reforms. The other, *Nynorsk*, is based on the old Norwegian dialects, particularly those of the Western region of the country. Although there have been some attempts to bring the two forms closer together they still retain their separate character and, in fact, the controversy continues.

According to Haugen, a distinction is sometimes made between *Bokmål* and *Riksmål*, where *Riksmål* is seen as being based on the prestigious spoken form, what Haugen terms the Colloquial Standard of upper class speakers, while *Bokmål* is seem as being a government-administered form of the language (1968: 682).

As far as the two forms, *Bokmål* and *Nynorsk*, are concerned, they have a very large common core. Haugen says they have identical phonemic systems; virtually identical syntax; and a very similar vocabulary, though *Nynorsk* draws more heavily on the dialects than *Bokmål* (1968: 683). The major difference is in morphology, the way words are formed e.g. prefixing and suffixing (Haugen, 1968: 683). Thus, as Haugen puts it:

> The conflict of the two languages in Norway is thus today reduced to a conflict over the writing of forms that are either felt by many to be vulgar or rustic or that are simply unfamiliar and strange, being either coined or otherwise of limited usage. The two languages are not really distinct languages, but might rather be called stylistic norms ... . (Haugen, 1968: 684)

Although the two forms are in theory equal in status the *Bokmål* form predominates. Newspapers almost exclusively use *Bokmål* as does business and advertising (Vikør, 1975: 66ff). Local newspapers, especially in the west, though, use *Nynorsk*. In Vikør's view, the situation between the two forms is that:

> The choice between the languages is less free than it may seem, mainly because [*Bokmål*] dominates in the big cities, especially the capital Oslo. In these major urban areas lie the 'word industries', i.e. the big papers, broadcasting and publishing houses. Through them, [*Bokmål*] dominates the life of every Norwegian. Administration, industry and commerce is also ... centred in the cities, and those who have gotten their jobs there are often more or less subtly (and not seldom explicitly) forced to adjust themselves to dominant linguistic usage and adopt [*Bokmål*]. In this way, [*Nynorsk*] and Norse popular speech (and their users!) are subjected to a strong discrimination by the power structure of the country. On the other hand, the very consciousness of this discrimination promotes a reaction against it by a number of people who therefore choose [*Nynorsk*] as their language and try to support it in various ways. (Vikør, 1975: 68)

In education, at present, only about one-sixth of Norway's children are taught *Nynorsk* as their main language, and most of these are in the western and midland areas of the country (Haugen, 1982: 16–17). However, all children must learn the other written form up to a certain level of proficiency, and a test in both languages is required for entry to institutions of higher education (Abrahamsen, 1965: 133).

In broadcasting

> parliament stated in 1971 that it wants at least 25% of all programmes to be
> broadcast in *Nynorsk*, for both speech and text subtitles, whether the pro-
> grammes are imported or not. (Berg, 1984: 244)

But, as Berg notes, only about one-fifth or one-sixth of programming is actually
in *Nynorsk* (1984: 244).

A complicating factor in broadcasting is the use of dialect. In 1982 new
internal language rules were adopted by the NRK (Norwegian Broadcasting
Corporation) which allowed for the use of dialects on radio and TV. These rules,
while they state that standard language, i.e. *Bokmål* or *Nynorsk*, should be used
for programmes directed to the entire population, allow for the use of dialect in
regional programmes. Also, there is considerable flexibility with dialect being
acceptable in, for example, a national programme on folk music whereas it may
not be so acceptable in a weather report (Berg, 1984: 244–5). The result of this
for the *Bokmål* and *Nynorsk* proportion is that

> every time a programme leader on radio or TV speaks dialect (and that is
> very often) one half of the programme is counted into the *Nynorsk* category
> and one half into the *Bokmål*. (Berg, 1984: 245)

The regional dialects of Norway can be divided into five major groupings:
Northern, Troudsk, Eastern, Central and Western. All these dialects are mutually
intelligible (Vikør, 1975: 66, 69). It is important to note that *Nynorsk* does not
have a community of native speakers since it is a synthesis of old Norwegian
dialects, though the western regional dialect is close to *Nynorsk* (Haugen, n.d.:
9; Marm & Sommerfelt, 1967: xi). *Bokmål*, on the other hand, is essentially the
speech of the urban educated élite which is spoken as a native dialect still often
referred to as *Riksmål* (Haugen, 1982: 16; Haugen, n.d.: 9).

There is, consequently, considerable variation in Norwegian speech, but all
forms are mutually intelligible. As far as prestige is concerned, it appears that
most, if not all, spoken dialects are relatively prestigious in present day Norway
where there is considerable tolerance towards dialectal speech (Haugen, n.d.: 9;
Vikør, 1975: 68; Berg, 1984: 245). For written expression and formal speech,
however, it seems that *Bokmål* is, if not more prestigious, at least more commonly used, since it is used by four-fifths of the population (Haugen, n.d.: 9).

References

ABRAHAMSEN, S. 1965, The linguistic controversy of modern Norway: A study in cultural
    change. In: C. F. BAYERSCHMIDT and E. J. FRIIS (eds) *Scandinavian Studies: Essays
    Presented to Dr H. G. Leach* (pp. 125–40). Seattle: University of Washington Press.

BERG, H. 1984, The Norwegian Broadcasting Corporation, minority languages and dialects. *Journal of Multilingual and Multicultural Development* 5 (3–4), 243–7.

HAUGEN, E. 1966, *Language Conflict and Language Planning: The Case of Modern Norway.* Cambridge: MA: Harvard University Press.

HAUGEN, E. 1968, Language planning in modern Norway. In: J. A. FISHMAN (ed.) *Readings in the Sociology of Language* (pp. 673–87). The Hague: Mouton.

HAUGEN, E. 1976, *The Scandinavian Languages: An Introduction to their History.* London: Faber and Faber.

HAUGEN, E. 1982, *Scandinavian Language Structures: A Comparative Historical Survey.* Minneapolis: University of Minnesota Press.

HAUGEN, E. n.d., The Scandinavian languages. *Wisconsin Introductions to Scandinavia* 1, 2.

KRISTENSEN, K.and THELANDER M. 1984, On dialect levelling in Denmark and Sweden. *Folio Linguistica* 18 (1–2), 223–46.

MARM, I. and SOMMERFELT A. 1967, *Teach Yourself Norwegian.* London: The English Universities Press.

VIKØR, L. S. 1975, *The New Norse Language Movement.* Oslo: Forlaget Novus.

Persian

Persian is a member of the South-Western sub-branch of the Iranian branch of Indo-European languages (Windfuhr, 1987: 523; Payne, 1987: 514). There are three major varieties of Persian: the Persian of Iran; the Persian of Afghanistan, usually called Dari, but sometimes known as Afghan Persian; and the Persian spoken in Soviet Tajikistan in Central Asia, usually called Tadzhik or Tajiki (Windfuhr, 1987: 523; Comrie, 1981: 163).

The Iranian languages show a very close relationship with Indo-Aryan languages, and are often grouped into an Indo-Iranian group of languages (Payne, 1987: 519; Encyclopaedia Britannica, 1985: 612ff). The Iranian and Indo-Aryan languages probably split into two groups around 2000 BC when the Indo-Aryans migrated into India (Encyclopaedia Britannica, 1985: 614). The Iranians probably moved into present-day Iran around 1000 BC (Payne, 1987: 519).

The earliest attested form of Persian is 'Old Persian' which dates from the sixth century BC (Comrie, 1981: 159). Old Persian was the language of the dynasty which ruled an empire stretching from Iran to Central Asia and north-western India (Payne, 1987: 523–4). Old Persian was written in the cuneiform script (Hodge, 1960: 1). At this time most Iranian forms were probably fairly close (Encyclopaedia Britannica, 1985: 624), but the dominant form was the dialect of the south-western province of Fars where the dynasty arose (Comrie, 1981: 159; Windfuhr, 1987: 523–4).

By the time Old Persian had evolved into what scholars term Middle Persian (from about 300 BC to 950 AD), the Iranian languages had begun to diverge considerably from each other (Encyclopaedia Britannica, 1985: 624). Nevertheless, Middle Persian, a direct descendant of Old Persian, was the main form used throughout the Persian empire as a written language (Payne, 1987: 518). Middle Persian, like Old Persian, was centred on the Province of Fars in south-western Iran (Comrie, 1981: 160; Payne, 1987: 518).

Because the political centre of the Persian empire was in the south-western province of Iran which was originally known as 'Parsa', later Arabicised to Fars, and called 'Perse' or 'Parsis' by the ancient Greeks, the names Persia, Persian and Farsi came to be used (Windfuhr, 1987: 524). The name Iran derives from the Old Iranian word 'aryanam' (Windfuhr, 1987: 524).

190

Middle Persian, as noted above, was used as a written and spoken language throughout the empire (Windfuhr, 1987: 524). The language was, however, not entirely homogeneous and there was a certain amount of regionalisation (Windfuhr, 1987: 524; Encyclopaedia Britannica, 1985: 624). Various forms of the Aramaic script were used to write Middle Persian (Encyclopaedia Britannica, 1985: 630). Perhaps the most important form of Middle Persian, as a direct descendant of Old Persian, is the form known as Pahlavi, or Pehlevi (Comrie, 1981: 159-160).

With the conquest of the Persian empire by the Arab Muslims during the seventh and eighth centuries, Persian declined and Arabic became an important literary language (Windfuhr, 1987: 524). According to Windfuhr, the period of Arabic conquest is also the period of the development of New, or Modern, Persian (1987: 524).

Although Comrie (1981: 160) considers that Modern Persian is a direct descendant of Old and Middle Persian, other scholars disagree. Windfuhr, for example, says that 'none of the known Middle Persian dialects is the direct predecessor of New Persian' (1987: 524). And

> Modern Persian does not represent a straightforward continuation of Middle Persian but is rather a koine (a dialect or language of a small area that becomes a common or standard language of a larger area), based mainly on Middle Persian and Parthian [a Middle Iranian language closely related to Middle Persian] but including elements from other languages and dialects. (Encyclopaedia Britannica, 1985: 624)

Whatever its origin, Modern Persian developed primarily, it appears, in the north-east, i.e. what is today Afghanistan and Soviet Central Asia. It was in this region, more distant from the Muslim capital of Baghdad, that Iranian nationalism reasserted itself (Windfuhr, 1987: 524). By the tenth century the Persian written in the north-eastern regions appears fairly standardised, and Modern Persian began to be used more and more as a written form throughout the Persian speaking area (Windfuhr, 1987: 524). The name 'Dari' was used to denote literary Persian in the tenth and eleventh centuries (Lazard, 1970: 75).

The thirteenth century marks the beginning of Classical Persian and also the shift of the centre away from the eastern regions; first back to Fars in south-western Iran, then north to Isfahan (1501–1731) and finally to Tehran. By this time most regionally marked features had disappeared and a fully standardised literary form was in use (Windfuhr, 1987: 525). Classical Persian continued to be the dominant form till the nineteenth century (Windfuhr, 1987: 525), and is still taught in schools (Hodge, 1960: 1; Lazard, 1970: 66). The Arabic alphabet, with some modifications, has been used to write Modern and Classical Persian since the ninth or tenth centuries (Hodge, 1960: 1). Arabic has also had a considerable influence on Persian vocabulary, with many

Arabic words being borrowed (Lazard, 1970: 76).

Since the nineteenth century political, economic and cultural forces have led to the development of new literary and formal styles of Persian which are closer to the colloquial spoken forms than Classical Persian is (Windfuhr, 1987: 525; Lazard, 1970: 66). The major influence on the new standard has been the educated speech of Tehran. This new standard is used in Iran and is also the norm in Afghanistan for Dari, though decreasingly so (Windfuhr, 1987: 525). As Lazard says:

> In Afghanistan ... where Persian is an official language side by side with Pashto, the traditional high style seems to be losing ground; although it is not clear yet which way the evolution will go and whether the literary language will stick to the Tehran standard or draw nearer the Kabul colloquial, people are conscious of the differences between their Persian, which they now call 'Dari' (an old and venerated name) and the language of Iran. (Lazard, 1970: 66)

Within Soviet Tajikistan a new contemporary standard based on local dialects and written in the Cyrillic alphabet has been developed recently (Windfuhr, 1987: 525; Comrie, 1981: 163–4).

In the spoken forms of Persian there are many sub-dialects, or colloquial forms which differ from the formal standard and from one another (Lazard, 1970: 70). The local forms of speech are not all mutually intelligible, but as is often the case, this is more a case of a continuum of local forms, the extremes of which are mutually unintelligible. Thus, spoken forms of Dari are relatively close to forms of Tadzhik and eastern forms of Persian spoken in Iran, but quite distinct from forms spoken in western Iran (Hodge, 1960: 1).

According to Comrie, Persian can be divided into two main dialectal groups: an Eastern group comprising eastern Iran, Afghanistan and Tadzhik; and a western group comprising forms spoken in western Iran (1981: 163). Windfuhr, though, classifies the dialect groups into three: Iranian, Afghani and Tadzhik, each of which has its own dialectal divisions (1987: 523). The major differences between the dialects lies in their phonology, the sound system (Comrie, 1981: 160; Windfuhr, 1987: 543), though Lazard notes that there are also grammatical and vocabulary differences (1970: 71).

Persian, therefore, has a long literary history, but Modern Persian dates from about the ninth century. And Classical Persian, which is still prestigious and taught in schools, dates from the thirteenth century. A new standard, closer to the spoken language, and most influenced by the educated speech of Tehran, grew up in the nineteenth and twentieth centuries. This form is still the standard in Iran and Afghanistan. However, the Kubuli colloquial form is influencing standard Dari and it appears to be moving away from the Iranian model. There are many local spoken forms of Persian which form a continuum from Soviet Tajikistan to western Iran, the extremes of which are mutually unintelligible.

It is worth noting that in 1936 Pashto was made the official language of Afghanistan in place of Dari. However, as MacKenzie notes, 'this official pre-eminence [of Pashto] was artifical' (1987: 547). Thus, Dari has once again been made an official language of Afghanistan.

References

COMRIE, B. 1981, *The Languages of the Soviet Union*. Cambridge: Cambridge University Press.

ENCYCLOPAEDIA BRITANNICA 1985, Indo-Iranian languages. In: *Macropaedia* Vol. 22, 612–30.

HODGE, C. T. 1960, *Spoken Persian: Part 1*. Washington, DC: The Centre for Applied Linguistics.

LAZARD, G. 1970, Persian and Tajik. In: T. A. SEBEOK (ed.) *Current Trends in Linguistics* Vol. 6 (pp. 64–96). The Hague: Mouton.

MACKENZIE, D. N. 1987, Pashto. In: B. COMRIE (ed.) *The World's Major Languages* (pp. 547–65). London: Croom Helm.

PAYNE, J. R. 1987, Iranian languages. In: B. COMRIE (ed.) *The World's Major Languages* (pp. 514–22). London: Croom Helm.

WINDFUHR, G. L. 1987, Persian. In: B. COMRIE (ed.) *The World's Major Languages* (pp. 523–46). London: Croom Helm.

Polish

Polish is a West Slavonic language, a member of the Slavonic branch of the Indo-European language family. It was for some time the prestige language of a large part of Central Europe, though perhaps less so in Poland itself. As Davies notes:

> In the kingdom [i.e. Poland], where many of the peasantry were frequently Polish-speaking themselves, the educated gentleman could best emphasise his quality by cultivating his Latin. But in the Grand Duchy [i.e. present-day Lithuania, Latvia and the Ukraine], where the masses spoke Latvian, Lithuanian or Ruthenian, a proper command of the Polish language became the mark of gentility and of social accomplishment. It was no accident that in the Romantic period Lithuania and Ukraine produced rather more great Polish writers than Poland itself. (Davies, 1984: 328)

In modern times, though, Polish has become more or less confined to the area enclosed by the borders of Poland drawn up after the second world war (Davies, 1984: 329).

Poland became a Roman Catholic country sometime in the ninth century and Catholicism was officially adopted in 966 AD, (De Bray, 1951: 589; Niedzielski, 1979: 135). In consequence, Latin became the language of all official documents and of education (Davies, 1984: 327–8).

Some documents, mostly religious, were composed in Polish from the late thirteenth century (De Bray, 1951: 590). According to Niedzielski, the writing system used was an adaptation of the system devised by the Czechs (1979: 136) and used the Roman alphabet. In 1364 an academy was set up in Krakow which began to teach in Polish and to propagate its use (Niedzielski, 1979: 136).

It was not until the Reformation and the advent of printing in the sixteenth century, however, that written Polish came into its own (De Bray, 1951: 590; Davies, 1984: 328). In 1543 Polish began to be used in official documents of the courts (Niedzielski, 1979: 136), and a literary form of the language began to be created.

The literary language was originally based on the dialects of western Poland, known as Wielkopolska, centred around Poznan (De Bray, 1951: 589). By the eighteenth century literary Polish had been more or less standardised

(Davies, 1984: 329). However, Latin was still extensively used, and in 1772 a National Education Board was established to teach Polish so that it could replace Latin in every field. However, the work of this board was terminated in 1795 by the partition of Poland by Russia, Prussia and Austria. From 1795 till 1918 Poland more or less ceased to exist and it was only in the Austrian controlled areas that Polish was allowed to be taught in schools with any degree of freedom (Niedzielski, 1979: 136–7). In the other areas the language of the occupiers became the official language and Polish was suppressed.

When Poland was resurrected in 1918 by the Treaty of Versailles each of the three parts of Poland, having managed, sometimes clandestinely, to maintain their language, had developed slightly different forms of the language. As a response to this, various organisations and societies were set up which looked into the problems of standardisation facing the Polish language (Niedzielski, 1979: 137ff).

In 1919 a lexical and orthographic reform of Polish was carried out to provide Poland with an official language. This official language was to be the standard, literary language for the whole of Poland. The dialectal basis of this reform, according to Niedzielski, was the Mazovian dialect spoken around Warsaw (1977: 130). Niedzielski, therefore, considers the Mazovian dialect to be the basis of the modern literary standard. De Bray, on the other hand, considers that the Wielkopolska dialects of western Poland, and the Malopolska dialects from around Krakow were the basis for the modern literary standard (1951: 605).

Whatever the basis of the literary standard may have been, there are, nowadays, several organisations and government bodies, such as the 'Commission for Language Culture' and 'language advising centres', which, taking the 1919 reforms as their basis, propagate 'correct' language, new terminology and so on (Niedzielski, 1979: 145ff). Language norms are thus established and published in book form as well as being disseminated via newspapers, radio broadcasts and conferences (Niedzielski, 1979: 146ff).

The use of these norms in the media is encouraged. As Niedzielski points out:

> The various branches of the government entrusted with some form of education — such as the Ministries of Education, of Culture, of Higher and Technical Institutions of Learning — encourage editors and program directors to avail themselves of the research and advice of language culture specialists. Special booklets are published for the use of specific institutions … [These booklets] offer lists of various types of phonologically, lexically, morphosyntactically, semantically, or stylistically erroneous expressions and their correct equivalents. (Niedzielski, 1979: 145)

However, this emphasis on standardisation does not mean that regional and social dialects have disappeared. De Bray lists five major dialect groups spoken in Poland. All of these dialects are mutually intelligible, though the Kashubian dialects spoken around Gdansk are more distinct from the literary standard than any of the others and some scholars have proposed that they should be considered as a separate language (De Bray, 1951: 601).

The large population movements brought about by the second world war and the repositioning of Poland's borders in 1945, as well as increased urbanisation, have influenced and occasionally destroyed regional dialects (Brooks, 1982: 92). But Brooks notes that

> while dialects are rapidly disappearing in villages, dialectal features present in the speech of the newcomers to cities from these villages influence the standard itself. (Brooks, 1982: 92).

As a consequence, according to Brooks,

> the decline in regional dialects has been compensated for by an increased differentiation in the standard, due either to stylistic distinctions or to newly emerging social dialects. (Brooks, 1982: 92)

Thus, it would appear that there is a formal standard propagated by organisations and government bodies whose use is encouraged in the media and publications. There would also appear to be what Brooks refers to as an 'informal standard' (1982: 91) which represents the spoken language of most of the population and is influenced by regional dialects as well as the formal standard. This 'informal standard' is, Brooks says, becoming more and more differentiated into newly emerging social dialects (1982: 92). The closer to the formal official language a speaker's dialect is, the higher the social prestige (Brooks, 1982: 97).

References

BROOKS, M. Z. 1982, Standardization and the acquisition of the standard language in Poland. *International Journal of Slavic Linguistics and Poetics* 25–26, 91–8.
DAVIES, N. 1984, *Heart of Europe: A Short History of Poland.* Oxford: Clarendon Press.
DE BRAY, R. G. A. 1951, *Guide to the Slavonic Languages.* London: J. M. Dent and Sons.
NIEDZIELSKI, H. 1977, The influence of society and environment on first language usage. *La Monda Linguo-Problemo* 6 (18), 129–39.
NIEDZIELSKI, H. 1979, Language consciousness and language policy in Poland. *Word* 30 (1–2), 134–59.

Portuguese

Portuguese is a Romance language, one of the languages descended from Latin. It is spoken principally in Portugal and Brazil, but it is also used in the former Portuguese colonies of Mozambique and Angola as well as in Macao, Goa, the Azores, Madeira and Timor.

When the Arabs invaded the Iberian Peninsula in 711 AD they quickly brought all but the north of the Peninsula under their rule. By the late tenth and early eleventh centuries, five dialect bands had begun to appear in the Christian north. These dialects were Galician, Leonese, Castilian (the forerunner of modern Spanish), Navarro-Aragonese and Catalan (Pei, 1976: 116). Of these five the two extremes, Catalan in the east and Galician in the west, tended to diverge most (Pei, 1976: 117).

In the eleventh century Galician speakers began to push southwards, reconquering territory from the Arabs. In 1143 Portugal was made a kingdom and by 1250 all of the land which constitutes present-day Portugal was in Christian hands (Elcock, 1975: 440).

However, the original territory of Galicia did not form part of the new kingdom of Portugal. Instead, Galicia remained politically part of Spain which eventually came to be dominated by the Castilians (Pei, 1976: 118–9).

As a consequence, the language of Portugal began to diverge from that of Galicia. As Hall says:

> After the political power and the language had become established farther south, Portuguese split from Galician in the fourteenth century. With the growing subordination of Galicia to Spain, the Portuguese standard lost its connection with the north, and came to be based, rather, first on the usage of Coimbra and then on that of Lisbon. (Hall, 1974: 122–3)

It should be noted, though, that even today, as Pei points out, 'the Galician language (or dialect, as we choose to view it) has far more points of contact with Portuguese than with Castilian' (1976: 118). Nevertheless, Galician is usually seen as 'a regional dialect, under the hegemony of Spanish' (Camara, 1972: 10).

Written literature in Portuguese probably began around the twelfth century (Hall, 1974: 101). The first grammars of literary Portuguese, however, did not appear till the sixteenth century (Camara, 1972: 11). By the eighteenth century modern literary Portuguese was more or less established (Camara, 1972: 11). The literary language was originally based on Galician, but the modern form is based on the dialect of Lisbon (Pei, 1976: 159).

Although there are many dialects of the spoken language in Portugal these are usually divided into three major groups. These are northern, including the dialects of Minho, Douro and Tras-os-Montes (this group is also sometimes considered to encompass the Galician dialects); central, including Beira, Estremadura and the dialects of the Lisbon area; and southern, including Alentejo and the Algarve. The differences between these dialects are relatively slight and would not appear to cause problems of comprehension (Hall, 1974: 23; Camara, 1972: 4). According to Hall the standard form of Portuguese is 'based on the speech of central Portugal, i.e. the territory from Coimbra to Lisbon' (1974: 22).

In Madeira and the Azores the spoken Portuguese differs from that in Portugal (Camara, 1972: 4). However, Hall considers that the differences are only slight, as are those between Portugal and Mozambique and Angola (1974: 22). No information was available to us on the form of Portuguese spoken in Timor.

Brazil is the other major country where Portuguese is the national language. Brazil was colonised by the Portuguese in the early sixteenth century, but it was not until the eighteenth century, with the discovery of gold, that large scale migration from Portugal began (Bortoni-Ricardo, 1985: 16). The migrants came from all areas of Portugal, and, as Camara notes,

> the coming together of such diverse dialects in a single overseas centre must have set up conditions leading to a sort of linguistic compromise, a new kind of dialect. (Camara, 1972: 20)

The élite who came also brought the 'standard' language of Lisbon. However, it was not until the Portuguese court fled to Brazil in 1808 to escape Napoleon's army that an urban centre, Rio de Janeiro, grew up and became the capital of Brazil (Bortoni-Ricardo, 1985: 18). This city

> experienced a rapid development and became a centre of diffusion for the standard language and for a cosmopolitan culture. (Bortoni-Ricardo, 1985: 18).

The Portuguese spoken in Brazil, though, has moved away from that spoken in Portugal. According to Camara the phonology has evolved differently and there are many vocabulary items used in Brazil which come from African (brought by slaves) and indigenous Indian languages which are not found in European Portuguese (1972: 21). And Pei points out that Brazilian Portuguese exhibits some archaic features and 'greater freedom of grammatical constructions' (1976: 165).

There are many dialects in Brazil. As Hall says

> there is variation over a wide spectrum between local dialects and the regional standard; the greatest dialectal differentiation is found in the North-East, but there are also marked variants in Rio Grande do Sul and in Rio de Janeiro ('carioca' dialect). (Hall, 1974: 23)

It appears, however, that prestige or stigmatised dialects are determined more by their grammar than their pronunciation. Bortoni-Ricardo says that

> it is worthwhile noticing that in the case of Portuguese ... there is no generally accepted phonetic standard to which one might refer. (Bortoni-Ricardo, 1985: 26)

She points out, though, that there are a few rural or regional phonetic features which are highly stigmatised (1985: 14).

Rural and lower class speech is, it seems, generally considered stigmatised whereas the speech of the major cities is relatively prestigious (Bortoni-Ricardo, 1985). As far as accent is concerned

> although the Rio de Janeiro accent is rather prestigious in a large area of the country, there are, in addition, many regional standard pronunciations and, furthermore, European Portuguese accents lack prestige in Brazil. (Bortoni-Ricardo, 1985: 14)

The written language of Brazil also differs from European Portuguese. Although there is an academy which attempts to regulate for a common orthography, with identical spellings and using the same diacritic marks such as accents, differences can be found (Camara, 1972: 21; Pei, 1976: 165). As Pei says 'it is often possible to distinguish a work written and published in Brazil from one done in Portugal by its orthography ...' (1976: 165–6).

References

BORTONI-RICARDO, S. 1985, *The Urbanization of Rural Dialect Speakers: A Socio-linguistic Study in Brazil*. Cambridge: Cambridge University Press.

CAMARA, J. M. 1972, *The Portuguese Language*. Chicago: Chicago University Press.

ELCOCK, W. D. 1975, *The Romance Languages*. London: Faber and Faber.

HALL, R. A. 1974, *External History of the Romance Languages*. New York: Elsevier North-Holland.

PEI, M. 1976, *The Story of Latin and the Romance Languages*. New York: Harper and Row.

Punjabi

Punjabi, often spelt Panjabi, is a member of the Indo-Aryan branch of the Indo-European family of languages (Tolstaya, 1981: 1). It is spoken in the State of Punjab in northern India, and in the province of Punjab in Pakistan.

The history of Indo-Aryan languages goes back to the arrival of the Aryan people in India probably about 4000 years ago (Yadav, 1966: 22). By about the fourth century BC a literary form of Indo-Aryan had been standardised and its fundamental norms had been formalised and consolidated in grammatical works (Zograph, 1982: 10). This form, known as Sanskrit, became the language of culture and tradition throughout most of India, and it is still in use, virtually unchanged, to this day (Zograph, 1982: 11).

Sanskrit, as a fixed literary language, soon became divorced from the constantly evolving spoken languages. As the spoken languages evolved they gradually diverged from each other to become separate languages. Most scholars consider that the Indo-Aryan languages passed through two distinct stages before the modern languages appeared. The two stages are known as *Prakrit* and *Apabhramsa*. As Yadav puts it,

> the spoken vernaculars (*Prakrits*) later became 'literary *Prakrits*' too, and in the course of time, passing through the *Apabhramsa* stage, gave birth to the modern Indian languages. (Yadav, 1966: 22)

And Zograph considers that 'the formative period of the new Indo-Aryan languages lies at the end of the first and the beginning of the second millennium AD.' (1982: 16).

The history of Punjabi as a separate language, therefore, goes back about one thousand years. However, as with most related language groups, there is no sharp dividing line between Punjabi and the neighbouring languages. Rather there is a continuum of dialects which form a transition from one language to the next. Zograph says:

> Local forms of speech change every few dozen kilometers, but not sufficiently to make them incomprehensible to close neighbours. As distances increase so too do dialectal variations, until the actual transition to another language is made. Thus, from the Panjab to Bangladesh, there is not one single sharply defined linguistic boundary ... . (Zograph, 1982: 22)

Spoken Punjabi today is made up of several dialects. Grierson considers that there are two major dialect groups which he calls 'Panjabi' and 'Dogri' (1968: 609). However, there appears to be relatively little difference between the two groups other than the fact that Dogri is spoken in the Indian state of Jammu.

Within the Punjabi group of dialects it seems to be generally agreed that the standard form is based on the Majhi dialect spoken around Amritsar (Grierson, 1968: 609; Bahl, 1969: 158). The Majhi dialect is also considered to be the basis of the standard written, literary language (Bahl, 1969: 157ff).

Bahl points out, though, that:

Standard Panjabi, both written and spoken (e.g. the language used by All India Radio in its broadcasts in Panjabi), though primarily based on the Majhi dialect of Amritsar has several grammatical features which can be identified with those of other dialects of the language.

And

The spoken form of Standard Panjabi employed by the masses (in discourses other than strictly formal) differs from the standard written Panjabi in several important respects. (Bahl, 1969: 158)

Bahl also considers that standard Punjabi 'as it is spoken today is not as uniform as is generally thought to be the case', and that the written language is not yet fully stabilised (1969: 158). A language department has been set up in Punjab to lay down rules and make recommendations for the written language (Bahl, 1969: 191).

The officially recognised system of writing used in the Indian State of Punjab at the present time is the Gurumukhi script (Bahl, 1969: 191). Grierson says that this script dates to the sixteenth century when it was developed to write down Sikh religious works (1968: 624). But G. B. Singh considers that the Gurumukhi script can be traced further back than the sixteenth century (quoted in Bahl, 1969: 191).

However, it is only relatively recently that the Punjabi language written in the Gurumukhi script has been officially recognised. In the thirteenth century most of northern India had been conquered by Muslims (Kini & Rao, 1962: 18ff). The Muslim conquerors eventually came to use Urdu, written in the Persian script, as the language of administration, and Punjabi was restricted to domestic and religious spheres (Pandit, 1978: 94–5). When the British arrived in the Punjab around the beginning of the nineteenth century, as well as introducing English they extended the use of Urdu into the British style education system (Pandit, 1978: 95).

As a consequence, the Persian script came to be used to write Punjabi, and, as Pandit notes, those Punjabi's educated prior to Indian independence in 1947 'even now are probably familiar only with Urdu [Persian] orthography' (1978: 100). In the Pakistani part of the Punjabi speaking region the Persian script is still the only one in use (Bahl, 1969: 191).

Another script used to write Punjabi is the Landa script. Grierson calls Landa 'the true alphabet of the Punjab' (1968: 624) since it was the original script used to write the Punjabi vernacular form. It appears, though, that its use has become restricted to the merchant community and is gradually dying out (Grierson, 1968: 624; Bahl, 1969: 191).

In pre-independance Punjab, therefore, Urdu and English were the official languages, though English was restricted to a relatively small élite (Pandit, 1978: 103). The Persian script was used to write Punjabi as well as Urdu, and the Gurumukhi script was used almost exclusively for religious instruction and sacred writing, particularly among the Sikhs. At this time Punjabi speaking Muslims, Hindus, and Sikhs were spread throughout the area.

After Independence and the partition of Punjab between India and Pakistan, considerable demographic changes occurred. Most Muslims migrated to the west into newly created Pakistan, and most Hindus and Sikhs migrated east-wards into Punjab State in India (Brass, 1974: 290). The Muslims who moved to Pakistan, according to Pandit, initially used Urdu almost exclusively, though they are now reviving the use of Punjabi (1978: 107).

In the Indian state of Punjab, language rivalry between Hindus and Sikhs, which had begun in the late nineteenth century but had previously been subordi-nated to a rivalry with Urdu, became much more intense (Das Gupta, 1970: 150ff). The Hindus were pushing for the use of Hindi, written in the Deva-nagari script, and the Sikhs for Punjabi, written in Gurumukhi (Brass, 1974: 286ff; Das Gupta, 1970: 150ff).

As a result of this language rivalry based on religious affiliation, it became common for Hindus to 'disown' Punjabi and declare that their mother tongue was Hindi. As Brass puts it:

> Sikhs in the Punjab came to attach increasing significance to Punjabi in Gurumukhi script as the language of the Sikhs and of the Sikh religion and Hindus developed a similar attachment to Hindi in the Deva-nagari script. There remained a fundamental difference in this respect, however, between Sikhs and Hindus in that the mother tongue of most Sikhs was, in fact, Punjabi, whereas the mother tongue of many Hindus in the Punjab was not Hindi, but was also Punjabi. (Brass, 1974: 326)

In 1966 the State of Punjab originally set up after independance was divided into three new states. One of these new states, the new Punjab, remained Punjabi speaking and predominantly Sikh, while the other two new states would be pre-dominantly Hindu and Hindi speaking (Brass, 1974: 322; Pandit, 1978: 96).

At the present time, therefore, Punjabi appears to be confined to a considerably smaller area than was the case only fifty years ago. It is possible though that Punjabi may still be used by Hindus in the two new states created in 1966, and it may also be being revived by Muslims in the Punjab region of Pakistan. Pandit, in his study of Hindu and Sikh students in Delhi, notes that the students could all speak Punjabi but the domains of usage differed according to religious affiliation (1978: 100f).

The population movements caused both by the partition of the region between India and Pakistan at independence, and the creation of the new Punjab State in 1966, have produced dialectal diffusion. Bahl points out that the original regional distribution of dialects no longer holds, and that it is even possible for different members of the same family to differ in their speech (1969: 194–5).

Punjabi nowadays appears to be predominantly the language of the Sikhs who use the Gurumukhi script. The Punjabi-speaking Muslims of Pakistan use Urdu as their official language, but may be reviving the use of Punjabi and use the Persian script to write it. Hindus seem to be 'disowning' Punjabi in favour of Hindi, but retain its use in certain domains, and, if they write Punjabi, tend to use the Deva-nagari script to write it. The original geographical distribution of dialects has been considerably altered by the mass population movements caused by partition and the setting up of the new Punjab State, but it appears that the Majhi dialect is still considered to be the basis for the standard spoken and written form of Punjabi.

References

BAHL, K. C. 1969, Panjabi. In: T. A. SEBEOK (ed.) *Current Trends in Linguistics* Vol. 5 (pp. 153–200). The Hague: Mouton.

BRASS, P. R. 1974, *Language, Religion and Politics in North India.* Cambridge: Cambridge University Press.

DASGUPTA, J. 1970, *Language Conflict and National Development: Group Politics and National Language Policy in India.* Berkeley: University of California Press.

GRIERSON, G. A. 1968, *Linguistic Survey of India* Vol. IX Pt. 1. Delhi: Motilal Banarsidass.

KINI, K. S. and RAO U. B. S. 1962, *Oxford Pictorial Atlas of Indian History.* Oxford: Oxford University Press.

PANDIT, P. P. 1978, Language and identity: the Panjabi language in Delhi. *International Journal of the Sociology of Language* 16, 93–108.

TOLSTAYA, N. I. 1981, *The Panjabi Language: A Descriptive Grammar.* London: Routledge and Kegan Paul.

YADAV, R. K. 1966, *The Indian Language Problem: A Comparative Study.* Delhi: National Publishing House.

ZOGRAPH, G. A. 1982, *Languages of South Asia: A Guide.* London: Routledge and Kegan Paul (*Languages of Asia and Africa* Vol. 3).

Romanian

Romanian (sometimes spelt Rumanian or Roumanian) is a Romance language, a member of the Indo-European family. It is descended from Latin which was introduced to the area by the Roman conquests of Trajan between 101 and 106 AD (Basdevant, 1965: 3–4).

After the Romans' withdrawal in 271 AD the area which makes up present day Romania was subject to successive invasions and domination by, among others, the Huns, the Magyars (ancestors of the present day Hungarians), the Tartars and the Turks (the Ottomans). In the thirteenth and fourteenth centuries, however, Romanians succeeded in setting up two principalities which now form part of modern Romania; the principalities of Wallachia in the south of the country, and Moldavia in the east (Basdevant, 1965: 16ff).

Nevertheless, it was not until the late sixteenth century that Romanian appeared in written form and then only in religious texts (Elcock, 1975: 284). During the seventeenth century this form of the language replaced Old Church Slavonic as the language of the local Orthodox Church, but only in the principality of Wallachia (Elcock, 1975: 284). In 1688 a new translation of the bible was produced in Wallachia and, according to Basdevant, this 'served as a model for the literary language' (1965: 30). Other texts composed in Moldavia used the same form of the language as the bible translation and consequently 'a literary standard was established' for both Wallachia and Moldavia (Elcock, 1975: 498).

The alphabet used for these texts was the Cyrillic alphabet. As well, there was in the language used a high proportion of words of Slavonic origin, though the grammar was entirely Romance (Elcock, 1975: 284–5).

In 1816 the first school which conducted classes in the Romanian language was opened in Bucharest, the capital of Wallachia (Basdevant 1965: 40). Then in 1859 Wallachia and Moldavia were united and the new state was given the name Romania (Elcock, 1975: 498; Close, 1974: 31). (Note: Basdevant (1965) gives the date as 1861). After the setting up of the school and with a reawakening of awareness that Romanian was a Romance language, a movement grew up to replace Slavonic and other foreign words with words from Latin, French and Italian (Pei, 1976: 141). This movement, it seems, was more successful among the intellectuals than the ordinary people. As Pei puts it, this importation of

Romance vocabulary 'gives the literary language ... a strongly Romance flavour that does not altogether coincide with the popular speech' (1976: 141).

One result of this movement, though, which was successful was the replacement of the Cyrillic alphabet by the Roman one. This was more or less accomplished by 1880 (Pei, 1976: 141). Close, in fact, considers that it was only during this period that a national literary language developed and that prior to this time there were 'marked regional variations ... in the written language' (1974: 31).

Thus, by the late nineteenth century a standard literary language using the Roman alphabet and incorporating new Romance words had developed. There were, however, still a considerable number of words of Slavonic origin and also some words of German, Greek and Turkish origin. Elcock considers that the Slavonic element comprised, and still comprises, about two-fifths of the Romanian vocabulary (1975: 285). Also, the third major area of Romanian speaking people, Transylvania, was still not part of Romania but was under Hungarian rule and, consequently, did not use Romanian as its standard written form. As late as 1910 only ten out of one hundred and sixty-nine schools in Transylvania taught in Romanian (Basdevant, 1965: 75). In fact, educational laws were passed which forbade the use of Romanian (Basdevant, 1965: 74). It was only in 1918 that Transylvania became a part of Romania and Romanian the official language (Basdevant, 1965: 82).

The standard written form of the language is based on the regional variety spoken around Bucharest in the province of Wallachia. Some Transylvanian and Moldavian forms, though, are admitted in the standard and so it cannot be identified solely with the language of the Bucharest area (Close, 1974: 31). There is a Romanian academy which 'legislates upon correct usage' of the literary language (Elcock, 1975: 498).

Spoken Romanian is usually divided into four main dialects; Daco-Romanian, Aroumanian (or Macedo-Romanian), Megleno-Romanian and Istro-Romanian (Nandris, 1966: xv–xvi). The last three of these dialects, however, are spoken outside of Romania: Aroumanian in northern Greece, eastern Albania and southern Yugoslavia; Megleno-Romanian in Greece near Salonika; and Istro-Romanian in Yugoslavia near Trieste (Pei, 1976: 138; Nandris, 1966: xv–xvi). These three dialects do not follow the literary standard of Romania and are not mutually intelligible (Close, 1974: 33).

The Daco-Romanian dialect is the one spoken in Romania and comprises three major sub-dialects; Transylvanian, Moldavian and Wallachian (Pei, 1976: 138). Speakers of Daco-Romanian would not understand any of the other three dialects, Macedo-, Megleno-, or Istro-Romanian without special study (Nandris, 1966: xvi). The three sub-dialects, though, are all mutually intelligible. As Nandris notes, in spite of small differences existing between the sub-dialects in various Daco-Romanian regions today, this North-Danubian dialect is so uniform that Romanians from all extremities of the country can understand and speak with each other without any difficulty. (Nandris, 1966: xv–xvi)

It should be noted that even though the Transylvanian, Wallachian and Moldavian sub-dialects are relatively uniform, there exist many local speech forms which differ from region to region (Close, 1974: 33). This is especially the case in the mountainous regions of Transylvania (Elcock, 1975: 495).

Of the three sub-dialects the Wallachian form spoken in and around Bucharest is considered to be the basis for the cultural 'standard' of the spoken language as it is for the written (Nandris, 1966: xv).

At the end of the Second World War a part of what was Romanian Moldavia became the Moldavian SSR and was incorporated into the USSR. The Soviet authorities have preferred to consider that languages spoken within the USSR are languages of the USSR. As a consequence they declared Moldavian to be a language distinct from Romanian (Bruchis, 1982; Comrie, 1981: 8). However, apart from changing the orthographic system back to the Cyrillic alphabet, 'the current standard language [of the Moldavian SSR] is extremely close to Standard Romanian' (Comrie, 1981: 188). But, as Comrie points out, it remains unclear to what extent the different alphabets, Latin in Romania and Cyrillic in Moldavia, affect pronunciation (1981: 188). Also, the influence of Russia has led to the incorporation of Russian words in Moldavia which are not found in Romania. This influence, and the political separation, may lead to increased differences over time between the language used in Romania and that used in the Moldavian SSR (Comrie, 1981: 188).

References

BASDEVANT, L. 1965, *Against Tide and Tempest: The Story of Rumania*. New York: Robert Speller and Sons (Translated by F. Dunham and J. Carroll).
BRUCHIS, M. 1982, *One Step Back, Two Steps Forward: On the Language Policy of the Communist Party of the Soviet Union in the National Republics (Moldavian: A Look Back, A Survey, And Perspectives, 1924–1980)*. New York: Columbia University Press (*East European Monographs* No. CIX).
CLOSE, E. 1974, *The Development of Modern Rumanian: Linguistic Theory and Practice in Muntenia 1821–1838*. London: Oxford University Press.
COMRIE, B. 1981, *The Languages of the Soviet Union*. Cambridge: Cambridge University Press.
ELCOCK, W. D. 1975, *The Romance Languages*. London: Faber and Faber.
NANDRIS, G. 1966, *Colloquial Rumanian*. London: Routledge and Kegan Paul.
PEI, M. 1976, *The Story of Latin and the Romance Languages*. New York: Harper and Row.

Russian

Russian is a an East Slavonic language, a member of the Slavonic group of Indo-European languages. It is spoken as a native, or first, language by nearly 59% of the population of the USSR (Comrie, 1981: 1). Up until the eleventh century A.D. it is probable that all Slavonic languages were mutually intelligible, but with the incursion of the Germanic speakers into what is today Austria and Magyar, Hungarian, speakers into Hungary, the Slavonic speaking areas were divided and began to diverge into separate languages (Vlasto, 1986: 2). However, the East Slavonic languages, i.e. Ukrainian, Byelorussian and Russian, remained fairly homogeneous until at least the thirteenth century, if not longer (Vlasto, 1986: 335ff).

When the first major East Slavic state, centered on Kiev, adopted Orthodox Christianity in the tenth century, a written language was also adopted. The written language was a Bulgarianised form of Old Church Slavonic using the Cyrillic alphabet (Vinogradov, 1968: xi; Vlasto, 1986: 7–8).

Old Church Slavonic, therefore, became the literary language of Russia. At this time, there were only relatively minor differences between the literary language and the spoken language. The literary language remained essentially fixed, even though it was superficially influenced by the spoken language (Vlasto, 1986: 31). The spoken language, however, continued to evolve and gradually diverged from Church Slavonic.

In the fifteenth century Moscow rose to power in Russia. Also, by the mid-fifteenth century the Turks had conquered Byzantium, Bulgaria and Serbia. In consequence, Moscow saw itself as 'the new Rome', the centre of the Orthodox Church, and many Serbian and Bulgarian scholars and churchmen fled from the Turks to Moscow (Andreyev, 1976; Vinogradov, 1968: xxii).

These scholars and churchmen had an almost mystical regard for the original form of Old Church Slavonic, and removed all local Russian characteristics from the Church Slavonic they encountered in Moscow. They therefore separated the language of literature, religion and education even further from the spoken language (Vinogradov, 1968: xxii).

The language of the Church remained the 'high', or prestigious, language form till the eighteenth century, though a radically different form of the written language was developing in government circles (Vinogradov, 1968: xxv). This 'chancery' form of the written language was based, for the most part, on the spoken language of Moscow, but it still contained numerous Church Slavonicisms (Vinogradov, 1968: xxv).

In 1708 Peter the Great introduced a new secular alphabet which, while still basically Cyrillic, simplified the forms of the symbols and reduced them slightly in number (Vlasto, 1986: 39). As Vinogradov notes:

> The reform of the alphabet in 1708 was a sharp blow to medieval attitudes toward the Church Slavonic language. It was a clear expression of the end of the hegemony of church ideology and an external, but very significant, symbol of the break between the church-book language and the secular speech styles. The new civic alphabet ... was a first step toward the creation of a national Russian written language. (Vinogradov, 1968: 47–8)

Along with the new alphabet, Peter the Great also introduced other modernising reforms of the language (De Bray, 1951: 27). Most of these reforms reflected the speech of Moscow, and consequently, because Moscow was the political and administrative centre of Russia, the Moscow dialect eventually became the basis of the standard literary language (De Bray, 1951: 27; Vlasto, 1986: 324).

However, Church Slavonic did not disappear altogether. Throughout the eighteenth and early nineteenth centuries different literary styles developed incorporating mainly Church Slavonic elements in the 'higher' styles such as liturgy and rhetoric, native Russian forms with almost no Church Slavonic for 'low' forms such as comedy, and a mixture of native and Church Slavonic forms for 'middle' styles such as drama (Comrie, 1979: 135). In the 1820s, with the works of Alexander Pushkin, Church Slavonic and native Russian elements were integrated. As Comrie puts it,

> in the work of ... Pushkin, usually considered the father of modern Russian literature, we find overall the same use of Church Slavonic and native Russian forms as in the language of today: in general, for a given word either the Church Slavonic or the native Russian form is used in all styles. (Comrie, 1979: 135)

Thus, Church Slavonic forms are still an integral part of the modern Russian literary language. But, as De Bray points out, it was the speech of Moscow which was used as the basis for the native Russian forms which made up the major part of the modern literary language (1951: 34).

The Russian literary language, therefore, was essentially standardised by the middle of the nineteenth century. The orthography, however, was revised in 1917, shortly after the Bolsheviks came to power. Apart from a few minor adjustments this orthography is still in use today (Comrie & Stone, 1978: 200ff).

The spoken language of Russia was originally divided into two major dialect areas, northern and southern. But, as Comrie says:

> Because of population movements northwards as a result of Tatar incursions, and because Moscow was a population magnet in the course of the consolidation of the Russian state ... the southern part of the northern dialect area was strongly influenced by features of the southern dialects, adopting some (but not all) of them, giving rise ultimately to a new dialect area, the so-called central dialects, including that of Moscow. (Comrie, 1979: 134)

The central dialects, therefore, combine elements of both the northern and southern dialects. One of them, the dialect of Moscow, emerged as the standard spoken dialect, primarily due to the political power of Moscow (Comrie, 1979: 134–5).

Though there are differences in pronunciation, vocabulary, and to some extent in grammar between northern, central and southern dialects, these differences are not so great as to cause any problems of comprehension (Vlasto, 1986: 305).

When the Bolsheviks took power in 1917 the standard literary and spoken varieties of Russian were primarily the preserve of the privileged classes (Comrie & Stone, 1978: 21). With the spread of education after the revolution the standard forms of Russian were disseminated to a much larger proportion of the population, and non-standard varieties have also affected the standard. As Comrie & Stone put it:

> One of the results of the Revolution has been the 'democratisation' of the Russian Language. On the one hand, the rise to power of new social classes led to the adoption of some features of their speech into the standard; on the other hand, the spread of education led to the adoption of standard features into the speech of those who had previously used non-standard varieties of the language. Over all, the latter has been the more powerful factor: except perhaps for the immediate post-Revolutionary years, there has been no trend to reject the traditional standard as a whole in favour of a norm closer to the actual usage of the working class ... . Non-standard (hence low-prestige) forms are still mainly found among workers, whose social prestige otherwise is high. (Comrie & Stone, 1978: 21)

The interaction of standard and non-standard features inevitably led to modification, albeit relatively slight, of the standard pronunciation. Comrie & Stone say that:

> The current standard is often referred to as Contemporary Standard Russian (CSR). The 'best' CSR is still considered that of educated Muscovites ... though it is much more widespread outside this circle than was [the

previous standard], and is normally insisted on for broadcasting purposes throughout the Soviet Union. (Comrie & Stone, 1978: 23)

The other dialects, however, are still used though they are becoming more restricted to the older generation (Krysin, 1979: 143). Also, the northern and southern dialect areas are tending to shrink as more and more speakers adopt central, or standard dialect features (Comrie & Stone, 1978: 12).

It is worth noting that the changes in the standard pronunciation and the orthographic reform of 1917 may be negatively perceived by some migrants. As Comrie & Stone note, 'in some emigré circles the belief is even now held that the Russian language has been somehow damaged by the Bolsheviks' (1978: 6).

References

ANDREYEV, N. 1976, Appanage and Muscovite Russia. In: R. AUTY and D. OBOLENSKY (eds) *An Introduction to Russian History: Companion to Russian Studies 1* (pp. 78–120). Cambridge: Cambridge University Press.

COMRIE, B. 1979, Russian. In: T. SHOPEN (ed.) *Languages and their Status* (pp. 91–151). Cambridge, MA: Winthrop Publishers.

COMRIE, B. 1981, *The Languages of the Soviet Union*. Cambridge: Cambridge University Press.

COMRIE, B. and STONE G. 1978, *The Russian Language since the Revolution*. Oxford: The Clarendon Press.

DE BRAY, R. G. A. 1951, *Guide to the Slavonic Languages*. London: J. M. Dent and Sons.

KRYSIN, L. P. 1979, Command of various language subsystems as a diglossia phenomenon. *International Journal of the Sociology of Language* 21, 141–51.

VINOGRADOV, V. V. 1969, *The History of the Russian Literary Language from the Seventeenth Century to the Nineteenth*. Madison: University of Wisconsin Press (Adapted into English by L. L. Thomas).

VLASTO, A. P. 1986, *A Linguistic History of Russia to the End of the Eighteenth Century*. Oxford: The Clarendon Press.

Scottish Gaelic

Scottish Gaelic, or Gaelic as it is more commonly known, is descended from the Goidelic branch of the Celtic language. In the fifth or sixth century AD. Gaelic was introduced into Argyll and the Isles on the west coast of Scotland by the Scoti, or Scots, who migrated from Ireland (Gregor, 1980: 90; Dorian, 1981: 10).

When the Goidelic, or Gaelic, speaking Scoti arrived, Scotland was inhabited by Pictish speakers in the north, and speakers of the other branch of Celtic, Brythonic, the precurser of Welsh, in the south (Gregor, 1980: 25). The Scoti gradually expanded eastward and northward, and Gaelic slowly supplanted Pictish and Brythonic, till, by the ninth century, Gaelic was the predominant language (Campbell, quoted in Dorian, 1978: 5).

In the eleventh century Gaelic reached the peak of its power and influence. It was the medium of government and administration (Durkacz, 1983: 4), and was the predominant spoken language from the Highlands in the north to the Lowlands in the south close to the present border between England and Scotland (Dorian, 1981: 15ff).

However, even though Gaelic was the dominant language during this period, it was never the only one (MacAulay, 1982: 25). In the south-east Anglo-Saxon was encroaching into the Lowlands; and the Hebrides, the Orkney and Shetland Isles, as well as the northernmost tip of the mainland, had been under Norse control and had been Norse speaking since at least the ninth century (Gregor, 1980: 26ff, 92). Also, in the south-west, Brythonic was still spoken to some extent (Dorian, 1981: 15).

At this time, it seems that the language form used for writing in Scotland was identical to that used in Ireland. MacAuley says that 'Gaelic Scotland and Ireland shared a high literary culture and a literary language ...' (1982: 27). And Agnew states that in the eleventh century there was a 'Gaelic standard common to Ireland and Scotland' (1981: 3).

The eleventh century, though, marks the beginning of the decline of Gaelic. In the latter part of the eleventh century the Scottish ruling house adopted English law and customs and brought in many Englishmen to fill high offices in Scotland (Gregor, 1980: 94; Dorian, 1981: 15). As a result Gaelic was gradually confined more and more to the Highlands. As Dorian puts it:

With both the Scottish nobility and the Scottish mercantile class ultimately English in speech, the position of Gaelic [in the lowlands] soon became unfavourable ... [By the fourteenth century] Gaelic had not only ceased to be socially dominant; it had ceased to be socially acceptable. It had come to be looked on as the language of a wild, even savage people; the Highlanders. (Dorian, 1981: 16)

In the Highlands, though, Gaelic was conserved and continued to develop an integrated culture (MacKinnon, quoted in Dorian, 1981: 16). Also, in the thirteenth century the Hebrides were recovered from the Norse and became Gaelic speaking once more (MacAulay, 1982: 25). Thus, while Gaelic lost considerable ground to the south it regained some territory to the west. The Orkney and Shetland Isles, however, never became Gaelic speaking even though they became part of Scotland in the fifteenth century (Gregor, 1980: 92).

Scotland was, therefore, divided linguistically into a Gaelic speaking area in the Highlands and an English speaking area in the Lowlands. It is worth noting that in the Lowlands there is a language form known as Scots, or sometimes as Lallans. This form is, according to Wood, 'an historical descendant of the northernmost varieties of the Anglian branch of Anglo-Saxon, with North Germanic, Scots Gaelic and other influences' (1977: 50). This form is still used today, and is variously considered to be a separate language or a differentiated dialect of English (Price, quoted in Wood, 1977: 48–9).

The Protestant Reformation in the seventeenth century had a considerable effect on Gaelic. Firstly, the literary contact between Scotland and Ireland was broken. As Wood puts it,

the loss of standardisation dates approximately from the period of the Protestant Reformation, when contacts with monasteries and other centres of literary activity in Ireland were broken off. (Wood, 1977: 47)

And Greene notes that it is from this time that the Gaelic literary language of Scotland 'must henceforth be reckoned as an independent language' (1972: 12). Secondly, the Lowland areas became Protestant, but significant areas of the Highlands remained loyal to Catholicism. In consequence Gaelic began to be seen by the authorities, who were predominantly Lowlanders, or English, as a prime symbol of disaffection (MacAulay, 1982: 26).

Even at this time, though, it seems that the Irish literary language was not intelligible to the majority of Scottish Gaelic speakers. Durkacz says that in the late seventeenth century an attempt was made to proselytise Protestantism through an Irish translation of the Bible. But 'its unfamiliar lettering, vocabulary and idiom ... rendered it unacceptable to Gaelic speakers' (1983: 18). Gregory also states that the Irish Bible 'would have been unintelligible even to literate Gaels' (1980: 322).

It is possible that the unintelligibility of Irish was due to the fact that the literary language of the Irish was accessible to only a very small minority in Scotland. MacAulay states that the literary culture in Scotland 'was vested largely in a professional literary caste' (1982: 27). Also, even in Ireland the literary language of this period was very far removed from the spoken language of the people and, as Durkacz notes, there were considerable dialectal differences between Ireland and Scotland by this time (1983: 19). Thus, it may be that this literary form was even further removed from spoken Gaelic than from spoken Irish.

It was not until the nineteenth century that a Bible translation in Gaelic was produced, and this suffered from the fact that there was, at this time, no 'broadly based tradition of printed Gaelic literature' (Durkacz, 1983: 20). Consequently dialectal problems arose since Gaelic was differentiated into many dialects (Durkacz, 1983: 20; Dorian, 1981: 8).

Gaelic, however, continued to decline in the nineteenth century. According to Van Eerde, the Church of Scotland and other organisations adopted education policies prejudicial to Gaelic, and the 1872 Education Act was opposed to the use of Gaelic in schools (Van Eerde, 1977: 33). As well, in what is known as 'the clearances', many Gaelic speakers were forcibly removed from their villages and relocated elsewhere to allow their land to be used for sheep or afforestation which would provide the landowners with more income (MacAulay, 1982: 26; Dorian, 1978: 7ff).

In the late nineteenth century, though, movements grew up for the preservation of Gaelic. Consequently, Gaelic is now officially allowed to be taught in schools; church services are conducted in Gaelic; and Gaelic is used on radio and television (Van Eerde, 1977: 33; Wood, 1977). Also, there is now a fairly wide range of publications in Gaelic (Thomson, 1984: 261).

As far as the spoken language is concerned, at the beginning of the twentieth century only about four percent of the population was still Gaelic speaking (Gregor, 1980: 272). However, even among this small number of speakers there was considerable dialectal variation. Dorian remarks that

it was proverbial in the Highlands even at the beginning of the twentieth century that every glen had a recognisably different form of speech from its neighbouring glens. (Dorian, 1981: 9)

And Oftedal says of a village in Lewis that,

the village ... is about two miles long, which is apparently enough for minor dialectal differences to manifest themselves from one end to the other. (quoted in Dorian, 1981: 9).

It appears that there is now a written form of the language which is used in education and printing. Dorian says:

A truly standardised Gaelic does not exist, but there is a generally accepted textbook norm for the written language. It is no one's native language, but many teachers adopt it for classroom use, rendering it in the pronunciation of their native dialect. (Dorian, 1981: 87)

The written norm, though, appears to be resisted by some speakers. Dorian, who investigated speakers in East Sutherland, in the north-east of Scotland, notes:

> speakers [from East Sutherland] who have tried the classes [in the written form of Gaelic] have given up rather than try to learn to speak a Gaelic which is unnatural to them and 'sounds foolish' coming out of their mouths. They recognise the prestige of this kind of Gaelic but do not aspire to speak it. (Dorian, 1981: 89)

There is also another form of Gaelic which has prestige, and that is the Gaelic used in religious services. According to Dorian, it is a rather archaic, conservative form which has higher prestige among East Sutherland Gaelic speakers than other regional dialects or the textbook form (1981: 90).

This 'Church' Gaelic was the form in which the Bible and other religious works were written. Consequently many Gaelic speakers were able to read it. However, in many cases it seems that this was the extent of their literacy in Gaelic (Dorian, 1981: 90).

Literacy in Gaelic, in fact, is confined to only one half of the Gaelic speaking population (MacKinnon, 1978: 34). MacAulay says that

> because of the history of the Gaelic language within the education system, many Gaelic speakers are illiterate, or only partially literate in Gaelic ... the result is that the vast majority of people who would not in normal circumstances speak English to each other would not even consider writing a letter to each other in Gaelic. (MacAulay, 1982: 29)

It is generally considered that all dialects of Gaelic are mutually intelligible, but Dorian presents evidence that this is not the case for speakers of East Sutherland Gaelic at least. According to a speaker of East Sutherland Gaelic, Stornoway girls from the Hebrides 'wouldn't understand us, and we weren't understanding [sic] them' (quoted in Dorian, 1978: 28). Also, the broadcasts in Gaelic, in which broadcasters use their own dialect but with extreme dialectal idiosyncracies removed, were difficult for East Sutherland speakers to understand (Dorian, 1978: 27). No information was available to us on other dialects and whether they also had problems of comprehension.

In Gaelic, therefore, there are several forms of the language: regional dialects, which appear to be markedly different and, according to Dorian's evidence, are not necessarily mutually intelligible; a mildly normalised variety, i.e. marked dialectal features are removed, used in broadcasting; a written form used in education and printing; and an archaic form used in religious services. It is difficult to discuss the relative prestige of these forms of Gaelic, though Dorian considers 'Church Gaelic' to have high prestige even though it has almost vanished from active use. She also notes that the local dialectal form has a formal style of speech which could also be considered prestigious in certain situations (Dorian, 1981: 93–4).

Gaelic speakers are today relatively few in number and the vast majority are bilingual in English. The 1971 census puts the figure at under 90,000 of whom less than 500 are monoglot (MacKinnon, 1978: 8). The areas where the majority of Gaelic speakers are found is known as the 'Gaidhealtachd' and comprises: the Western Isles Region, including the Hebrides where in some areas up to 98% of the people are Gaelic speaking (Wood, 1977: 43); parts of the Highlands; and parts of Strathclyde in the west of the country (MacKinnon, 1978: 17).

References

AGNEW, J. A. 1981, Language shift and the politics of language: the case of the Celtic languages of the British Isles. *Language Problems and Language Planning* 5 (1), 1–10.

DORIAN, N. C. 1978, *East Sutherland Gaelic: The Dialect of The Brora, Golspie, and Embo Fishing Communities*. Oxford: Dublin Institute for Advanced Studies.

DORIAN, N. C. 1981, *Language Death: The Life Cycle of a Scottish Gaelic Dialect*. Philadelphia: University of Pennsylvania Press.

DURKACZ, V. E. 1983, *The Decline of the Celtic Languages*. Edinburgh: John Donald Publishers.

GREENE, D. 1972, *The Irish Language*. Cork: Mercier Press (The Cultural Relations Committee of Ireland).

GREGOR, D. B. 1980, *Celtic: A Comparative Study*. Cambridge: The Oleander Press.

MACAULAY, D. 1982, Register range and choice in Scottish Gaelic. *International Journal of the Sociology of Language* 35, 25–48.

MACKINNON, K. 1978, *Gaelic in Scotland 1971: Some Sociological and Demographic Considerations of the Census Report for Gaelic*. The Hatfield Polytechnic.

THOMSON, D. S. 1984, Publishing in Scottish Gaelic. *Journal of Multicultural Development* 5 (3–4), 259–65.

VAN EERDE, J. 1977, Gaelic in Scotland. *Language Problems and Language Planning* 1 (1), 32–40.

WOOD, R. E. 1977, Linguistic organizations in Scotland. *Language Problems and Language Planning* 1 (1), 41–53.

Serbian

Serbian is a South Slavonic language spoken in the Serbian Republic of Yugoslavia. It is a member of the Slavonic group of Indo-European languages. The ancestor of the South Slavonic languages was brought to the Balkan region in the sixth and seventh centuries, and evolved, over time, into Serbian, Croatian, Slovene, Macedonian and Bulgarian (Corbett, 1987: 391). According to Corbett the main linguistic divisions in South Slavonic were evident by the ninth century (1987: 391). It should be noted that Serbian and Croatian are often treated as one language with two varieties, or major dialects, but, as Corbett notes:

> The whole question of the status of the two varieties is very sensitive, because of the cultural and political implications. To the outside linguist, the numerous shared features between the varieties added to the ease of mutual comprehension suggest one language with two varieties, and many Yugoslavs concur. But we must accept that some Yugoslavs feel it important, often for non-linguistic reasons, to recognise Croatian and Serbian as distinct languages. (Corbett, 1987: 396)

The earliest Slavonic literary language was developed after the Slavs were converted to Christianity in the ninth century. This language, Old Church Slavonic, was originally written in two alphabets, the Glagolitic and the Cyrillic. Though the Cyrillic alphabet, based on the Greek alphabet, soon came to predominate (Comrie, 1979: 129), it was originally used solely for religious works but, after a time, also came to be used for secular writing.

In the eleventh century political rivalry between Byzantium and Rome led to a division of Christianity in the region into Roman Catholic and Eastern Orthodox (Comrie, 1979: 130). Serbia remained orthodox and consequently retained the Cyrillic alphabet, but Croatia became Roman Catholic and adopted the Latin alphabet. In the nineteenth century both alphabets were reformed, and there is today an exact letter for letter correspondence between the Cyrillic alphabet used in Serbia, and the Latin alphabet used in Croatia. Also, it seems that the Latin alphabet is now being used to some extent in Serbia as well (Corbett, 1987: 392ff).

In the fourteenth century Serbia came under the control of the Ottoman Turks. In consequence many words of Turkish, Arabic and Persian origin came into the language. Croatia, though, was tied to Hungary and later the Austro-Hungarian Hapsburg empire and thus adopted many German words.

These differences in religion, alphabet and political history led to a divergence in vocabulary between Serbian and Croatian which continues to the present day. Thus, the vocabulary of Serbian borrows from Russian, incorporates a fairly large number of words of Ottoman origin and has a different religious terminology (Franolić, 1984).

Three main dialects are spoken in the Serbian and Croatian region of the Balkans. These are štokavian, kajkavian and čakavian (Kalogjera, 1985: 94; Babić, 1981: ix). In Serbia there is also a fourth dialect called torlakian (Kalogjera, 1985: 94; Magner, 1978: 473). Within these dialects, however, there is considerable variation. For example, Kalogjera notes that there are local dialects which show many features of one dialect but also use features of another (1985: 94). Also, as Magner points out, up until recently many villages 'were little worlds to themselves, very distinct in speech and manner from neighbouring settlements' (1978: 465). This variation between local areas has by no means completely vanished, though

> rural dialects are slowly disappearing under the pressure of literacy, education, mass information, population contacts and mobility, and, finally, the effect of the horizontal and vertical expansion of standard languages. (Radovanović, 1983: 59).

The standard form of the language, which was adopted in the nineteenth century, is a variety of the štokavian dialect. The štokavian dialect has three major varieties based on the spelling and pronunciation of Old Slavic *e*. These varieties, or variants as they are sometimes called, are ekavian, often referred to as što-e; ijekavian, or što-ije; and ikavian, or što-i (Babić, 1981: ix; Franolić, 1984). For example, 'a nice flower' would be *lep cvet* in što-e; *lijep cvijet* in što-ije; and *lip cvit* in što-i (Babić, 1981: ix). The Serbian standard literary language uses the ekavian, or što-e, variety of the štokavian dialect, whereas the Croatian standard literary language uses the ijekavian variety, or što-ije (Corbett, 1987: 395).

The što-e variety is, it appears, also the basis for the standard spoken language in Serbia. However, it is by no means the only form used. Kalogjera (1985), in fact, considers that 'pure' standard što-e or što-ije is found only in writing, whereas in the spoken language a certain amount of colouring from local dialects is present.

In Nis, the third largest city in Serbia, the local dialect is torlakian, though Magner notes that this dialect is perceived as being of low status and that dialect loyalty is practically non-existent. Consequently most speakers in this area are moving to an approximation of standard što-e and torlakian is gradually disappearing (1978: 477, 480 note 10).

It would appear that rural dialects are also perceived to be of relatively low prestige. According to Kalogjera evidence for the claim that rural speech is inferior

> seems to be the readiness with which speakers of a rural vernacular try to dispose of their type of speech and exchange it for an approximation to standard štokavian when living permanently in large centres like Zagreb and Belgrade. (Kalogjera, 1985: 98)

However, dialects which differ from the standard are still in use and are not always stigmatised. Their use, though, tends to be restricted. As Tezak says,

> explicit statements recognising the useful function of both nonstandard dialect and standard language for appropriate topics and situations now appear in school textbooks. (Quoted in Kalogjera, 1985: 107)

The linguistic situation in the urban areas which are usually centres of prestigious speech forms is summed up by Magner. He says:

> The cities of Zagreb, Split and Nis are like many other cities in Yugoslavia in two respects: they have distinctive dialects — what we might call the dialect of the old settlers in each city, and they have experienced considerable population growth in the post-war era. The inundation of these cities with masses of immigrants from neighbouring and distant regions has created a battleground of linguistic systems. At one pole is the traditional dialect of the old settlers and at the other pole is the textbook version of the official language, i.e. Textbook Croatian or Textbook Serbian. In between is a swirling amalgam of imported dialects whose speakers are torn between loyalty to their regional dialects, pressure to adapt to the dialect of the old settlers and a still greater pressure to adapt to the textbook language. (Magner, 1978: 476)

Thus, while the ekavian variety of the štokavian dialect is the 'standard' form it is not the only form used. Also, it would appear that a 'pure' ekavian is rarely used in speech, rather a new linguistic amalgam approximating to the standard but 'still peculiar to the particular city and its surrounding region' is emerging (Magner, 1978: 477–8).

As noted above it must be remembered that the situation in Serbian and Croatian is not merely linguistic but social and political also. It is mainly for non-linguistic reasons that Serbian should be seen as a separate language from Croatian. Dunatov (1978) argues that while there is 'no question' that Serbian ekavian and Croatian ijekavian are dialects of the same language in linguistic terms, there are sociolinguistic and political considerations which 'can equally well be used to argue for the autonomy of the Croatian standard *vis-a-vis* the Serbian' (1978: 265).

References

BABIĆ, S. 1981, *Serbo-Croatian for Foreigners*. Beograd: Kolariev Norodni Univerzitet.

COMRIE, B. 1979, Russian. In: T. S. Shopen (ed.) *Languages and their Status* (pp. 91–151). Cambridge, MA: Winthrop Publishers.

CORBETT, G. 1987, Serbo-Croat. In B. COMRIE (ed.) *The World's Major Languages* (pp. 391–409). London: Croom Helm.

DUNATOV, R. 1978, A sociolinguistic analysis of the recent controversy concerning the Croatian/Serbian standard language(s). In: H. BIRNBAUM (ed.) *American Contributions to the Eighth International Congress of Slavicists* Vol. 1 (pp. 256–67). Columbus, OH: Slavica Publishers.

FRANOLIĆ, B. 1984, *A Historical Survey of Literary Croatian*. Paris: Nouvelles Editions Latines.

KALOGJERA, D. 1985, Attitudes toward Serbo-Croatian language varieties. *International Journal of the Sociology of Language* 52, 93–109.

MAGNER, T. F. 1978, City dialects in Yugoslavia. In: H. BIRNBAUM (ed.) *American Contributions to the Eighth International Congress of Slavicists* Vol. 1 (pp. 465–81). Columbus, OH: Slavica Publishers.

RADOVANOVIĆ, M. 1983, Linguistic theory and sociolinguistics in Yugoslavia. *International Journal of the Sociology of Language* 44, 55–69.

Sinhalese

Sinhalese, sometimes spelt Singhalese and sometimes referred to as Sinhala, is a member of the Indo-Aryan branch of the Indo-European family of languages (Zograph, 1982: 26). It is spoken in Sri Lanka by the Sinhalese who form the majority of the population of the island (De Silva, 1969: 235).

The ancestors of the Sinhalese came to Sri Lanka probably around the fifth century BC (De Silva, 1969: 241). There is, however, some controversy among scholars as to the place of origin of the Sinhalese settlers. Some scholars believe they came from the eastern part of North India, while others believe they came from the western part (De Silva, 1979: 14ff).

Sinhalese, like other Indo-Aryan languages, can be traced back to Sanskrit (De Silva, 1979: 13). Due to its isolation from the North Indian languages, though, it has developed along independent, if broadly similar lines (Zograph, 1982: 107). Archaeological evidence points to Sinhalese being used as a written language since the third century BC (De Silva, 1979: 13).

The arrival of Buddhism in the third century BC brought Pali to Sri Lanka (Obeyesekere, 1974: xv). Pali is one of the forms of Indo-Aryan known as Prakrit, the earlier of two distinct stages of development of the Indo-Aryan languages between Sanskrit and the modern forms (Zograph, 1982: 10ff). Because Pali was considered to be the language of the Buddha, it was sacred and relatively fixed at an early date (Obeyesekere, 1974: xv; Godakumbure, 1976: 11).

Originally the Pali texts of the Buddhists were handed down orally, but Sinhalese was used to write explanations and commentaries on these texts, and as an aid to memory (Obeyesekere, 1974: xv; Godakumbure, 1976: 4–5). When Pali, and also Sanskrit, began to be written in Sri Lanka, the practice of writing commentaries and explanations in Sinhalese continued. As well, Sinhalese began to be used for translations of the Pali and Sanskrit works (Godakumbure, 1976: 13ff).

Over the centuries, as the Sinhalese spoken language evolved, some of the early writing became difficult for the Sinhalese to understand even though works were revised to bring them closer to the spoken form whenever they were copied (Godakumbure, 1976: 13). Geiger posits four stages for Sinhalese: Sinhalese-Prakrit, from 200 BC to the fifth century AD; Proto-Sinhalese, fifth to eighth centuries; Mediaeval Sinhalese, eighth to thirteenth centuries; and Modern Sinhalese, thirteenth century to the present (Geiger, cited in De Silva, 1969: 242–3).

By the thirteenth century a classical literary form of Sinhalese had been codified and standardized (Zograph, 1982: 107). De Silva, though, says that written Sinhalese shows a gradual evolution up to the fourteenth century (1967: 10). This 'classical' form is sometimes called Elu and borrowed vocabulary from Sanskrit and also from Pali (Geiger, cited in De Silva, 1979: 29; Godakumbure, 1976: 36ff). However, although the literary language eschewed the use of non-Aryan forms, it appears that the spoken language was influenced by the Dravidian languages of South India to some extent (De Silva, 1979: 21ff). Also, the alphabet used to write Sinhalese, which is derived from the Brahmi script, was also influenced by South Indian scripts (De Silva, 1979: 23).

When Europeans came in the early sixteenth century, Sinhalese literature declined (De Silva, 1967: 10–11). The Portugese, the Dutch and finally the British succeeded each other in Sri Lanka, but it was not until 1815 that the British gained control of the entire island (Obeyesekere, 1974: xxx). As a result English became the prestigious language and a new, small English educated bureaucracy became the élite (Obeyesekere, 1974: xxxiii).

However, some official documents were produced in Sinhalese under the Portugese, Dutch and early in the British period. These documents were written in a form of literary Sinhalese which was much closer to the spoken language than was classical Sinhalese (De Silva, 1967: 11). And, according to De Silva, a written form of Sinhalese closer to the spoken form was also used at the beginning of the literary revival in Sri Lanka in the late eighteenth century (1967: 11).

By the nineteenth century, though, the majority of scholars had taken as their model for literary Sinhalese the classical form codified and standardized in the thirteenth century (De Silva, 1967: 11–12). This 'purist' movement had a lasting effect on the language.

In the mid-nineteenth century vernacular schools were established in Sri Lanka, and from about the same time there was a considerable upsurge in interest in Sinhalese (Obeyesekere, 1974: xxxiii–xxxiv). The late nineteenth century saw magazines and newspapers in Sinhalese, and the printing of classical Sinhalese texts. As puts it,

> the latter part of the nineteenth century was thus characterized by a burst of literary activity, a spate of publications of old classical works, and a lively and controversial interest in questions political, religious, and literary. (Obeyesekere, 1974: xxxiv)

The form of language used for most of these writings was the 'pure' literary Sinhalese from the thirteenth century. There was some writing in the grammar of the spoken language, though, particularly dialogue in novels, popular from the early twentieth century (De Silva, 1967: 14). Nevertheless, the language of virtually all written works up till the present is literary Sinhalese (Gair, 1968: 1–2).

Literary Sinhalese is taught in schools as it is no one's first language. It differs from colloquial, or spoken, Sinhalese in pronunciation when read aloud, in vocabulary and in grammar (Gair, 1968: 2ff). As De Silva says, 'the written language, therefore, has the qualities of a second language in many respects' (1967: 6). There is, however, some debate in Sri Lanka over the literary form (De Silva, 1979: 42), and in some writing, such as newspapers, although a grammar akin to the classical is used, some of the strict rules are violated (De Silva, 1967: 15–16). Literary Sinhalese, though, continues to be perceived as the 'correct' form for all writing (De Silva, 1967: 6) and this form has high prestige (Gair, 1983: 57).

With independence in 1946 and Sinhalese being proclaimed the sole official language of Sri Lanka in 1956, the role of Sinhalese in the island has increased, perhaps especially in administration and education, while that of English has decreased (Gair, 1983). A knowledge of English is, though, still considered prestigious and is of practical value (Gair, 1983: 49). The increased use of Sinhalese does not appear to have altered the status or form of literary Sinhalese, even though a greater number of people are now called on to write a greater number of texts in Sinhalese (Gair, 1983: 57).

The written literary form of Sinhalese is never used in conversations, while the colloquial variety is virtually never used in writing. Sinhalese, therefore, exhibits what is known as diglossia: two distinct codes, one for writing and one for speaking (Gair, 1983: 54–5). Even when being read aloud, a literary text or a newspaper would sound different to any spoken dialect in Sri Lanka. That is, as well as differing in grammar and vocabulary, literary Sinhalese requires a different phonology (De Silva, 1967: 6–7; De Silva, 1969: 238–9). However, De Silva also notes that Sinhalese speakers who cannot read or write can usually understand the literary form when it is read aloud (1979: 41).

According to Gair, spoken Sinhalese can be divided into two varieties: formal spoken and colloquial (1968: 10; 1983: 55). Formal spoken Sinhalese merges elements of the literary form with elements of the colloquial. Gair says that the formal spoken variety makes use of one, and usually more, grammatical features of the literary variety and shares a considerable amount of vocabulary with the literary variety, but is nonetheless fundamentally closer to the colloquial spoken form (Gair, 1968: 10; 1983: 55). The colloquial form is 'the language of ordinary conversation' (Gair, 1983: 55).

The formal spoken variety is used for such situations as public speaking, radio talks, lectures, and formal discussions (Gair, 1968: 9). It should be noted, though, that as is usual in language there is no sharp dividing line between these varieties. However, as Gair points out, in Sinhalese the division between the written and spoken varieties is clearer than that between the formal and colloquial spoken varieties (1983: 55ff).

It would appear, therefore, that in Sinhalese there are two continua: one for spoken Sinhalese, with colloquial at one end and formal spoken at the other; and one for written Sinhalese. It seems that the formal end of the spoken continuum and the 'informal' end of the written continuum, e.g. letters and newspapers, converge but do not quite touch (De Silva, 1979: 40; Gair, 1983: 55ff). Thus, as Gair puts it,

> whatever the uncertainties may be as to the precise and proper form to be written, there is little feeling that writing does not call for a special, markedly distinct form of the language... . (Gair, 1983: 56)

There are several spoken dialects in Sri Lanka, but apart from a few vocabulary items they are all mutually intelligible (De Silva, 1967: 6). These dialects, though, 'are not only geographical, they are also social so that caste, rank, etc. bear distinguishing features throughout the country' (De Silva, 1979: 49). But, the speech of educated Sinhalese differs little from region to region. (De Silva, 1967: 6).

In Sinhalese, therefore, there are two distinct varieties: one for writing and one for speaking, i.e. Sinhalese exhibits diglossia. The spoken language forms a continuum between colloquial, used for everyday conversation, and a formal variety used for public speaking, radio talks, sermons and so on. There are various mutually intelligible dialects both geographical, and perhaps more important, social. The social, educated dialect appears to be very similar throughout the island, and is possibly towards the formal end of the spoken continuum. The written language is based on the literary form of the thirteenth century and differs considerably from the spoken language.

It is worth noting that while Sinhalese is the official language in Sri Lanka, there are two national languages: Sinhalese and Tamil. According to Brann, 'official' in this context means that Sinhalese has a political identity while 'national' gives Sinhalese and Tamil territorial identity (1985: 34). Tamil is used in the Tamil areas as a medium of instruction in education, for certain administrative purposes, and in some other areas (Brann, 1985).

As well as Tamil and Sinhalese, another language, known as Vedda, is also spoken in Sri Lanka. Vedda, though, has been so influenced by Sinhalese that it is now very close to colloquial Sinhalese. It can still cause problems of comprehension, though, for some Sinhalese. Sinhalese, or a form very close to it, is spoken in the Maldive Islands (De Silva, 1979: 18ff).

References

BRANN, C. M. B. 1985, Sinhala and English: a clarification. *Language Problems and Language Planning*. 9 (1), 31–6.

DE SILVA, M. W. S. 1967, Effects of purism on the evolution of the written language: case history of the situation in Sinhalese. *Linguistics* 36, 5–17.

DE SILVA, M. W. S. 1969, Sinhalese. In: T. A. SEBEOK (ed.) *Current Trends in Linguistics* Vol. 5 (pp. 235–48). The Hague: Mouton.

DE SILVA, M. W. S. 1979, *Sinhalese and Other Island Languages in South Asia*. Tubingen: Gunter Narr Verlag (*Ars Linguistica* 3).

GAIR, J. W. 1968, Sinhalese diglossia. *Anthropological Linguistics* 10 (8), 1–15.

GAIR, J. W. 1983, Sinhala and English: the effects of a language act. *Language Problems and Language Planning* 7 (1), 43–59.

GODAKUMBURE, C. E. 1976, *Literature of Sri Lanka*. Sri Lanka: Department of Cultural Affairs (*The Culture of Sri Lanka* — 3).

OBEYESEKERE, R. 1974, *Sinhala Writing and the New Critics*. Colombo: Gunasena.

ZOGRAPH, G. A. 1982, *Languages of South Asia: A Guide*. London: Routledge and Kegan Paul (Translated by G. L. Campbell).

Slovak

Slovak is a West Slavonic language, a member of the Indo-European family of languages (Comrie, 1987: 322). It is spoken in the Slovak Federal Republic, part of the state of Czechoslavakia. Slovak is also spoken in other Central European countries such as Hungary as a result of migration and the altering of political boundaries throughout history, and in several other countries around the world because of political and economic migration (Short, 1987: 367). Short notes, though, that the form of Slovak spoken outside of the Slovak Federal Republic may differ through physical separation and the influence of the dominant languages in other countries (1987: 367).

The Czech and Slovak Slavs may have arrived in what is now Czechoslovakia during the sixth century AD, possibly from the north-east (Bradley, 1971: 1). The Slovaks of the central regions of Slovakia, though, are thought to have come from the south, from what is now Hungary (Short, 1987: 389; De Bray, 1969: 524). The separate tribes formed into three major groups: in Bohemia in the west, Moravia in the central area, and Slovakia in the east (Bradley, 1971: 2ff). In the ninth century the most powerful group at that time, the Moravians, adopted Christianity in its Eastern form (Bradley, 1971: 4–5).

Writing in the Cyrillic alphabet was introduced along with Christianity (De Bray, 1969: 435). However, from the early stages of Christianity in this area, the Western Church was also active in Bohemia and Moravia, and by the end of the ninth century the Eastern Church had been expelled from the region (Bradley, 1971: 6).

By early in the tenth century the Moravian state had collapsed, the kingdom of Bohemia and Moravia, centred on Prague, was founded, and Slovakia came under Hungarian rule (Bradley, 1971: 6ff; Brock, 1976: 4). In consequence, Latin became the written, and official, language of Slovakia (Brock, 1976: 4; Short, 1987: 369).

Because Slovakia, as an integral part of Hungary, lacked any significant political or cultural centre, no local dialect assumed the function of a literary language (Salzmann, 1980: 41). Instead, literary Czech came to be used, from about the fifteenth century, as a literary language in Slovakia, alongside Latin, German and Hungarian (Salzmann, 1980: 41; De Bray, 1969: 513). However, as Brock notes,

[Czech] was not written usually in quite the same form as in Bohemia and Moravia, a strong tendency to 'Slovakise' being understandable in view of the distance of the Slovak area from the important Czech cultural centres. (Brock, 1976: 4)

The arrival of the Reformation in northern Hungary, and particularly the adoption by Slovak Protestants of the Czech literary language used for the translation of the Bible, led to a reversing of the tendency to 'Slovakise' the Czech literary language in Slovakia (Brock, 1976: 4). As Brock puts it,

> for Protestants during the long period of its use, and particularly after the suppression of Protestantism in the Czech lands following the lost battle of the White Mountains in 1620 ... this Biblical language was transformed into something almost sacred which only profane hands would attempt to alter. (Brock, 1976: 4)

Catholics, on the other hand, particularly during and after the Counter-Reformation, did not hold the Czech literary language of the Bible in such high regard. Rather they saw it 'merely as a convenient vehicle of expression' (Brock, 1976: 4). And, as Salzmann notes, 'Slovakisation of the local literary language was ... strongly noticeable in the Catholic works produced in the service of the Counter Reformation' (1980: 41–2). It should be noted, too, that 'Slovak Protestants continued to Slovakize when the vigilant eyes of the church press's proofreaders, who were often Czech immigrants, were absent' (Brock, 1976: 4).

The desire of the Catholics to win back the Slovak masses from Protestantism, and to hold them once reconverted, led the Catholics to introduce more and more Slovak elements into their writings since it was found that Czech was comprehensible only to the better educated (Brock, 1976: 5). In the mid-seventeenth century, consequently, a form known as 'Jesuit Slovak' began to be used. This form was based on Czech and the West Slovak dialects (Salzmann, 1980: 42). According to Short, various hybrids of Czech and local dialects came into use during the seventeenth and eighteenth centuries, and these are nowadays referred to as 'cultured western, central and eastern Slovak' (1987: 369–70). Jesuit Slovak is, therefore, nowadays usually called cultured western Slovak.

In the late eighteenth century a Catholic priest, Anton Bernolak, took what Salzmann calls 'the first step of any significance' in the codification and standardisation of an independent Slovak literary language (Salzmann, 1980: 42). Bernolak took Jesuit, or cultured western, Slovak as his point of departure and brought it much closer to the West Slovak dialects, with some elements from the Central dialects (Salzmann, 1980: 42; Auty, quoted in Brock, 1976: 9).

Although Bernolak's version of literary Slovak gained limited acceptance, even among some Protestants, it was viewed negatively by most intellectuals, Catholic as well as Protestant, and the Protestant liturgy continued, for the most part, to be conducted in Czech (Brock, 1976: 15; Short, 1987: 369; De Bray, 1969: 514).

Some Slovak Protestants, particularly the younger intellectuals, began to reappraise their adherence to Czech in the early part of the nineteenth century, since the ordinary people, especially the Catholic majority, could not understand it (Brock, 1976: 30ff). As well, the idea of the modern cultural and linguistic nation was being brought to Slovakia by those who had studied in the Protestant universities in Germany (Brock, 1976: 36). When, in the 1840s, the Hungarian authorities attempted to make Hungarian the sole language of religion, education and administration throughout Hungary (thus including Slovakia) (Brock, 1976: 38ff), matters came to a head.

In 1843 a decision was taken by a small group of Protestant Slovaks to adopt written Slovak as a counter to Hungarian, and as a means to advance Slovak nationalism (Brock, 1976: 45; De Bray, 1969: 514). The dominant figure in this group was L'udovit Stur, and it is he who is generally credited with developing a new literary Slovak based on the dialects of Central Slovak (Salzmann, 1980: 42; Brock, 1976; Short, 1987: 369). However, as Brock points out, no single dialect formed the basis of this new literary language, and it is generally regarded as a codification of the speech of educated people from central Slovakia (1976: 47).

According to Short, Stur's work, based on Central Slovak, found immediate favour (1987: 369). There were, nevertheless, some Protestant elements who still preferred to use Czech, and also some Catholics who maintained their use of the previous form of literary Slovak developed by Bernolak (Brock, 1976: 53; De Bray, 1969: 514). By the mid 1860s, though, a modified form of Stur's work had been accepted by nearly all the Slovak intelligentsia, and it is this form which is today the basis of modern Slovak (Brock, 1976: 53; De Bray, 1969: 514).

When Slovakia joined Bohemia and Moravia to form the new Czechoslovakia in 1918, Czech and Slovak were declared to be two 'versions' of one language: Czechoslovak (Salzmann, 1980: 42–3). During the first half of the twentieth century, as Salzmann puts it, 'the Czechs made no attempt to hide their conviction that Czech culture — its language and literature in particular — was far superior to that of the Slovaks' (1980: 43). This, coupled with the fact that there was still in Slovakia a continuous current which favoured the use of Czech, or a mutation to a common Czechoslovak (Short, 1987: 370), led to attempts to promote Czech and bring the two literary languages closer together at the expense of Slovak (Salzmann, 1980: 44).

After the Second World War, although the individuality and equality of Slovak was recognised in the 1948 constitution, efforts to bring Czech and Slovak closer together continued (Salzmann, 1980: 46ff). In the 1960s, though, the situation began to change, and, with the federalisation of Czechoslovakia in 1969 into a state comprising the Czech Federal Republic and the Slovak Federal Republic, the Slovak literary language became fully self-sufficient and able to develop according to its own laws (Salzmann, 1980: 48ff). However, as Short notes:

> Although there has been a strong tendency ... to keep Slovak maximally distinct from Czech and free of Bohemicisms, there are some signs of a reverse tendency, due in part to the shift of the languages' centre of gravity away from the high literary towards the technical. Both languages resort to neologisms, and standardisation to international norms often means coincidence rather than further division. Added to that, Slovak, despite the opposition of purists, remains open to influences from Czech. (Short, 1987: 370)

During this century there have been several orthographic and other reforms in Slovak designed to bring the spoken and written forms of the language closer together (Salzmann, 1980: 49ff). Modern Slovak, in its continuing development, draws heavily on Slovak dialects, though the basis remains the Central dialects (Salzmann, 1980; Short, 1987: 388).

Slovak dialects are usually divided into three major groups, each comprising numerous subdivisions (De Bray, 1969: 524; Short, 1987: 388). It would appear that although there are quite considerable differences between the dialects, they are all mutually intelligible. The Central dialects seem to form the basis of the standard spoken form of Slovak, as they do for the written form (Short, 1987: 388).

Slovak, then, has a standard literary form developed in the nineteenth century and based on the educated speech of the Central dialects area. From the time of independence up till the 1960s there were attempts to bring literary Slovak closer to Czech, but after the 1960s literary Slovak became more self-sufficient, although there are still areas of convergence, particularly in vocabulary, between Slovak and Czech. There are three major dialect groups in Slovak, each with numerous sub-dialects, though it seems that the educated speech of the Central area is considered standard.

As regards the relationship between Czech and Slovak at the present time, Short says:

> The similarities are highest, and increasing, at the lexical level (where there are also some of the most striking differences), while phonologically and morphologically the differences affect most words, though not enough to inhibit comprehension. The overall distinctiveness is, however, great enough for translations between the two languages to be a meaningful exercise. (Short, 1987: 368)

References

BRADLEY, J. F. N. 1971, *Czechoslovakia: A Short History*. Edinburgh: Edinburgh University Press.

BROCK, P. 1976, *The Slovak National Awakening: An Essay in the Intellectual History of East Central Europe*. Toronto: University of Toronto Press.

COMRIE, B. 1987, Slavonic languages. In: B. COMRIE (ed.) *The World's Major Languages* (pp. 322–8). London: Croom Helm.

DE BRAY, R. G. A. 1969, *Guide to the Slavonic Languages*. London: J. M. Dent and Sons.

SALZMANN, Z. 1980, Language standardization in a bilingual state: the case of Czech and Slovak, two closely cognate languages. *Language Problems and Language Planning* 4 (1), 38–54.

SHORT, D. 1987, Czech and Slovak. In: B. COMRIE (ed.) *The World's Major Languages* (pp. 367–90). London: Croom Helm.

Slovenian

Slovenian is a South Slavonic language which is the official language of the Socialist Republic of Slovenia, part of the Socialist Federal Republic of Yugoslavia. It is a member of the South Slavonic sub-branch of the Slavonic branch of the Indo-European family of languages (Comrie, 1987: 322). According to Darby, the Slovenes first arrived in the area they now occupy in the second half of the sixth century AD (1966: 13).

By the ninth century the Slovenes were subjects of the Franks and they were converted to the Roman Catholic Church (Darby, 1966: 13). As a consequence, the Roman, rather than the Cyrillic, alphabet was, and still is, used to write Slovenian. With the Franks began a period of German influence which lasted almost uninterrupted till the twentieth century.

The German influence was greatest under the Habsburgs who, between 1278 and the late fourteenth century, acquired the whole of Slovenia (Singleton, 1985: 50–1). Under the Austrian Habsburgs German was the official language of the state; the language of the upper and, to some extent, the middle classes; and the language of education (Darby, 1966: 16, 21). Nevertheless, although many Slovenes were absorbed into the dominant German culture, 'the mass of the Slovene peasants retained their Slav culture and language' (Singleton, 1985: 51).

In the sixteenth century the Reformation came to Slovenia. A major consequence of the Reformation was the establishment of Protestant churches and schools in which Slovenian was extensively used (Singleton, 1985: 51; Darby, 1966: 15).

At this time there were four major dialect groups in Slovenian. These were: Upper Carniolan, Lower Carniolan, Styrian, and Carinthian (Paternost, 1985: 9). These dialects appear to have been mutually intelligible though exhibiting considerable variation (Lencek, 1976: 118). The use of Slovenian by the Protestants meant that several works, almost all religious texts, were printed in the second half of the sixteenth century. However, not all the dialect groups were used for these works. According to Lencek, the most important Slovenian writer of that time used the Lower Carniolan dialect with a few features from Upper Carniolan; and the most important work, a translation of the Bible, was also primarily written in the Lower Carniolan dialect but with elements of other dialects from the central parts of Slovenia (Lencek, 1976: 114).

The texts produced at this time are generally associated with the beginning of the Slovenian literary language. Paternost says that the written variety of Slovenian was first codified in the sixteenth century (1985: 9). And Lencek asserts that the language of the Bible translation 'became the foundation of the literary language' (1976: 114).

The early form of the literary language, therefore, drew on essentially one regional base, the Lower Carniolan dialect (Paternost, 1985: 10). However, the Catholic Counter-Reformation, led by the Jesuits under the policy of the Austrian rulers, restored Catholicism as the religion of Slovenia by the beginning of the seventeenth century. Much of the literature produced by the Protestants was declared heretical and was burnt, and book production declined significantly (Darby, 1966: 16; Lencek, 1976: 114). Nevertheless, the literary language survived. As Lencek notes, 'the few books that were produced sustained the [Protestant] norm' (1976: 114).

Towards the end of the eighteenth century, despite the general Germanising policy of the Austrian rulers, the Age of Enlightenment spreading through Europe led to a considerable increase in the production of works in Slovenian (Darby, 1966: 17; Lencek, 1976: 116). As well as an increase in the number of books published, secular subjects were also broached in literature for the first time, and the first newspaper in Slovenian was founded in Ljubljana (Darby, 1966: 17; Lencek, 1976: 116).

The form of the language used for most of these writings was based on the literary language codified in the sixteenth century. However, some of the major writers of the time introduced Upper Carniolan features into their writings, while others attempted to establish literary forms based on the Styrian or Carinthian dialects (Lencek, 1976: 117, 124). By the middle of the nineteenth century, though, a fusion of Upper and Lower Carniolan features was accepted as the literary norm throughout Slovenia (Lencek, 1976: 117).

After 1850 there was considerable debate about the form the literary language should take. Lencek enumerates four factors which influenced the written language; Slavisation, archaisation, purism, and vernacularisation (1976: 128ff). Slavisation refers to the borrowing of words from other Slavonic languages, perhaps especially Serbian and Croatian, either to replace Germanisms or to provide neologisms. It has been estimated that approximately one third of the words in the 'Slovenski Pravopis', a Slovenian dictionary, are borrowed from other Slavonic languages. The borrowing, however, was not confined to vocabulary but affected the grammar also (Lencek, 1976: 128).

Archaisation refers to the attempt to consciously structure the written language after Old Church Slavonic which was seen as a direct ancestor of

Slovenian. Consequently, grammatical categories and formal classes which had disappeared from the spoken language were reintroduced into literary Slovenian (Lencek, 1976: 129).

Purism and vernacularisation are virtually the opposite of Slavisation and archaisation. In this case vocabulary items and elements of grammar from Slovenian dialects rather than other Slavonic languages are incorporated into the literary language (Lencek, 1976: 130ff).

The consequence of all these various elements being incorporated into the literary language meant that this form moved further and further away from the spoken language. In fact, the Slovenian orthographic dictionary defines the literary language as 'an independent artificial structure which does not agree in details with any of the living dialects although it is based on the central dialects' (quoted in Paternost, 1985: 9). Also, Paternost notes 'its norm (e.g. pronunciation, grammar, spelling) is modeled on an idealised Slavic pattern, and differs somewhat from the vernacular' (1985: 9).

The literary form is also used as a spoken language which, while differing from any of the dialects, represents a common standard throughout Slovenia. According to Lencek: 'This spoken form of the literary language is a model speech of contemporary Slovene' (1976: 113). However, it seems that this 'cultivated, literary' style of speech reached a peak of prestige by 1945 and has since, though it is still used for written literature, been superceded by new forms of the spoken language.

Since 1945 there has been considerable population movement in Slovenia, both from region to region and from rural to urban areas (Lencek, 1976: 134). This has resulted in a significant shift in the geographical distribution of the dialects and, in fact, has accelerated the retreat of dialectal speech in general. According to Lencek a new system of regional interdialects are being generated, especially around the large urban centres (1976: 135).

The important factor in the generation of the new regional interdialects, Lencek says, is the 'democratisation' of the literary language. By 'democratisation' Lencek means that there is a general merging of the standard of usage of the élite with the standard of speech of the semi-educated speaker as they begin to participate in situations where formal language is required, such as public forums, administration and so on (Lencek, 1976: 135). This leads to a new form of the language, somewhere between the 'pure' rural dialects and the former élite literary standard; in other words, a 'regional interdialect' as Lencek calls it.

It appears that the mass media is tending to use the interdialects rather than the older literary speech style for both written communication, newspapers and magazines, and spoken, radio and television. Consequently, the interdialects, especially the forms used in the media are becoming the new prestige forms (Lencek, 1976: 136; Paternost, 1985: 11). In fact, Lencek states that there has been a complete reversal of prestige forms in Slovenian since 1945. The language of the media, administration and the spoken language in general are now considered prestigious, whereas the 'literary' style of speech is considered archaic (1976: 136).

The interdialects, however, are not uniform throughout the country, but differ from region to region. Although they avoid the dialectal, they are based on the speech of urban societies and, consequently, do not pursue any artificial trends in vocabulary and grammar in the way the literary language did (Lencek, 1976: 137). Lencek believes that it is only a matter of time before these new interdialects enter the written language of Slovene 'belle-lettres' (1976: 137).

It would appear, though, that even with the growth of the interdialects, that regional varieties have not disappeared. Paternost notes that 'regional varieties and their many dialects' are still spoken in Slovenia (1985: 9). However, he does not make it clear whether these local dialects are becoming more confined to the older generation, or to more intimate situations, as would be expected if these varieties were dying out.

Slovenian continues to borrow from other languages, though it appears that English is now a major source of loanwords (Paternost, 1985: 13–14). Serbian and Croatian are also sources of loanwords and are compulsory subjects in schools (Tollefson, 1980: 237). But it appears that Slovenians are concerned that their language is being threatened by the use of Serbian and Croatian ('Slovenely Speaking' 1982: 76) and they have recently set up a special Language Arbitration Tribunal to advise the Slovenian public on the 'proper use of language' (Paternost, 1985: 14).

In sum, therefore,

> whereas literary Slovene still represents the highest form of the educated language in Slovene society, the post war evolution of new interdialects of at least three major urban communities (Ljubljana, Maribor, Trieste) distinctly indicates a spontaneous growth of a less formal and a less rigid form of an urban speech of unequivocal social prestige which might be leading the evolution toward a new modern standard Slovene. (Lencek, 1976: 145)

It is perhaps worth noting that many migrants who left Slovenia before, or only shortly after, 1945 may not have had any exposure to this new form of the language, and may experience some problems of comprehension, or may not consider it to be prestigious.

References

DARBY, H. C. 1966, Slovenia. In: S. CLISSOLD (ed.) *A Short History of Yugoslavia: From Early Times to 1966* (pp. 13–22). Cambridge: Cambridge University Press.

LENCEK, R. L. 1976, On dilemmas and compromises in the evolution of modern Slovene. In T. F. MAGNER (ed.) *Slavic Linguistics and Language Teaching* (pp. 112–52). Cambridge, MA: Slavica Publishers.

PATERNOST, J. 1985, A sociolinguistic tug of war between language value and language reality in contemporary Slovenian. *Internationl Journal of the Sociology of Language* 52, 9–29.

SINGLETON, F. 1985, *A Short History of the Yugoslav Peoples*. Cambridge: Cambridge University Press.

Slovenely Speaking 1982, *The Economist* May 8, London.

TOLLEFSON, J. W. 1980, Types of language contact and the acquisition of language. *Language Sciences* 2 (2), 231–45.

Spanish

Spanish is a Romance language, part of the Indo-European family of languages. It is spoken in Spain, Latin America including some Caribbean Islands, especially Cuba and Puerto Rico, and in the southwestern United States. This chapter will look first at variation in Spain, secondly at variation in Latin America, and thirdly at variation between the two.

Latin, from which Spanish is descended, was introduced to Spain when the Romans conquered the area between 218 and 15 BC and eventually supplanted the indigenous languages of Iberia with the sole exception of Basque (Green, 1987: 237–8). By the middle-ages several dialects had arisen in what is now Spain, and one of them, Castilian, was used by the leaders of the Reconquest of Spain from the Arabs. As Penalosa puts it:

> When the Christians of the far north rallied to drive out the Arabs, one of the north Spanish dialects, Castilian, spoken in the tiny kingdom of Oviedo in the Cantabrian Mountains, became the language of the Reconquest. With the political consolidation and hegemony of the kingdom of Castile, this dialect became the language of the new Spanish state. (Penalosa, 1980: 17)

As well, Castilian, which had a flourishing tradition of oral literature was used in the thirteenth century as a written literary language for translations into Spanish of literary, historical and scientific works written in Latin, Greek, Arabic and Hebrew, and thereby consolidated its national and international position (Green, 1987: 238–9). As Green says, 'since that time, the pre-eminence of Castilian has never been challenged, though there have always been local norms of pronunciation' (1987: 239)

Thus, by 1492 when the Reconquest was completed, Castilian was the most prestigious and powerful language of Spain, and it has remained so till the present: Castilian is now the official language of Spain. However, the other north Spanish dialects, especially Asturian, Leonese, Navarrese, and Aragonese, though they were displaced from official and formal situations, continued as vernaculars, especially in the remoter areas (Entwhistle, 1936: 217). These dialects still exist today and diverge quite considerably from Castilian (Penalosa, 1980: 16).

As well as these dialects there is also variation in the south of Spain, but, unlike the [northern] dialects those of southern Spain are not variants of the common tradition of Spanish Romance, but of its particular Castilian variety. (Entwhistle, 1936: 217)

These varieties are found principally in Andalusia, particularly around Seville and Granada.

It should also be noted that Spanish is not the only language spoken in Spain. Basque, Catalan and Galician are also spoken. Basque, a language apparently unrelated to any known language family, is spoken in the north around San Sebastian and the Pyrenees; Catalan, a Romance language, is spoken in the north-east around Barcelona and as far south as Valencia; and Galician, more closely related to Portuguese than to Spanish, is spoken in the northwest. Although the vast majority of speakers of these languages are bilingual in the regional language and Castilian (in 1976 they represented over 29% of the population of Spain (Lopez-Aranguren, 1981: 270)), Basque and Catalan are now recognised as official languages alongside Castilian, with their own parliaments and use of the regional language in education and the media (Vallverdu, 1984: 25–6). Galician, too, is now taught in schools though it does not have as much autonomy as the others (Williamson & Williamson, 1984).

In a language attitude study in Valencia, it was found that Castilian had higher status than Catalan (Garcia, 1984: 73). The same result was found in Galicia, where Galician is seen as the low code and Castilian as the high, or prestigious, code (Williamson & Williamson, 1984: 412). In both studies a regional variety of Castilian is also discussed which, while prestigious, is not as highly regarded as Castilian spoken without a regional accent (Garcia, 1984; Williamson & Williamson, 1984).

The linguistic situation in Spain, therefore, is complex. There are several languages, e.g. Spanish, Basque, Catalan; several dialects of 'Old Spanish', e.g. Asturian, Castilian, Aragonese; and several varieties of Castilian, or 'new' Spanish, e.g. the southern varieties, the Galician and the Valencian varieties. But, as Stevenson notes:

> In European Spain, even among the more cultured people, certain differences are noticeable. A kind of artificial norm is based on what are considered the best speech forms of Castile (especially Old Castile) and many people from dialect-speaking areas, as well as those from the regions where separate languages, such as Catalan-Valencian, Galician and Basque are current, use their local speech-forms in their home area and the more standardised forms elsewhere. (Stevenson, 1970: 5)

However, Stevenson also points out that although these 'standardised forms'

> sufficiently approach a norm or standard to make them mutually intelligible … no recognised standard really exists

and

> it would be more correct to say that there are a number of standards accord-
> ing to district, class, literature, age group and mere fashion, which suffi-
> ciently approximate to an ideal but not a strictly determined standard.
> (Stevenson, 1970: 5)

The conquest and colonisation of Latin America began in 1492 when
Columbus discovered 'the New World'. Since Castilian had become the principal language of most of Spain by this time, it was most probably Castilian which
was taken to the new colony. Malkiel argues that the majority of early colonists
were from Andalusia and consequently 'the strong South Spanish flavour of the
primitive layer of American Spanish ... must ... be unquestioningly accepted'
(1972: 41). Penalosa says that 'regardless of what dialect or language the
Spanish conquerors and settlers spoke, only Castilian has survived in the New
World' (1980: 19); and Entwistle, when discussing the characteristics of
'Spanish-American', concludes that they are 'all forms of the Castilian pattern
of Spanish' (1936: 249).

Thus, the Spanish, or Castilian, of Latin America is more homogeneous
than the situation in Spain. This does not mean, however, that there is no variation. Penalosa makes this clear when he says,

> Although mutually intelligible, the Spanish spoken in such places as
> Mexico City, Havana, Buenos Aires, or Bogota, for example, are noticeably
> different, and hence we are justified in speaking of Latin American dialects
> of Spanish, though dialectal differences in Spain are still more extensive
> than those in the Americas. (Penalosa, 1980: 25)

However,

> it has become increasingly evident that attempts to delineate geographical
> dialect zones on a phonological basis for Spanish America have met with
> little success. (Canfield in introduction to Resnick, 1975: xi)

This means that

> for example, at least two dialectal features of Costa Rica are also to be
> found in western Argentina, and things thought of as Mexican are also
> heard in Bolivia. (Canfield, 1981: 1–2).

It is, therefore, difficult to talk about any uniformity in Latin American
Spanish, though 'it is Castilian' (Canfield, 1981: 1). Stevenson says that:

> On the other side of the Atlantic [i.e. Latin America] no determined norm
> exists. But the educated classes of the principal towns speak a well-defined
> variety of American-Spanish intelligible throughout the Spanish-speaking
> world, though it would be too much to say that even the well-educated
> Mexican uses the same pronunciation as his distant cousin from Buenos

Aires, Santiago or Bogota. (Stevenson, 1970: 5)

There is, unfortunately, a problem of data when dealing with Latin American dialects. Resnick points this out when he notes that it is virtually impossible to obtain comparative information on dialects (1975: 4), and Lipski makes the same point for Central America where, as he says, 'in recent years, Central America has fared little better, for the area has remained virtually untouched in linguistic studies' (1985: 143).

Consequently, although there is certainly dialectal variation and 'considerable sociolinguistic stratification exists, especially in urban areas' (Lipski, 1985: 143), it is virtually impossible to find any data concerning it. The best information is from Resnick (1975) who numbers over 200 dialects associated with regions (countries, cities) or levels of society, but he gives no indication of their relative prestige or whether there is a 'standard' form or not.

Perhaps the greatest difference between the Castilian of Spain and the Castilian of Latin America is in the lexicon. As Trend notes 'where the influence of Indian languages [on Spanish] is undoubted is in the vocabulary' (1953: 168), and Penalosa says, 'the most important effect on the Spanish language of the indigenous element has been felt in the lexicon' (1980: 23). Thus, for example, for a Mexican 'turkey' is *quajalote*, from the Nahuatl indian language, in Spain it is *pavo* (Penalosa, 1980: 18). In different regions of Latin America, different indigenous languages have influenced Spanish. Thus, the vocabulary may differ both from region to region and transatlantically.

The phonology and syntax of Spanish in Latin America, however, has not perceptibly been affected by the indigenous languages (Penalosa, 1980: 23).

The variation between Spain and Latin America is summed up by Penalosa:

> The more educated the speaker, the smaller are the differences between his speech [i.e. Latin American] and that of educated speakers in the other country [i.e. Spain] ... On the other hand, the less educated the speaker, the more likely that his speech is influenced by local or regional dialects, particularly rural ones. There is certainly more linguistic variability along the social-class continuum in each country than there is transatlantically. (Penalosa, 1980: 18)

To sum up the situation, then, in Spain there is considerable linguistic diversity but Castilian is the official language and the language of prestige and power. Castilian appears to be prestigious no matter what regional variety or accent is used, e.g. in Valencia, Castilian spoken with regional variation was still seen as prestigious. In Latin America, a form of Castilian is spoken but with variation depending on region and social class. Unfortunately, no data were available to us to indicate what the prestigious varieties are or even whether there are any. However, from the information available, it is possible that the educated, urban speech will be relatively similar throughout the whole area and will be prestigious. Variation in vocabulary due to the influence of indigenous languages is also found. As far as variation between Spain and Latin America is concerned, it seems to be the case that for educated speech there is only minor variation, but there is considerably greater variety along the 'social continuum' in each country.

References

CANFIELD, D. L. 1981, *Spanish Pronunciation in the Americas*. Chicago: The University of Chicago Press.

ENTWHISTLE, W. J. 1936, *The Spanish Language — Together with Portuguese, Catalan and Basque*. London: Faber and Faber.

GARCIA, M. R. 1984, Speech attitudes to speakers of language varieties in a bilingual situation. *International Journal of the Sociology of Language* 47, 73–90.

GREEN, J. N. 1987, Spanish. In: B. COMRIE (ed.) *The World's Major Languages* (pp. 236–59). London: Croom Helm.

LIPSKI, J. M. 1985, /S/ in Central American Spanish. *Hispania* 68 (1), 143–9.

LOPEZ-ARANGUREN, E. 1981, Linguistic consciousness in multilingual society. The case of Spain. *Language Problems and Language Planning* 5 (3), 264–78.

MALKIEL, Y. 1972, *Linguistics and Philology in Spanish America: A Survey (1925-1970)*. The Hague: Mouton.

PENALOSA, F. 1980, *Chicano Sociolinguistics: A Brief Introduction*. Rowley, MA: Newbury House Publishers.

RESNICK, M. C. 1975, *Phonological Variants and Dialect Identification in Latin American Spanish*. The Hague: Mouton.

STEVENSON, C. H. 1970, *The Spanish Language Today*. London: Hutchinson.

TREND, J. B. 1953, *The Language and History of Spain*. London: Hutchinson.

VALLVERDU, F. 1984, A sociolinguistic history of Catalan. *International Journal of the Sociology of Language* 47, 13–28.

WILLIAMSON, R. C. and WILLIAMSON, V. L. 1984, Selected factors in bilingualism: the case of Galicia. *Journal of Multilingual and Multicultural Development* 5, 401–13.

Swedish

Swedish is an offshoot of the Germanic branch of Indo-European languages. Between about 550 and 800 AD all Scandinavian languages, Icelandic, Danish, Swedish, Norwegian and Faroese constituted a single language known as Common Scandinavian (Haugen, 1976: 90–2). This language was written in the runic alphabet, the origins of which are unclear (Walshe, 1965: 27).

In the eleventh century Scandinavia was christianised and the Latin alphabet was introduced, though the runes did not disappear till much later, even surviving till modern times in some areas (Haugen, 1976: 191). At about the same time Common Scandinavian began to split and

> by 1350 the main characteristics of the various dialects [i.e. what we now know as Danish, Swedish, Norwegian etc] had already emerged, and towards the end of the middle ages, around 1500, the linguistic diversification of Scandinavia was reaching its peak. (Kristensen & Thelander, 1984: 223).

During this period of linguistic diversification trade in Scandinavia was dominated by the German Hanseatic League. The domination of the Germans had a considerable effect on the language. As Haugen says:

> In ... cities and in their commerce with the Germans, many Scandinavians were forced to become bilingual in Low German. From this language they adapted quite literally thousands of words for the many and varied crafts that were introduced or dominated by the Germans.
>
> The borrowing of terms extended to the point where even German prefixes ... became part of the productive apparatus of the Nordic languages. Nor is it too improbable to speculate that the general breakdown of case and personal endings was due to the same bilingual influence. (Haugen, 1982: 14)

With the advent of printing and the new bible translations brought about by the Reformation, a standard Swedish was developed in the sixteenth century. This meant that

> even while the spoken dialects of the common people were becoming ever more fragmented because of their isolation and inbreeding, a countercurrent was setting in that reversed this trend by setting up language models that

were valid wherever the central government could establish its authority. (Haugen, 1976: 323).

The standard language, however, 'did not agree with anyone's speech, but was a species of idealised form for everyone' (Haugen, 1976: 328). This written norm was developed around the region of Stockholm and Uppsala which was the main centre of government and learning (Haugen, 1976: 41). By 1800 it had developed into a standard of considerable stability which has had only a few revisions since, mostly in spelling, the last being in 1906 (Walshe, 1965: 65–6).

While the written language was standardised to a very large extent several centuries ago this is not the case with the spoken language. The written language was based on the speech of the educated élite and their familiarity with formal language in turn influenced their speech. At the time of development of the written language, however, the majority of Swedes were rural and spoke a variety of dialects. This rural population had little or no access to the élite standard (Haugen, 1976: 1982).

As well as the élite standard dialect and the rural dialects there were also urban dialects. These, according to Haugen

> usually retain many traits from the surrounding rural communities, but interaction within the new community has levelled out differences and created new norms, primarily associated with the working classes ... . (Haugen, 1982: 3)

Thus, 'Stokholmska', the dialect of Stockholm, is more likely to be a pejorative term than a complimentary one (Haugen, 1976: 58).

It was only in the nineteenth century with the spread of schooling that the standard written form of Swedish was extended to the whole population, but as Haugen notes,

> the new literacy did not at once mean a change in speech, only that a basis of passive knowledge of the written norm was established throughout the population. (Haugen, 1976: 360).

During this century the increasing mobility of the population and the advent of radios, televisions and other mass media, as well as education has caused a levelling of dialects within Sweden. This, however, has not led to the acceptance of the élite speech of Stockholm as the standard everywhere. What appears to have occurred, rather, is the emergence of regional standards or norms. These norms 'still compete with those of the capital and characterise their speakers without branding them as inferior' (Haugen, 1976: 60). Also, as Haugen says:

> The teaching of correct *speech* has so far been of less concern to the schools of [Sweden] than the teaching of the literary language. There is reluctance to uniform pupils into a standard pronunciation in view of the

great regional variations and the natural resistances of local pride. (Haugen, 1976: 60)

Kristensen and Thelander conducted a study of the speech in Burtrask in northern Sweden. They found that the population used both dialect and an approximation to the Stockholm standard which, they say, is causing dialect levelling and has 'played a vital part in the dawning of a regional standard language' (1984: 246).

Thus, dialects are, for the most part, being replaced by regional standards, at least outside of the home. Haugen says it is now difficult to find genuine speakers of dialects close to urban centres and that even if people speak dialect at home they are 'ashamed or unwilling' to speak it to strangers since 'today the use of local dialects marks a speaker as rural or untutored' (Haugen, 1976: 56–7).

Nevertheless, there are areas, particularly areas far removed from the capital, where dialects are still used and can cause problems of comprehension for outsiders. For example, Dalarna, Skane, northern Norland and the Island of Gotland have dialectal forms which are difficult for others to understand (Haugen, 1982: 3, 55; Kristensen & Thelander, 1984: 223).

Also, the Swedish spoken by a Swedish minority on the Baltic coast of Finland has developed its own dialect due to its isolation from the mainland of Sweden. This dialect too can cause some problems of comprehension (Loman, 1980: 207).

Thus, although 'there is no universally accepted standard speech norm' (Haugen, 1976: 59) for the whole of Sweden, there are a number of regional varieties which are reasonably closely related and act as the accepted prestige forms. Some Swedes, though, still speak a dialect other than a regional standard, and these may be considered more or less stigmatised (Haugen, 1976: 57–8).

A further point to note is the intrusion of English into the Swedish language. There appear to be two positions on this; the first is to consider the use of English words and phrases as a barbarisation of the language; and the second is to accept English freely. The first position is upheld by language purists and the second is upheld by young people via their literature and newspaper articles depicting the youth culture. Also, journalists, who receive a large proportion of news in English, and those whose professional models write in English such as social scientists and industrialists find it hard to use a form of Swedish free of anglicisms (Haugen, 1976: 69–70).

References

HAUGEN, E. 1976, *The Scandinavian Languages: An Introduction to their History.* London: Faber and Faber.

HAUGEN, E. 1982, *Scandinavian Language Structure: A Comparative Historical Survey.* Minneapolis: University of Minnesota Press.

KRISTENSEN, K. and THELANDER, M. 1984, On dialect levelling in Denmark and Sweden. *Folia Linguistica* 18 (1–2), 223–246.

LOMAN, B. 1980, A literary aspect of the hidden language conflict of Finland. *Journal of Multilingual and Multicultural Development* 1 (3), 207–16.

WALSHE, M. O'C. 1965, *Introduction to the Scandinavian Languages.* London: Andre Deutsch.

Tamil

Tamil is a Dravidian language from South India. It is spoken in the southern Indian state of Tamilnadu (formerly Madras), where it is the official language, and in Sri Lanka. Also, there are large Tamil speaking Indian communities in Malaysia, Fiji and South Africa (Meenakshisundaran, 1965: 17). Tamil has its own script mainly derived from the old Brahmi script but incorporating elements of other southern Indian scripts (Gaur, 1984: 106ff).

The Tamil literary language dates back to at least the second century BC (Shanmugam, 1975: 55). And according to Arooran the best literature was written between 850 and 1200 AD (1980: 14).

With the arrival of Europeans in the sixteenth century Tamil began to be influenced by western languages and culture (Shanmugam, 1975: 55). The greatest influence was that of English. The British arrived in India and Sri Lanka in the eighteenth century, and English was soon the prestige language of education, administration and the law, as well as other such fields (Kandiah, 1978: 61). Tamil, therefore, tended to be reserved for the more domestic spheres of life. Arooran, in fact, considers that Tamil was to a large extent neglected and that the élite became 'incapable of formal Tamil speech' (1980: 15).

In the late nineteenth century the publication of some of the major works of ancient Tamil literature in Tamilnadu led to a resurgence of interest in Tamil (Arooran, 1980: 19–20). This resurgence of interest was not confined to language alone, but extended into cultural and religious aspects as well.

Until this time, the religious and social system had been subject to a rigid caste system. At the top of the caste hierarchy were the Brahmins. For all religious purposes the Brahmins maintained the superiority of Sanskrit, an ancient Indo-European language of northern India, in which the bulk of the scriptures were written. (Arooran, 1980).

However, with the rediscovery of the old Tamil texts 'the educated non-Brahmins by the beginning of the twentieth century began to question the inferior position assigned to the Dravidian [Tamil] civilisation in history' (Arooran, 1980: 36). This led to the formation of non-Brahmin social and political groups, attempts to revive and establish what was felt to be the original religion of the Dravidians, and the purging of Sanskrit elements from Tamil (Arooran, 1980; Shanmugam, 1975: 61). Shanmugam notes that in 1900

244

it was estimated that 50% of the words in written Tamil were of Sanskrit origin, or at least influenced by Sanskrit, but that by 1950 this had been reduced to 20% and the process is still continuing so that nowadays the percentage must be relatively small (1975: 61).

In Sri Lanka the situation is somewhat different. It appears that the Brahmins and Sanskrit were not as influential as they were in India. The influential caste among Sri Lankan Tamils is the Vellala. According to Fernando, Brahmins exist but are few in number and almost exclusively priests whereas the 'de facto' high caste are the Vellala, the landlords (1979: 31). Also, even though English was the exclusive language of the administration, legislation and so on during the colonial period, there was a group of traditionalist scholars, known as the pandits, who maintained and upheld a literary language based on a grammar written in the fifth century AD, if not considerably earlier (Kandiah, 1978: 60; Meenakshisundaran, 1965: 51). Shanmugam, (1975: 55), in fact, dates the grammar to the second century BC. According to Kandiah, this literary language was seen as standard Tamil and has been maintained unchanged by the pandits throughout Sri Lankan Tamil history since the grammar was first produced (1978: 60–1).

The ancient literary language, therefore, has considerable prestige in both Tamilnadu and Sri Lanka. In Tamilnadu it provided justification for the rise of the non-Brahmin movements, which, as Arooran says ,

> not only provided the catalyst to a new cultural awakening among the Tamils but also brought a new sense of Dravidian consciousness and cultural pride which led to the rise of linguistic sub-nationalism in Tamilnad. (Arooran, 1980: 26f)

And in Sri Lanka the pandits had maintained the ancient literary language as an 'eternal standard', and provided Sri Lankan Tamil with 'one of the longest unbroken traditions of any among the world's living languages' (Friedrich, quoted in Kandiah, 1978: 67). This literary tradition, according to Kandiah, is used as a symbol of Tamil nationalism and has the power to

> compel acquiescence in so many of the institutions that wield influence in matters relating to Standard Lankan Tamil, such as the University, the Training Colleges, the Official Languages Department, and so on. (Kandiah, 1978: 60, 67).

Shanmugam considers that in Tamilnadu 'the modernisation of Tamil seems to have started only from the beginning of this century' (1975: 55). The modernisation being discussed, however, concerns the written language only. According to Shanmugam the modernisation entailed some spelling reforms; the coining of new scientific, technical and cultural terms, often based on classical elements; the elimination of foreign words, for example Sanskrit words; and some minor grammatical changes (1975: 55ff).

None of these modernisations, however, has removed the 'modern' written language very far from the ancient written language. In fact, Schiffman considers that for Tamil in Tamilnadu 'no serious movement [towards modernisation] has been attempted, or to my knowledge, even proposed' (1973: 131).

In Sri Lanka modernisation began slightly later, but appears to have gone further. According to Kandiah, in the last few decades the élite have developed, and are in fact still developing, a written standard which is based on the 'eternal standard' of the ancient literary language, but which differs from it in several important respects (1978: 68). Kandiah notes that the modern élite declare their allegiance to the traditional standard, thereby attracting to themselves the prestige and status of that standard, but in practice use it only to develop a kind of idealisation of their own usage (1978: 68). A new form of 'educated' Tamil, therefore, appears to be developing which, while still distinct from the spoken colloquial forms, is not as divergent as the traditional standard.

It is the 'modern' literary languages of Tamilnadu and Sri Lanka (which, at least in Tamilnadu, appears,in effect, to be only slightly different from the ancient literary language) which represent the standard languages for formal spoken situations. As Shanmugam says for Tamilnadu 'Modern standard written Tamil ... is not only used for writing but also for making public speeches and reading radio news, etc.' (1975: 57). And Kandiah says for Sri Lanka:

> [The written standard] is generally used by educated Tamils in writing and in formal speech (at lectures, political meetings and so on) and even, at times, as a supplementary style, in less formal situations, when less 'domestic' subjects (like politics, literature, history and so on) are being discussed. Moreover, it is being spread by the mass media (the Sri Lanka Broadcasting Corporation, as well as the two largest Tamil daily newspapers in Sri Lanka ... use it as their base language, and so do various journals, government notices, advertisements and such publications) to all Tamil-using corners of the country. (Kandiah, 1978: 69)

The two literary standards differ from one another, though it would appear that they are mutually intelligible, probably because they are both based on the same ancient texts. Kandiah notes that the standard from Tamilnadu is influencing the standard in Sri Lanka through the importation of books, journals, newspapers and films, and through Sri Lankans receiving Tamilnadu radio broadcasts, but 'there is no doubt at all that this standard [i.e. the Sri Lankan standard] is a distinct entity, and will continue to remain so' (1978: 70).

The literary standards, which, as noted above, are also used for formal speech, do not correspond to anyone's spoken dialect (Shanmugam, 1975: 77; Meenakshisundaran, 1965: 194; Schiffman, 1973: 129; Subbiah, 1966: 1). The literary language differs from the spoken dialects in phonology (sounds), vocabulary and grammar (Shanmugam, 1975: 58; Schiffman, 1973: 129). Consequently, a diglossic situation exists in Tamilnadu and Sri Lanka. This diglossic situation means that there are at least two codes, or ways of speaking, used in Tamil speaking communities. The formal code, often called the 'high' code in linguistic literature, may differ to a considerable extent from the informal, colloquial code. It is usual for the 'high' code to be the only one with a written form. In many cases of diglossia an 'educated' form evolves which maintains many of the features of the formal code but is more flexible and is used in more varied situations.

The differences between the literary standard and colloquial Tamil speech are so great that Subbiah considers educated Tamils to be 'bilingual' (1966: 1). And Schiffman remarks that 'no other spoken language has a written form so different from the spoken' (1973: 130). He also says,

> so different are the two dialects of Tamil [i.e. the literary and colloquial] that illiterates can understand only a fraction of the spoken form of the literary language. (Schiffman, 1973: 129).

However, it appears that colloquial speech is generally looked down upon. As Kandiah notes:

> ... the notion of a standard language is, especially because of the strength of traditionalist opinion, too much identified in the minds of Tamil users with writing to permit it to have the kind of relevance to spoken usage that it normally would have. Certainly, a mere description of the colloquial usage of the élite (or of any group, for that matter) would be rejected out of hand as representing 'bad Tamil', and the rejection would be almost universal. (Kandiah, 1978: 69)

Nevertheless, many dialects of spoken Tamil exist and are widely used. Subbiah (1966) notes that there are several dialects in Tamilnadu differentiated by the use of certain vocabulary items. And Zvelebil states that there are at least four major dialects in Sri Lanka: North, with Jaffna as the centre; north-east, around Trincomalee; south-east, around Batticaloa; and a mixed variety in Colombo (1969: 356). Zvelebil also notes that in Tamilnadu there are 'vertical' or social dialectal differences, such as, for example, between the speech of Brahmins and the speech of non-Brahmins (1969: 358). Subbiah, however, states that 'there is no Standard Colloquial Tamil at present.' (1966: 1).

The dialects of Tamilnadu, though, appear to differ more from those of Sri Lanka than they do from each other, and vice-versa (Zvelebil, 1969: 356). According to Steever, the formal, literary, variety of the Central dialect of the cities of Tanjore, Tirichirapalli and Madurai is emerging as the standard spoken dialect for Tamilnadu (1987: 731).

In Tamil, therefore, there are many spoken dialects (it would appear that they are all mutually intelligible) with the major differences being between Sri Lanka and Tamilnadu. There are also 'vertical' or social dialects of the spoken language, e.g. the Brahmin and non-Brahmin dialects in Tamilnadu. The standard, however, is not based on any of the spoken dialects, but rather on the literary language. The literary language itself is based, it seems, on the ancient Tamil texts dating back to perhaps the second century BC and has changed only slightly since then. The standard literary language differs between Sri Lanka and Tamilnadu though it seems that there are few problems of comprehension between the two varieties. However, the standard differs considerably, in sound, in grammar and vocabulary from the colloquial spoken dialects, and for the illiterate it poses considerable problems of comprehension.

The problem of diglossia is a major one for Tamil. It must be assumed that for different situations a different level of formality will be required; for example, a discussion on religion, politics, or literature would probably be conducted in the most formal code, whereas an interview with a farmer or factory worker would probably be in colloquial Tamil. It is necessary, therefore, to have a knowledge of all codes of Tamil in order not only to have command of the relevant code, but also to know precisely which code to use in what situation.

References

AROORAN, K. N. 1980, *Tamil Renaissance and Dravidian Nationalism: 1905–1944*. Madurai: Koodal Publishers.

FERNANDO, T. 1979, Aspects of social stratification. In: T. FERNANDO and R. N. KEARNEY (eds) *Modern Sri Lanka: A Society in Transition* (pp. 29–42). Syracuse: Syracuse University (*Foreign and Comparative Studies/Asian Series* No. 4).

GAUR, A. 1984, *A History of Writing*. London: The British Library.

KANDIAH, T. 1978, Standard language and socio-historical parameters: standard Lankan Tamil. *International Journal of the Sociology of Language* 16, 59–75. The Hague: Mouton (*Aspects of Socio-linguistics in South Asia*).

MEENAKSHISUNDARAN, T. P. 1965, *A History of Tamil Language*. Poona: Linguistic Society of India.

SHANMUGAM, S. V. 1975, Modernization in Tamil. *Anthropological Linguistics* 17 (3), 55–63.

SCHIFFMAN, H. 1973, Language, linguistics, and politics in Tamilnad. In: E. GEROW and M. D. LANG (eds) *Studies in the Language and Culture of South Asia* (pp. 125–34). Seattle: University of Washington Press.

STEEVER, S. B. 1987, Tamil and the Dravidian languages. In: B. COMRIE (ed.) *The World's Major Languages* (pp. 725–46). London: Croom Helm.

SUBBIAH, R. 1966, *A Lexical Study of Tamil Dialects in Lower Perak*. Kuala Lumpur: University of Malaya.

ZVELEBIL, K. V. 1969, Tamil. In: T. SEBEOK (ed.) *Current Trends in Linguistics* Vol. 5 (pp. 343–71). The Hague: Mouton.

Turkish

Turkish is a member of the Turkic family of languages. It is spoken in Turkey where it is the official language. Turkish is also the co-official language, with Greek, in Cyprus, and it is used by a large number of Turkish speakers in Bulgaria, Yugoslavia and Greece (Kornfilt, 1987: 620).

Turkish was brought to Anatolia from the east when the Turks invaded the area in the eleventh century (Kornfilt, 1987: 621). The Turks were converted to Islam sometime prior to the thirteenth century, and probably used Arabic and Persian as their literary language when they first arrived in Anatolia (Kornfilt, 1987: 621). From the thirteenth, and especially in the fourteenth, century works in Turkish began to be produced. From the beginning, though, these works were written in the Arabic script and heavily influenced by Arabic and Persian (Kornfilt, 1987: 621–2).

By the fifteenth century Ottoman Turkish, the language of the Ottoman rulers of the Turkish empire, had evolved out of the older form of the language (Kornfilt, 1987: 620–1). But, as Kornfilt notes,

> in the literature written for scholarly, administrative and literary purposes, the Persian and Arabic components became so prevalent that 'Ottoman' became a mixed language, having lost some of its characteristic Turkic properties to the point of not being usable as a medium of communication common to all social classes. (Kornfilt, 1987: 622)

However, there were also some works written for the less educated in a form much closer to the spoken language and which was influenced very little by Persian and Arabic. And from the eighteenth century there was a movement calling for the official literary language to be 'purified' of foreign elements and made into a language with local features (Kornfilt, 1987: 622–3).

At the beginning of the twentieth century, though, the official written language of Turkey was still 'Osmanlica', as the 'synthetic amalgam of Arabic, Persian, and Turkish, with grammatical and syntactic features of each' was called (Gallagher, 1971/1975: 161). Osmanlica was restricted to the élite and was unintelligible to the majority of Turks who spoke what was derisively known as 'crude Turkish'. There was thus a considerable gap between the official language used by the educated class and the vernacular.

Osmanlica continued to be written in the Arabic script which reflected the fact that Islam was central to the political and social organisation of the Ottoman empire. As Lewis says, 'in many societies there is a close link between religion and writing — nowhere more clearly than in the Ottoman world' (1961: 419). Lewis also points out, though, that the Arabic script was 'peculiarly inappropriate to the Turkish language' (1961: 420) despite the heavy borrowing from Persian and Arabic.

The movement to reform literary Turkish also continued into the twentieth century, and from 1909 journals and some literary works began to be published in a 'purified' form of literary Turkish (Kornfilt, 1987: 622–3). In the 1920s Mustafa Kemal (Ataturk) came to power and instituted a number of political and social reforms designed to modernise, westernise and secularise the country.

One of the major areas of reform was concerned with the language and orthographic system. A new writing system based on Latin letters was devised and made the official system of Turkey in laws passed in 1928. The Arabic script was forbidden from the beginning of 1929. The new script was designed to reflect, as closely as possible, the pronunciation, and, as Lewis puts it, 'the new Turkish alphabet, though not perfectly phonetic, is a good deal more so than that of most European languages' (1960: 96).

Along with the major reform of the writing system the vocabulary of Turkish was also reformed. In 1932, at Ataturk's suggestion, the Turkish Linguistic Society was formed. This society had three essential tasks:

> to collect Turkish words from the popular language and from old Turkish texts; to define the principles of word formation and to create words from Turkish roots; and to encourage the use of true Turkish words in replacement of foreign words used in the written language. (Gallagher, 1971/1975: 165)

The Turkish Linguistic Society initially attempted to expurgate all Persian and Arabic words from the language. After a time, however, a more relaxed attitude was taken and some of the more 'familiar and indispensable Arabic and Persian words were granted reprieve and naturalisation' (Lewis, 1961: 429).

The language reform is still taking place to this day with new words being coined and borrowing still going on. The borrowing these days, though, is mainly from the West, especially from French.

So the linguistic situation is that Turkish has undergone considerable change over the past fifty years and, as Hotham remarks,

> people today cannot understand the early speeches of Ataturk, the originator of the reform, and one sees the strange phenomenon of Turkish writers 'translating' their own books from the old Turkish into the new. (Hotham, 1972: 18)

It is important to note that the language reforms instituted by Ataturk were, in part, designed to move Turkish society away from the Islamic countries and re-orient it towards the West. In consequence, the form of language used by a Turkish speaker has considerable religious, social and political overtones. In this regard it is worth quoting at length from Gallagher:

> If, as has been remarked, language is close to the heart of the culture but functions as an autonomous part of it, it is natural that it should mirror the problems, conflicts, and value differences of a society with some faithfulness. This is true in Turkey today, where much may be known about the fundamental outlook of a man by the language he uses. His vocabulary may give him away before the content of his utterances has been digested. To take an example from one of the borrowings mentioned above, the word 'international' can be expressed in four ways. The traditional, Arabic-derived term is *beyenelmilel*, an Arabic pronoun put together with the broken plural form of the Turkified form of the Arabic noun *millet* (people, nation), all of which create an air of fusty and elegant literarism-cum-piety [sic]. Another widely accepted, neo-traditional Turkish coinage is *milletlerarasi*, where the preceding noun has been given indigenous suffixes to express the same concept of 'between nations'. A more recent and national invention of the language planners is *uluslararasi*, where the Turkish noun *ulus* has replaced the Arabo-Turkish *millet*, found now in textbooks and government publications as well as being given broad usage. Finally, a popular modern word found in much advertising and throughout the mass media is *enternasyonal*. In the process of listening to this example and many similar ones of multiple choice, one learns much about who has accepted which of the alternatives. The struggle for primacy among such words and expressions is a view in miniature of the still bitterly contested struggle for the cultural and social future of Turkey. (Gallagher, 1971/1975: 175)

It is also important to note that many of the vocabulary changes have been reflections of government policy and, since the radio, TV and education are government controlled, different generations of Turks may have access to only one variety. That is, for example, younger speakers of Turkish may only be able to understand the most recent version of Turkish and find the vocabulary changes promulgated in the 1940s or 1950s unintelligible. There may also be an element of bias engendered by the way people react to one form or another of the language. For example, a devoutly religious person may react adversely to the 'modern' Turkish, and a secularist may automatically be put off by Turkish spoken with a heavy concentration of Arabic and Persian words.

Very little information was available to us on dialectal variation in spoken Turkish. However, since the orthography of Turkish is relatively phonemic, that is, each letter represents one sound (Kornfilt, 1987: 625), it is probable that as Turkish speakers learn to read and write they also learn a standard pronunciation.

According to Kornfilt, Modern Standard Turkish represents a standardisation of the Istanbul dialect of the Anatolian group of dialects (1987: 620).

References

GALLAGHER, C. F. 1975, Language reform and social modernization in Turkey. In J. RUBIN and B. JERNUDD (eds) *Can Language Be Planned?* Honolulu: The University Press of Hawaii.

KORNFILT, J. 1987, Turkish and the Turkic languages. In: B. COMRIE (ed.) *The World's Major Languages* (pp. 619–44). London: Croom Helm.

HOTHAM, D. 1972, *The Turks*. London: John Murray.

LEWIS, B. 1961, *The Emergence of Modern Turkey*. London: Oxford University Press.

LEWIS, G. L. 1960, *Turkey*. New York: Frederick A. Praeger.

MARDIN, Y. 1976, *Colloquial Turkish*. Routledge and Kegan Paul.

Ukrainian

Ukrainian is grouped with Byelorussian and Russian in the East Slavonic branch of the Slavonic group of Indo-European languages (Matthews, 1951: 115). It is written in the Cyrillic alphabet.

It is difficult to determine exactly when Ukrainian, Byelorussian and Russian became separate languages, though Shevelov notes that in the sixth and seventh centuries AD certain phonological changes took place in Ukraine and that from this time on it is possible to speak of the emergence of a separate Ukrainian language (Shevelov, 1979: 29ff). Vlasto, however, considers that East Slavonic remained fairly homogeneous till at least the thirteenth century (1986: 335ff).

The name 'Ukrainian' was originally used to designate the form of the language in only one region of Ukraine. It came into use nationally only in the seventeenth century, and in the Transcarpathian region only after 1938 (Shevelov, 1979: 30) Up until the seventeenth century the name '*Rus'kyj*' was used for the language spoken in Ukraine, and the name '*Russkij*' was used for the language of Russia (Shevelov, 1979: 30). The similarity of name stems from the original name, '*Rus*', used during the time of the first East Slavic state, centred in Kiev in Ukraine. As Shevelov puts it:

> The geographical nucleus of the term '*Rus*' was the Kiev land, but ... the term was ambiguous because Kiev applied it to all Slavs which it had or aspired to have under its sway, i.e. to the ancestors of Ukrainians, Russians, and Belorussians [sic]. (Shevelov, 1979: 30)

When Kiev adopted Christianity in the tenth century, it also adopted a written language. The written language which it adopted was a Bulgarianised form of Old Church Slavonic, written in the Cyrillic alphabet (Shevelov, 1979: 213; Szporluk, 1979: 7). Christianity, and Old Church Slavonic, soon spread to all East Slavic regions, and, according to Shevelov, the literary language of Kiev from the eleventh to the fourteenth century was 'ideally one and the same with that of other East Slavic principalities' (1971: 31).

Thus, although the spoken languages had diverged and split into three separate languages, only one written form was introduced. However, even though Old Church Slavonic remained relatively fixed, there was, nevertheless, a certain amount of infiltration of dialectal features into the written language. By the late fourteenth century Old Church Slavonic had evolved into a number of different varieties, which were the result of its adaptation to local speech habits (Shevelov, 1979: 215; 1981: 218).

From the fourteenth to the nineteenth centuries the history of the literary and prestige language forms used in Ukraine is, to a large extent, the history of the foreign powers which ruled in Ukraine. In the thirteenth century much of eastern Ukraine had been overrun by the Tatars and much of the population fled to the west or to Russia (Shevelov, 1981: 218). In the fourteenth century the western regions were partitioned, principally between Poland and Lithuania though Moldavia and Hungary also gained small areas of Ukrainian lands (Shevelov, 1981: 218; Szporluk, 1979: 12ff).

As a result Polish and Latin were introduced into the Polish ruled areas, and Ruthenian, a language form based on Byelorussian but incorporating some Ukrainian features, was introduced in Lithuanian ruled areas (Shevelov, 1981: 219). In the sixteenth century, after the constitutional union of Poland and Lithuania, the Lithuanian areas of Ukraine became part of the Kingdom of Poland and Polish and Latin replaced Ruthenian (Szporluk, 1979: 13; Shevelov, 1981: 220).

In the Polish areas many of the upper strata of society converted to Roman Catholicism, the religion of Poland, and adopted the Polish language and culture. Thus, according to Szporluk, 'Ukrainian society ... was transformed into a predominantly peasant folk' (1979: 16).

Church Slavonic, too, was becoming more remote from spoken Ukrainian. This was due to what is known as the Euthymian recension brought to Ukraine and other East Slavic states by Bulgarians fleeing the Turkish conquests of the Balkans. The Bulgarians were hostile to any vernacularisation of the Church language and consequently 'purified' it. This resulted in Church Slavonic becoming artificial and divorced from the spoken language (Shevelov, 1979: 394ff).

In the sixteenth century, the Tatars were pushed back and areas of eastern Ukraine were recolonised. In these areas Ukrainian dialects took the upper hand and the mixing of the dialects of the settlers produced what are known as the south eastern dialects. These dialects are the most uniform of all Ukrainian dialects and formed the basis of a vernacular literary language, known as *prostaia mova*, which was widely used in the eastern part of Ukraine in the seventeenth century (Shevelov, 1979: 38; 1981: 222).

Ukraine was again divided, this time between Poland and Russia, in the seventeenth century. Poland retained its territories in the west and Russia took over the eastern areas (Szporluk, 1979: 22ff). By the eighteenth century Polish and Russian were the two major prestigious and literary languages of Ukraine. Church Slavonic was replaced by Russian and the *prostaia mova* had broken up into dialectal forms (Shevelov, 1979: 570, 703).

UKRAINIAN

255
From the eighteenth to the mid-twentieth centuries Ukraine suffered further partitions. At various times Austria, Russia, Czechoslovakia, Romania, Hungary, and Poland were in control of parts of Ukraine (Szporluk, 1979). Nevertheless, from the late eighteenth, and particularly in the nineteenth, century a Ukrainian literary language began to develop.

By the late eighteenth century Ukrainian was preserved as a spoken language primarily among a peasant population in the rural areas, the educated classes spoke either Russian or Polish in everyday life, and the cities had virtually become 'de-Ukrainianised' in favour of Russian or Polish (Wexler, 1974: 41). The advent of the so-called Age of Romanticism, however, led some writers to turn to spoken Ukrainian since 'language was considered the expression of the nation's aspirations and soul and the sum of its historical experience' (Shevelov, 1981: 224).

At this time there were a considerable number of dialects spoken in rural areas. As well, the influence of Polish in the west and Russian in the east, had led to considerable divergence, especially in vocabulary, of the eastern and western regions (Wexler, 1974: 71). According to Shevelov, though, 'the modern Ukrainian literary language ... stems from the popular language which is based on the dialect of the southeast' (1981: 224). This language, Shevelov notes, is related to the *prostaia mova* which grew up in the seventeenth century (1981: 224).

In 1863 and again in 1876 Russia forbade the use of Ukrainian in its areas. As a result most of the development of a standard Ukrainian took place in the Austrian controlled part, especially the area known as Galicia (Shevelov, 1981: 225). Under the Austrians Ukrainian was allowed in administration, education, and the law among other areas of usage (Szporluk, 1979: 51). But the Austrian controlled areas had previously been Polish, and so many Polish elements entered the standard literary language (Wexler, 1974: 69ff; Shevelov, 1981: 226).

During the period of development of the standard language, there was considerable debate and controversy about the use and influence of Polish and Russian. As a rule, it seems, only Ukrainian forms were desired, though this may not always have been the case in practice (Wexler, 1974; Shevelov, 1981: 225). It is generally agreed, however, that the standard language is based on the south-eastern, Kiev-Poltava dialect (Shevelov, 1981: 224; Wexler, 1974).

By the 1930s, then, a standard form of Ukrainian had been developed, free, as far as possible, of Polish and Russian influence and based on the Kiev-Poltava dialect. This form of the language represented the spoken standard, used in public offices, schools, broadcasting and so on, as well as the literary standard (Luckyj & Rudnyckyj, 1950: 4).

After the Second World War all of the Ukrainian lands became part of the USSR as the Ukrainian SSR. The dialectal basis of the standard language has remained the same, but Russian elements, particularly in vocabulary, but also in syntax and grammar, are once more entering the standard (Wexler, 1974: 313–4).

It is worth noting that many emigré Ukrainians prefer to adhere to the standard form developed by the 1930s which excluded Russian and Polish forms (Koscharskij, 1988). It is highly probable, therefore, that there will be apparent differences between the standard language as it is used in Ukraine today, and the language used by emigre Ukrainians.

As far as the spoken language is concerned there are still many dialects in Ukraine. Shevelov divides the dialects into three major areas, northern, south-western and south-eastern. Of these, the most important and the most uniform are the south-eastern. The other two major areas can be sub-divided into several sub-dialects (Shevelov, 1979: 38ff). The standard spoken form is, as noted above, the same as the literary standard and is based on the south-eastern, Kiev-Poltava dialect. Halyna Koscharskij (1988) pointed out that 'Russification' of the spoken language, as well as the literary language, is occurring on all levels, from the local dialects to the standard form.

In Ukraine, at the present time, Russian is a very important language. Ukrainian language schools are declining while Russian language ones are increasing proportionately. Also, Russian language periodicals and publications are replacing Ukrainian ones (Szporluk, 1979: 122). Many Ukrainians, especially in urban areas, are bilingual in Russian (Wexler, 1974: 317), and Russian is the language of instruction in universities (Koscharskij, 198X). Halyna Koscharskij (198X) has also pointed out that the issue of the prestige of the Ukrainian language is a very pertinent one in Ukraine today, and that many writers and poets have raised their voices in protest at the increasing use of Russian.

References

KOSCHARSKIJ, H. 1988, School of Modern Languages, Macquarie University, personal communication.
LUCKYJ, G. and RUDNYCKYJ, J. B. 1950, *A Modern Ukrainian Grammar*. Minneapolis: The University of Minnesota Press.
MATTHEWS, W. K. 1951, *Languages of the U.S.S.R.* Cambridge: Cambridge University Press.
SHEVELOV, G. Y. 1979, *A Historical Phonology of the Ukrainian Language*. Heidelberg: Carol Winter Universitatsverlag.
SHEVELOV, G. Y. 1981, Evolution of the Ukrainian literary language. In: I. L. RUDNYTSKY (ed.) *Rethinking Ukrainian History* (pp. 216–31). Edmonton: University of Alberta (The Canadian Institute of Ukrainian Studies).
SZPORLUK, R. 1979, *Ukraine: A Brief History*. Michigan: Edwards Brother.
VLASTO, A. P. 1986, *A Linguistic History of Russia to the end of the Eighteenth Century*. Oxford: The Clarendon Press.
WEXLER, P. 1974, *Purism and Language: A Study in Modern Ukrainian and Belorussian Nationalism (1840–1967)*. Bloomington: Indiana University Publications.

Urdu

Urdu is an Indo-Aryan language, a branch of the Indo-European family. It is the official language of Pakistan, and in India it is the state language of the states of Jammu and Kashmir (Kachru, 1987: 470). Urdu and Hindi are linguistically very similar, differing mainly in their learned vocabulary and script; the chapters on Urdu and Hindi are, therefore, also similar.

The Indo-Aryan languages have their origin in the migration of the Aryan peoples into India which began around 2000 years BC. As Zograph notes,

> it would seem that the groups of Aryans who entered India were neither ethnically nor linguistically homogeneous, and that they brought with them not one single language but rather a collection of related dialects. (Zograph, 1982: 9)

The most ancient form of the Aryan's language which was written down was Vedic. Vedic, though, appears to reflect the spoken dialects of that time and, consequently, was not unified in its form (Zograph, 1982: 10).

During the first millenium BC a form known as Sanskrit evolved, and by about the fourth century BC a written form of Sanskrit had been standardised and codified, particularly in the work of the grammarian Panini (Zograph, 1982: 10–11). Once Sanskrit had been standardised it remained fixed and is still in use today in virtually the same form. The constitution of India lists Sanskrit as one of the most important languages of the country (Zograph, 1982: 11).

The spoken language, however, was not fixed and continued to evolve. Two major stages in the development of the Indo-Aryan languages from Sanskrit to the modern languages are usually discussed by scholars. These are the Prakrit and Apabhramsa stages. The Prakrits, meaning 'natural', 'ordinary' speech, are attested in several forms in different regions of northern India. These Prakrits were also used for literature and one of them, Pali, became the language of Buddhism (Zograph, 1982: 12ff). The Prakrit known as Sauraseni, spoken in the western part of northern India, is considered by Grierson to be the ancestor of Urdu (1968: 2).

The Apabhramsas, meaning 'corrupted language', also developed different-ly in different regions. They formed the transition between the Prakrits and the modern Indo-Aryan languages (Zograph, 1982: 14). Like the Prakrits, the Apabhramsas were also used for literature (Zograph, 1982: 14).

The modern Indo-Aryan languages, often called New Indo-Aryan, evolved from about 1000 AD (Kachru, 1987: 470). These New Indo-Aryan languages did not evolve identically or discretely. The linguistic situation in northern India thus became, and has remained, complex. The distinction between language and dialect is often difficult to draw in this area (Kachru & Bhatia, 1978; Rai, 1984: 287ff). And as Zograph says:

> Local forms of speech change every few kilometers, but not sufficiently to make them incomprehensible to close neighbours. As distances increase so too do dialectal variations, until the actual transition to another language is made. Thus, from the Punjab to Bangladesh, there is not one single sharply defined linguistic boundary, although, according to [the Linguistic Survey of India], six languages represented by dozens of dialects merge, one into another, across this vast territory. (Zograph, 1982: 22)

At about the same time as the New Indo-Aryan languages were emerging from the Apabhramsa stage India was invaded by Persian Muslims (Rai, 1984: 285). Under the Muslims Persian, with a heavy mixture of Arabic, the language of Islam, became the language of law, administration and élite culture (Kachru & Bhatia, 1978: 48). However, the Muslims also used the speech of the indigenous Indian population in the area around their capital, Delhi, as a common language of communication with the Indians under their rule (Kachru, 1987: 471).

The form of New Indo-Aryan which was used is variously termed 'Hindi', a Persian word meaning Indian, or connected with northern India (McGregor, 1974: 62), 'Hindustani', which Grierson says was first used in the seventeenth century to mean the *lingua franca* of northern India (1968: 3; also Zograph, 1982: 32), and 'Khari Boli' the name of the New Indo-Aryan language or dialect spoken around Delhi (Kachru, 1987: 471). Whatever it was called, this form gradually adopted Persian and Arabic vocabulary and came to be written in the Perso-Arabic script (McGregor, 1974: 62).

In the eighteenth century Khari Boli, or Hindustani, was adopted by the Muslim court as their language of literature and the influx of Persian and Arabic vocabulary intensified (Zograph, 1982: 32; McGregor, 1981: 3). According to Rai, the eighteenth century also saw a 'purifying' of this form by the Muslims to reject or discard Sanskrit elements from their literature (1984: 285).

The literary form which developed, written in the Perso-Arabic script, became the language of the Muslim élite all over the north of India (Mobbs, 1981: 205). It was also used by Hindus, especially in the cities (McGregor, 1980: 3–4). This form came initially to be known as 'Rexta' or 'Rekhta', mixed language, and from the nineteenth century it was known as 'Urdu', a name which apparently derives from a Turkish or Farsi (Persian) word meaning 'camp' (Kachru, 1987: 471; Mobbs, 1981: 205).

By the early nineteenth century, then, Urdu was the literary language of the Muslim élite and of some Hindus, it was also, according to Kachru and Bhatia, used informally for legal and administrative purposes (1978: 48). The official language remained Persian (Kachru & Bhatia, 1978: 48), though some Persian Muslims and Indian Muslims by this time spoke Hindustani, or Khari Boli, or, as it was now called, Urdu, as their mother tongue (McGregor, 1981: 3). When the British took over northern India in the nineteenth century, Urdu was recognised as the language of the law and as an official language of administration (Kachru & Bhatia, 1978: 48).

However, throughout the period of Muslim rule Hindus had used other New Indo-Aryan languages related to Khari Boli, such as Braj or Brajbhasa, and Rajasthani, as literary languages and these were written in the Devanagari script (Kachru & Bhatia, 1978: 48; McGregor, 1981: 4). According to Rai, during the eighteenth century Hindus had begun writing a form of Hindustani, or Khari Boli, in Devanagari script (1984: 285). It seems that because of the currency of Khari Boli throughout the north of India there was a tendency to see in it the basis of a standard form which Hindus could adapt to their own cultural purposes (McGregor, 1974: 62–3). Consequently, in the early nineteenth century,

> another style of Khari Boli, written in Devanagari script (with lexical borrowings mainly from Sanskrit), known as Hindi, was developing rapidly and was extensively used by the general population but had as yet no official or administrative sanction. (Kachru & Bhatia, 1978: 48)

This represents the beginning of modern Hindi, based, as is Urdu, on Khari Boli, or Hindustani.

When Urdu was recognised as an official language by the British, a movement began to obtain for Hindi similar offical recognition, and by 1900 Hindi had been granted official status in the states of United Provinces (now Uttar Pradesh) and Bihar (Kachru & Bhatia, 1978: 48).

Thus, on the same base, that of Hindustani or Khari Boli, two literary forms had arisen. One, Urdu, heavily influenced by Persian and Arabic, written in the Perso-Arabic script, and mainly used by Muslims. The other, Hindi, developed mainly in the nineteenth century, drawing its literary vocabulary mainly from Sanskrit, and excluding Persian and Arabic forms, written in the Devanagari script, and used principally by Hindus. It is worth noting, though, that many prose writers used both Urdu and Hindi in their writing (Kachru & Bhatia, 1978: 48).

The association of Hindi with Hindus and Urdu with Muslims led to rivalry and antagonism between supporters of the two forms (Rai, 1984: 285–6; Kachru

& Bhatia, 1978: 49). As a result, Hindi and Urdu came to be seen by some as two different languages (Mobbs, 1981: 205). On religious, social and political grounds there may be a case for considering Hindi and Urdu as different languages (Rai, 1984: 287ff), but on purely linguistic grounds there is far less of a case. As Zograph says, 'such grammatical differences as exist between Hindi and Urdu are insignificant' (1982: 33). The major differences are found in the vocabulary, and even here it is in the 'high' or literary forms that these differences are mostly manifest (Zograph, 1982: 33).

In their spoken forms Hindi and Urdu differ very little. As Mobbs puts it,

Urdu and Hindi may differ, in the spoken mode, in the selection of lexical items for certain word classes [e.g. nouns]; but the majority of words and all the grammatical elements in a text are common to both styles. (Mobbs, 1981: 209)

Also, many words of Persian origin were naturalised in Khari Bholi before Hindi and Urdu split and still remain in the base form of both styles (Mobbs, 1981: 210 fn10).

In colloquial speech it appears that an inter-regional form, also based on Khari Boli was in use. This form, which was known as Hindustani, did not make use of either Persian/Arabic vocabulary or extensive Sanskrit borrowing (Zograph, 1982: 32; Kachru & Bhatia, 1978: 49). In the early twentieth century an attempt was made to use this form as a bridge between the rival Hindi and Urdu forms. Although this did not succeed because Hindustani was seen as merely a colloquial variety, it was, apparently, used as a *lingua franca* throughout northern India (Kachru & Bhatia, 1978: 49).

The situation in India in the early twentieth century, therefore, was complex. There was a colloquial variety, known as Hindustani, used as an inter-regional variety for colloquial speech throughout northern India, and which exhibited neither heavy Persian, nor heavy Sanskrit borrowing. For writing, though, Urdu, sometimes called High Urdu, was used by Muslims, and Hindi, or High Hindi, was used by Hindus. These two forms were often seen as different languages for religious, political and social reasons, and because of the different scripts used to write them.

At the time of independence Urdu became the official national language of Pakistan, and the state language of the Indian states of Jammu and Kashmir. It is not clear from the literature available whether the name Hindustani is still used in these areas to denote the colloquial form of the language. From Mobbs' (1981) evidence, though, it would appear that at the spoken level few differences between Urdu and Hindi are present today.

It is important to note that Urdu is, for many of its speakers, learnt in school as a second language. Mobbs points out that many Urdu speakers have

Punjabi, Gujarati or even Bengali as their mother tongue, and as he puts it,

> Urdu and Hindi are in most cases subsequently acquired, high languages for Muslims and Hindus respectively, though mother tongue learning of these is increasing among later generations. (Mobbs, 1981: 205)

And Rai notes that Urdu has no geographical region of its own. He says that

> the 'region' it has is a metaphorical region or, to put it differently, a psychological or emotional region, this being another name for the language loyalty of Muslims, no matter of which linguistic region, to Urdu. (Rai, 1984: 286).

As a consequence, it is difficult to find information on variation in Urdu, though it is probable that such variation is beginning to occur within Pakistan. It is presumed that a spoken form close to the written literary form will be considered prestigious.

References

GRIERSON, G. A. 1968, *Linguistic Survey of India* Vol. IX Pt. 1. Delhi: Motilal Banarsidoss.

KACHRU, Y. 1987, Hindi-Urdu. In B. COMRIE (ed.) *The World's Major Languages* (pp. 470–89). London: Croom Helm.

KACHRU, Y. and BHATIA, T. K. 1978, The emerging 'dialect' conflict in Hindi: a case of glottopolitics. *International Journal of the Sociology of Language* 16, 47–58.

McGREGOR, R. S. 1974, *Hindi Literature of the Nineteenth and Early Twentieth Centuries*. Weisbaden: Otto Harrasowitz (Vol. VIII of J. Gonda (ed.) *A History of Indian Literature*).

McGREGOR, R. S. 1981, *A New Voice for New Times: The Development of Modern Hindi Literature*. Canberra: The Australian National University Press.

MOBBS, M. C. 1981, Two languages or one? The Significance of the Language Names 'Hindi' and 'Urdu'. *Journal of Multilingual and Multicultural Development* 2 (3), 203–11.

RAI, A. 1984, *A House Divided: The Origin and Development of Hindi/Hindavi*. Delhi: Oxford University Press.

ZOGRAPH, G. A. 1982, *Languages of South Asia: A Guide*. London: Routledge and Kegan Paul (*Languages of Asia and Africa* Vol. 3).

Vietnamese

There does not appear to be consensus among scholars as to the origin of Vietnamese. D. H. Nguyen says that the 'true genetic relationship of Vietnamese' is as a member of the Mon-Khmer group (1987: 778). But DeFrancis notes that the origin of Vietnamese 'is a matter of some uncertainty' and that it may be a Tai language which has adopted a considerable amount of vocabulary from Mon-Khmer languages, or a Mon-Khmer language which has adopted tones from Tai (1977: 5). K. V. Nguyen also points out that Vietnamese shares many characteristics with both Tai and Mon-Khmer languages and he says that linguists are still divided on the question of which group Vietnamese belongs to (1977: 14).

Vietnamese is spoken in Vietnam and in countries such as France, the USA, and Australia, among others, by over one million overseas Vietnamese (Nguyen D. H., 1987: 777). Within Vietnam there are a large number of non-Vietnamese ethnic groups. About 60 different languages are spoken in Vietnam by ethnic groups which include Chinese, Cambodians, Indians, and many highland groups known as Montagnards. All of these ethnic groups, though, know and can use Vietnamese (Nguyen D. H., 1987: 777; Nguyen K. V., 1977: 13).

According to DeFrancis, 'the Vietnamese people entered recorded history when they were conquered and incorporated into the Chinese empire in BC 111' (1977: 3). During the thousand years of Chinese rule in Vietnam the Chinese introduced Buddhism and Confucianism, as well as the Chinese language and writing system. Chinese was the official language of administration, education, philosophy, historical and medical studies, and literature in cultivated circles (Nguyen K. V., 1977: 15). During this period, though, very few Vietnamese had access to power or an education in Chinese (DeFrancis, 1977: 12).

When Vietnam gained its independence in 938 AD, it maintained the use of Chinese and patterned its institutions and administration after those of China (Nguyen K. K., 1972: 13; Nguyen K. V., 1977: 15). Thus, as DeFrancis notes, while Chinese political dominance was eliminated, Chinese cultural influence was increased since the new scholars, administrators and political élite were now primarily Vietnamese (1977: 13–14).

At the time of independence Vietnam consisted only of territory around the valley of the Red and Black rivers in the north. Over succeeding centuries the

Vietnamese conquered and incorporated areas to the south, till, by the late eighteenth century, the whole area of present-day Vietnam had been assimilated (DeFrancis, 1977: 39; Brick & Louie, 1984: 1).

As Vietnam expanded southwards, so too did the influence of Chinese, which had been adopted as the official writing of the state in 1174 (DeFrancis, 1977: 18–19). Chinese continued to be used for official purposes until the late nineteenth century in the south and into the twentieth century in the central and northern areas (DeFrancis, 1977). According to K. V. Nguyen, Chinese was used in villages in northern and central Vietnam in religious services and for writing land deeds until 1945 (1977: 15). Chinese characters are known in Vietnamese as Sino-Vietnamese, or as *Chu nho* 'scholars script' or *chu han* 'Han (Chinese) script' (DeFrancis, 1977; Nguyen D. H., 1987: 778).

However, the number of Vietnamese who possessed a good command of spoken and written Chinese was probably never more than about 3 to 5% of the population (DeFrancis, 1977: 19). The majority of the population spoke only Vietnamese, and the élite also used Vietnamese in ordinary conversational situations (DeFrancis, 1977: 20). As well, there was a rich oral literature in Vietnamese (DeFrancis, 1977: 20).

By the thirteenth century a system for writing Vietnamese using Chinese characters had been invented (DeFrancis, 1977: 20ff; Nguyen K. K., 1972: 25). This system, known as *Chu nom* 'demotic writing' used Chinese characters in two main ways: one was the use of a character purely for its phonetic value, e.g. the character which is read as *ban* 'half' in *Chu nho* (Sino-Vietnamese) was used for the word pronounced *ban* in Vietnamese but with the meaning 'to sell'; the other was to use a combination of characters, one for its meaning where the pronunciation was irrelevant and another for its pronunciation with the meaning irrelevant (DeFrancis, 1977: 24–5).

Chu nom was used primarily for literature and only rarely for official purposes. It played a secondary role to *Chu nho*. Use of *Chu nom* declined rapidly after the First World War and is apparently not in use today (DeFrancis, 1977: especially 205 and 227).

The alphabetic, or romanised writing system in use nowadays was originally devised by Catholic missionaries in the seventeenth century as an aid for learning Vietnamese (Nguyen D. H., 1987: 779). Initially this system was used only in Catholic circles which K. V. Nguyen says represented only 'a tiny minority' of the population (1977: 17).

When the French conquered the southern part of Vietnam, which they called Cochinchina, in the 1860s, they introduced the romanised script, called *Quoc ngu*, and French into the administration system and into education (DeFrancis, 1977; Nguyen K. V., 1977: 17). In 1885 the French took over the central and northern areas of Vietnam, which they called Annam and Tonkin respectively (DeFrancis, 1977: 112). They soon began to introduce *Quoc ngu* and French into these areas as well (DeFrancis, 1977: 129ff). However, there was considerable opposition to French rule and to the use of *Quoc ngu*, especially in the central and northern areas, because it was seen as 'a tool of foreign aggressors' (Nguyen K. V., 1977: 17; DeFrancis, 1977: 148ff).

Leaders of the opposition to French rule, however, began to make use of *Quoc ngu* early in the twentieth century. This was because the romanised script took only a few months to learn, rather than the years needed to learn *Chu nho* or *Chu nom*. Consequently, *Quoc ngu* could be used to propagate education and as a propaganda weapon against the French (Nguyen K. V., 1977: 17; DeFrancis, 1977: 163).

In 1945 when the Democratic Republic of Vietnam was founded, Vietnamese became, for the first time, the official language of administration and was used at all levels of education (Nguyen K. V., 1977: 17). The French, though, attempted to regain control after the Second World War, and, although they did not succeed, the influence of French, and later English, remained strong in the southern areas, Cochinchina (DeFrancis, 1977: 238). Thus, while French was quickly replaced by Vietnamese, written in *Quoc ngu*, in the north, this was not so in the south where French, and later English, were the media of instruction in many subjects at universities till reunification in the 1970s (DeFrancis, 1977: 238). As well, more transliteration of earlier *Chu nho* and *Chu nom* texts into *Quoc ngu* has been carried out in the north than in the southern areas (DeFrancis, 1977: 234).

According to D. H. Nguyen the Hanoi dialect of Vietnamese 'has served as the basis for the elaboration of the literary language' and 'the written medium, which one can qualify as literary style, is uniformly used in the press and over the radio and television' (1987: 781). Vietnamese has been heavily influenced by Chinese due to the centuries during which Chinese was the official language. As a result, Chinese words make up about a third of Vietnamese vocabulary as a whole and 'in formal writing up to sixty per cent of the vocabulary may be of Chinese origin' (Nguyen D. H. cited in DeFrancis, 1977: 8).

As far as the spoken language is concerned, there are several dialects in Vietnam. D. H. Nguyen says:

> Most dialects form part of a continuum from north to south, each of them different to some extent from the neighbouring dialect on either side. Such major urban centres as Hanoi, Hue and Saigon represent rather special dialects marked by the influence of educated speakers and of more frequent contacts with the other regions. (Nguyen D. H., 1987: 781)

The dialects differ only slightly, according to DeFrancis, and there are no problems of intelligibility between them. The differences are found, though, in grammar, phonology and vocabulary. For example in the Hanoi dialect there are six tones whereas in the Saigon dialect there are five (note: tones are changes in pitch used to distinguish separate meanings of words otherwise identical in sound) (DeFrancis, 1977: 5ff).

It appears that efforts have been made to standardise the spoken language. The standard, it seems, is taken as the Hanoi dialect which forms the basis of the written language (DeFrancis, 1977: 253–4; Nguyen D. H., 1987: 781). D. H. Nguyen, though, considers that dialects are still used throughout the country (1987: 781).

References

BRICK, J. and LOUIE, G. 1984, *Language and Culture: Vietnam*. Sydney, NSW: Adult Migrant Education Service.

DEFRANCIS, J. 1977, *Colonialism and Language Policy in Vietnam* The Hague: Mouton (*Contributions to the Sociology of Language* No. 19).

NGUYEN, D. H. 1987, Vietnamese. In: B. COMRIE (ed.) *The World's Major Languages* (pp. 777–96). London: Croom Helm.

NGUYEN, K. K. 1972, *An Introduction to Vietnamese Culture*. Saigon: The Vietnamese Council on Foreign Relations.

NGUYEN, K. V. 1977, *Glimpses of Vietnamese Literature*. Hanoi: Foreign Languages Publishing House.

Welsh

Welsh is a Celtic language brought to Britain (i.e. what is today England, Scotland and Wales, but excluding Ireland) by Celtic tribes sometime before the Christian era (Williams, 1972: 3). Tolkien suggests that the Celts may have arrived in Britain as early as 1000 BC (1963: 14). The early Celtic language was divided into two varieties, or branches: Goidelic, the precursor of Irish and Scottish Gaelic; and Brythonic, or British. Welsh is descended from the Brythonic branch (Jones, 1973: 18).

In the first century AD the Romans conquered Britain, and by the time they left, nearly four centuries later, it is probable that Brythonic had largely disappeared except in the north (i.e. what is today southern Scotland and northern England) and the west (Williams, 1972: 4). Also, the influence of Latin had brought considerable changes in the Brythonic still spoken in these areas. The subsequent invasions of the Germanic speaking Angles and Saxons, who brought the precursor of English with them, and the advance of the Scoti in Scotland, displaced Brythonic from its northern territories (Jackson, 1963; Dorian, 1978: 5). Consequently, Brythonic was gradually restricted more and more to what is today Wales and Cornwall (Jones, 1973: 18; Gregor, 1980: 67).

The Brythonic spoken in Wales and that spoken in Cornwall gradually diverged and ultimately became separate languages. Cornish though, died out as a native language towards the end of the eighteenth century. As well, another descendant of Brythonic, Breton, is still spoken in the north-west of France, where some British Brythonic speakers fled at the time of the invasions of the Angles and Saxons (Williams, 1972: 4).

The earliest literature in Welsh is dated to the sixth century and was probably written in the northern Brythonic territories of southern Scotland and northern England (Williams, 1972: 5; Jones, 1973: 19). This early form of the language is known to scholars as Early or Primitive Welsh (Jones, 1973: 19).

The history of the Welsh literary language is broken into several periods by scholars. Primitive Welsh refers to the period between the middle of the sixth century and the end of the eighth century; Old Welsh extends to the beginning of the twelfth century; Middle Welsh continues to the end of the fourteenth century; Early Modern Welsh is the period from the late fourteenth century to the third quarter of the sixteenth; and Modern Welsh brings the history of the literary language from the sixteenth century to the present day (Jones, 1973: 19ff).

From the early times of the literary language considerable attention was devoted to it, particularly by a group of scholars known as 'the bards'. As Evans puts it:

[The bards] held official positions in the courts of the Welsh princes and were required to perform certain ceremonies. The rules they had to master at bardic schools involved not only the intricacies of Welsh metrics but also a thorough study of Welsh grammar, syntax and vocabulary. In addition they were required to commit to memory the works of earlier poets and important events in history, together with legends, folk tales and genealogies. (Evans, 1978: 8)

And Williams notes that 'the bardic pupils had to spend years studying the works of their ancestors from the sixth century onwards ...' (1972: 7).

Thus, even though the Welsh literary language went through various periods, there is a literary tradition which maintained a degree of standardisation throughout its history. Consequently, 'Welsh is a very conservative language. Sounds that have changed over a thousand years are still represented in writing' (Williams, 1972: 6).

Since much of the literary tradition was oral, the standardisation of the language extended to the spoken language also. According to Williams:

poets ... were concerned not only with the literary language as such, but also with the style of their spoken Welsh. Of course, there were dialects in Wales in medieval days, but it is quite clear that there was also a standard form of spoken Welsh among the poets and also in the courts of the princes, and that this prevailed in every part of the country. (Williams, 1972: 6)

The culmination of the Welsh literary tradition came in 1588 with the translation of the Bible. Williams says; 'the language as it had been perfected in the bardic schools, became the language of the Welsh bible' and '[this language] has set a standard which all writers have followed ever since' (1972: 9). However, by this time the literary language had become divorced from the everyday spoken language and was quite far removed from the speech of the people. As Evans puts it, 'it must be remembered that the literary language of the bards used in translating the Bible was archaic even in the middle ages' (1978: 9).

Nevertheless, the Bible, together with a major grammar and a dictionary published in the first half of the seventeenth century, provided 'a permanent model of the best Welsh' (Jones, 1973: 22).

This 'model of the best Welsh' is of considerable importance in the subsequent history of Welsh since the Bible came to serve as the major, if not the only, counterbalance to the anglicisation of Wales. Evans considers that the Bible

> also gave the language a standard literary form which enabled it to with-
> stand tendencies to disintegrate into mutually unintelligible dialects.
> (Evans, 1978: 9).

Even though Welsh had had no official status in Wales since the late thir-teenth century (Evans, 1978: 8), the bardic tradition had maintained the literary language. But in 1536 the Act of Union was passed in the English parliament. This Act of Union forbade the use of Welsh in any official capacity whatsoever. A Welshman who wanted to hold a legal office therefore had to speak English. English thus became the language of government, law, and administration (Mathias, 1973: 40; Jones, 1970: 33).

In consequence, the gentry, who had supported the bardic traditions through their patronage, became more and more anglicised in order to maintain their power. The anglicisation of the gentry meant that support for the bards began to wane, and the bardic order, and the literary tradition it upheld, began to decay (Jones, 1970: 34).

Because the learning of the bards took years to acquire, and the literary lan-guage was far removed from the speech of the people, the decay of the bardic order meant that 'it seemed as if Welsh learning would disappear and the lan-guage would degenerate to become a mere *patois*' (Williams, 1972: 7). The translation of the Bible ensured that this did not happen. Welsh, proscribed in government, law and administration, became the language of religion (Mathias, 1973: 42). In the seventeenth century

> the religious fervour of the Reformation and Counter Reformation led to
> the restriction of the content of books written in Welsh to religious matters.
> (Evans, 1978: 9)

In the eighteenth century the spread of Methodism led to a considerable revival of interest in Welsh, sparked by the desire to learn the literary language in order to read the Bible (Williams, 1972: 11). The nineteenth century saw social and political developments which fostered the appearance of literary Welsh in domains other than religion (Evans, 1978: 9).

In spite of the fact that Welsh was proscribed as an official language by the Act of Union, the vast majority of ordinary Welsh citizens were monoglot Welsh speakers into the nineteenth century. Thomas, in fact, states that more than 90% of the population were Welsh speakers at this time (1982: 87).

The Act of Union, however, eventually resulted in the considerable decline of the use of Welsh. In the latter half of the nineteenth century education was brought to Wales. Because Welsh had no official status, education policy was for English to be the only language in the classroom. J. L. Williams states that:

In the course of two generations whole communities changed their natural language from Welsh to English. They had no choice — the English language was 'stuffed down their throats', and not always without a measure of cruelty. The next generation did not receive their national language from parents or school. Whole communities virtually lost contact with Welsh as a result of government policy. (Williams, 1973: 95)

The decline in the use of Welsh led to the fact that in 1971 only 21% of the population were still Welsh speaking (McAllister & Mughan, 1984: 322). This decline was probably made more rapid by the use of English on radio and TV. In the early 1970s, out of nearly ninety five hours per day of programming on radio and TV less than four hours was in Welsh, whereas over ninety hours was in English (Rees, 1973: 180).

However, Welsh was never without its champions and it appears that the decline has recently been halted, if not turned around. In 1967 the Welsh Language Act restored a measure of official recognition to Welsh (Thomas, 1982: 88–9). Also, there has been a steep increase in the number of bilingual schools; in 1960 there were 28 such schools, and by 1981 this had grown to 56 schools (Edwards, 1984: 250). In the media too there is now far more time devoted to programs in Welsh, with one TV channel being devoted primarily to Welsh (Edwards, 1984: 249). All this helped to generate a 40% increase in the numbers of children speaking Welsh between 1971 and 1981 (Howell, 1982: 51).

In Welsh today there are a number of regional dialects. The primary dialect division is between the north and the south (Griffen, 1980: 190). A. R. Thomas divides Welsh into two core dialect areas, north and south, and then into six smaller areas. He also notes that the northern dialect areas are less fragmented internally than the southern areas (1980: 15).

Dialectal differences exist on all levels of linguistic structure; phonology, vocabulary, and syntax, with the greatest differences being in vocabulary (M. Jones, 1973: 120). However, it is unusual for a speaker of one dialect to be unable to understand any of the others even though the differences may be quite considerable, and they may not be able to speak another dialect. In other words, a speaker of Welsh will usually have an active command of only one dialect, i.e. will be able to speak and understand only his/her local dialect, but will have a passive knowledge of dialects other than his/her own, i.e. will be able to understand those dialects but not speak them (M. Jones, 1973: 122).

As far as a standard form of spoken Welsh is concerned, it appears that in Welsh the development of such a standard is based on the filtering of local dialects rather than on the emergence of a particular regional dialect. The dialects, though, are not uniformly filtered and so it is not unusual for there still to be differences in the vocabulary and syntax of two speakers in a radio discussion, for instance. This form of filtered Welsh tends to be context dependent and is used in situations which are semi-formal, such as education, public speaking, and the media. Thus, as M. Jones puts it:

> Whereas ... some filtering does take place many dialect features are still used in public contexts. What emerges, therefore, is that — at this time at any rate — we do not have a homogeneous, uniform spoken standard where only one sound, syntactic pattern, word or meaning is used where a choice is available in the dialects. Rather, we have variations within the standard ... and the Welsh standard itself involves various regional choices. (M. Jones, 1973: 122)

For very formal speech a form close to the literary standard is used. Consequently, like the literary standard, formal spoken Welsh has its origins in the language of the Bible translation of the sixteenth century (Thomas, 1982: 102). According to Thomas,

> there is no received pronunciation of formal spoken Welsh: in its phonetics and phonology, the region of origin of the speaker can easily be determined, but at all other linguistic levels it shows very few regional differences. (Thomas, 1982: 102)

Formal Welsh, though, since it is based on the literary language of the Middle Ages is considerably different from the spoken dialects which have developed into modern forms. It is used, therefore,

> only by formally educated speakers in schools and universities, broadcast studios, poetry competitions, and other contexts in which the topics are elevated and the audience trans-dialectal. (Griffen, 1980: 190).

In the past twenty or thirty years a new form of Welsh has been developed. This form, known as *Cymraeg Byw* (living Welsh), was designed primarily for learners of Welsh under the auspices of the Welsh Joint Education Committee. It set out

> to establish a 'model of spoken Welsh which would be acceptable throughout all Wales' and also 'to bridge the gap between the literary language and the spoken language'. (M. Jones, 1973: 123)

Cymraeg Byw is based on the spoken dialects of Wales, not on the literary language. According to Griffen it is based, for the most part, on the dialects of the south of Wales (1980: 191). This form is apparently gaining ground extremely rapidly in Wales (Griffen, 1980: 191). However, according to Thomas, 'one matter for concern is that adult learners [of *Cymraeg Byw*] are beginning to notice that their Welsh seems to worry native speakers' since it is sometimes seen as a 'contrived' kind of Welsh (1982: 112). This form is also, it seems, intended to provide a written form of Welsh close to the spoken form (Thomas, 1982: 111).

Another point to note is the intrusion of English, particularly English words, into Welsh. Since the majority, if not all, Welsh speakers are bilingual in English, and since many new terms and concepts are introduced via English, there is a tendency for Welsh speakers to give the English form currency rather than to find a Welsh equivalent. As M. Jones says:

> there is no 'practical' need for [a speaker of Welsh] to 'Welshify' the English term or expression. Indeed, in some respects it is unreal to expect him to distinguish what is Welsh and what is English: he possesses fluent control over two vocabularies and, to some extent, they must blend into one vehicle of expression. (M. Jones, 1973: 125)

In Welsh today, then, there are several varieties of the language, one or other of which is used depending on the context or situation. In informal contexts local dialects, which may exhibit considerable differences from each other, are used. For more formal usage these dialects are filtered to produce a semi-standardised variety which nonetheless exhibits marked variation. A form of the language close to the literary standard, and extremely different from any of the dialects, is chosen for the most formal and elevated contexts. These varieties, though, are not discrete entities, but rather form a cline or continuum along which speakers choose the relevant form depending on the context and, as they move further towards the formal end of the continuum, their level of education. As well, there is a new form of the language, which has been developed in the second half of this century, designed for learners of Welsh, and to provide a new spoken and written standard somewhere between local dialect and the formal literary standard.

References

EDWARDS, D. G. 1984, Welsh-medium education. *Journal of Multilingual and Multicultural Development* 5 (3–4), 249–57.

GREGOR, D. B. 1980, *Celtic: A Comparative Study*. Cambridge: The Oleander Press.

GRIFFEN, T. D. 1980, Nationalism and the emergence of a new standard Welsh. *Language Problems and Language Planning* 4 (3), 187–94.

HOWELL, W. J. Jr 1982, Bilingual broadcasting and the survival of authentic culture in Wales and Ireland. *Journal of Communication* 32 (4), 39–54.

EVANS, E. 1978, Welsh. In: C. V. JAMES (ed.) *The Older Mother Tongues of the United Kingdom*. London: Centre for Information on Language Teaching and Research.

JACKSON, K. 1963, Angles and Britons in Northumbria and Cumbria. In: *Angles and Britons — The O'Donnell Lectures*. Cardiff: University of Wales Press.

JONES, M. 1973, The present condition of the Welsh language. In: M. STEPHENS (ed.) *The Welsh Language Today* (pp. 110–26). Llandysul: Gomer Press.

JONES, R. B. 1970, *The Old British Tongue*. Cardiff: Avalon Books.

JONES, R. B. 1973, A brief history of the Welsh language. In: M. STEPHENS (ed.) *The Welsh Language Today* (pp. 18–31). Llandysul: Gomer Press.

MATHIAS, R. 1973, The Welsh language and the English language. In M. STEPHENS (ed.) *The Welsh Language Today* (pp. 32–63). Llandysul: Gomer Press.

McALLISTER, I and MUGHAN, A. 1984, The fate of the language: determinants of bilingualism in Wales. *Ethnic and Racial Studies* 7 (3), 321–41.

REES, A. D. 1973, The Welsh language in broadcasting. In: M. STEPHENS (ed.) *The Welsh Language Today* (pp. 174–94). Llandysul: Gomer Press.

THOMAS, A. R. 1980, *Areal Analysis of Dialect Data By Computer: A Welsh Example.* Cardiff: University of Wales Press.

THOMAS, C. H. 1982, Registers in Welsh. *International Journal of the Sociology of Language* 35, 87–115.

TOLKIEN, J. R. R. 1963, English and Welsh. In: *Angles and Britons — The O'Donnell Lectures* (pp. 1–41). Cardiff: University of Wales Press.

WILLIAMS, G. J. 1972, *The Welsh Language: Its Origins and History.* Wales: National Museum of Wales.

WILLIAMS, J. L. 1973, The Welsh language in education. In: M. STEPHENS (ed.) *The Welsh Language Today* (pp. 92–109). Llandysul: Gomer Press.

Yiddish

Yiddish is the language of Ashkenazic Jews, often called Ashkenazim. Ashkenazim refers to those Jews who settled in Central and Eastern Europe many, if not most, of whom spoke Yiddish (or Judeo-German as it is sometimes called) as their mother tongue, as opposed to Sephardim which refers to Jews who settled originally in Spain and spoke mainly Ladino (or Judeo-Spanish) as their mother tongue. After their expulsion from Spain in 1492 the Sephardic Jews migrated mainly to North Africa, the Balkans and Turkey. Weinreich says 'the ninth century is the birth period of Ashkenazic Jewry and of the Yiddish language' (1980: 340). But Birnbaum puts the origins of Yiddish around the tenth century (1979: 34); and Fishman dates it to the eleventh century (1965: 1).

Whatever the exact date may be, the fact is that a group of Jews migrated from areas of what are now France and Italy to an area of the Lorraine in Germany known as Loter among the Jews (Weinreich, 1980: 39). Their spoken language was Loez (sometimes called Laaz) the 'Jewish correlate of Old French and Old Italian' (Weinreich, 1980: 39). They also used Hebrew which was, and remains, 'the Jews' language of prayer and religious ceremonies' (Rosten, 1968: 447).

When the Jews arrived in Loter they came into contact with regional varieties of German which they adopted and adapted as their new spoken language. However, many elements of Loez and Hebrew were incorporated into this new language. As Fishman puts it, 'In the case of Yiddish the major early constituents consisted of Middle High German, Romance [i.e. Loez], and Hebrew elements ...' (1965: 1). Yiddish thus began as a fusion language (i.e. the mixing together of elements from different languages to form one new language) drawing elements from three major sources, with German being the pre-eminent one. It should not, though, be seen as being identical to German; as Weinreich notes, 'there was no Jewish community speaking "pure German"' (1980: 350). Also, Yiddish has always been written from right to left using the Hebrew alphabet.

Between the thirteenth and sixteenth centuries there was a great migration of Jews from Germany to the east; to countries such as Czechoslovakia, Poland, and the Ukraine among others, where various Slavonic languages were spoken. As a consequence many Slavonic elements entered the Yiddish language. But, as Weinreich says:

When the Slavic component began to enter Yiddish, the language as a whole was already constituted by the primary fusion in Loter. The fourth component could therefore only modify the language; its essence, the fusion character, was already established. (Weinreich, 1980: 526)

Nevertheless, each Slavonic language influenced Yiddish, principally the vocabulary, but also to some extent the phonology and syntax. Thus, for example, the Yiddish of those Jews who settled in Poland was influenced by Polish, and those who settled in Czechoslovakia by Czech or Slovak. The Yiddish spoken in any one country, therefore, began to differ slightly from the others.

Consequently, several dialects of Yiddish developed, depending on the area in which it was spoken. Most studies say there were four or five major dialect groups. For example, Gold (1980) discusses Western, Central, Southern, South-Eastern, and North-Eastern Yiddish; Birnbaum says there was West, Central and East Yiddish, with East Yiddish divided into three sub-dialect areas (1979: 94ff); and Weinreich distinguishes four: Western, Central, North-Eastern, and South-Eastern (1980: 40, 578). All of these dialects, however, were similar enough for Jews from one area to understand all others, except, perhaps, for a few vocabulary items.

By the sixteenth century, then, Yiddish was spoken over most of central and eastern Europe. It should be noted, though, that 'Yiddish speakers represented a socio-cultural grouping not in control of an independent national-territorial unit' (Fishman, 1965: 2). In other words, although Yiddish was spoken in virtually every country from France and Italy in the west to the borders of Russia in the east, the political, educational and legal apparatus was never in the Jews' control and Yiddish was not the official language of any country.

Towards the end of the eighteenth century Russian began to have an influence on Yiddish. Russia had 'resisted Jewish settlement in her territory with all her might' (Weinreich, 1980: 591), but, with the annexation of Poland and other Slavic countries, Jewish communities came under the authority of Russia. Russian became the language of the administration, the school, and the printed word in these countries. Its influence, as a consequence, was felt in Yiddish (Weinreich, 1980: 592). The influence was again mainly in vocabulary.

By about the middle of the nineteenth century West (or Western) Yiddish, i.e. that dialect spoken in what is today Western Europe, had all but died out (Fishman, 1965: 3). The speakers of West Yiddish had either migrated east or been linguistically assimilated into the language of whichever country they were living in. In the east, however, Yiddish was still the mother tongue of the vast majority of Jews.

During the late nineteenth and early twentieth centuries there was considerable debate amongst different factions of Jews on the status of Yiddish. One group wanted all Jews to speak only Hebrew; another desired linguistic assimilation; and a third felt that Yiddish should be maintained as the Jews' native tongue and become the vehicle of literature (Goldsmith, 1976). Ironically, those factions who wished to get rid of Yiddish were forced to use it in order to reach the majority of Jews, and

> their earnest campaigns [against Yiddish] served to strengthen the attachment of the Jewish masses to that vernacular [i.e. Yiddish] they already called 'the people's tongue' or 'the language of the masses'. (Rosten, 1968: 448)

Also, as Goldsmith puts it,

> Although they despised [Yiddish] and viewed it solely as a temporary means to enlightenment, many of the propagandistic and didactic works ... possessed literary merit and became foundations on which modern Yiddish literature was established. (Goldsmith, 1976: 40).

Yiddish consequently gained in strength and prestige and, by the time of the First World War, was an extremely vital language with a growing body of literature and a press. It became, for a brief period, the official language of Jews in Russia; it was used at all levels of religious life except the written scholarly and liturgical, and was the usual everyday language of most Ashkenazic Jews (Fishman, 1965: 9). In 1939, according to Weinreich, there were nearly seventeen million Jews in the world, 92% of them were Ashkenazim and therefore Yiddish speakers (1968: 384).

From the late nineteenth century many Jews began to migrate to other parts of the world, particularly America. Thus Yiddish began to spread across the world. In America, and most probably in other countries as well,

> the intensity of Jewish cultural interests and the social-material needs of Jewish immigrants were such that a number of imposing organised efforts were launched — via Yiddish and on behalf of Yiddish — many of which continue to function to this very day. (Fishman, 1965: 13)

As a result of the massacres in the Second World War the number of Yiddish speakers in Europe was drastically reduced. Continuing migration, nowadays mainly to Israel, has also reduced the number of Yiddish speakers in Europe. As Birnbaum puts it, 'In the greater part of this territory [i.e. Europe], Yiddish is no longer spoken — as a result of emigration, war, annihilation and assimilation' (1979: 94).

In Israel, where many Yiddish speakers now migrate, Yiddish tends to be negatively perceived and Hebrew is the recognised, official language (Cooper & Danet, 1980: 11). In other countries, such as America, although the position of Yiddish has been weakened due to assimilation, it is still in use and is taught in 'Yiddish secular schools' (Fishman, 1965: 21–2). And, according to Birnbaum:

The language is still very much alive. It is cultivated assiduously by many
... In addition, there is still a religious core among whom there has not
been a break in the generations and whose mother tongue is Yiddish.
(Birnbaum, 1979: 43)

As far as the literary language is concerned, there is a standard form.
Birnbaum says that the modern literary language is based on the form of East
Yiddish (1979: 101). Gold (1980) states that there is also a 'Modern Standard
Yiddish' spoken form which has been developed by language planners and
draws on all dialectal forms except the extinct Western form. Birnbaum, however, disagrees. He says, 'there is no standard pronunciation in Yiddish' (1979:
100). Nor does there appear to be a preferred or prestigious dialect.

References

BIRNBAUM, S. A. 1979, *Yiddish: A Survey and a Grammar*. Manchester: Manchester
    University Press.
COOPER, R. and DANET, B. 1980, Language in the melting pot: the sociolinguistic context
    for language planning in Israel. *Language Problems and Language Planning* 4 (1),
    1–28.
FISHMAN, J. A. 1965, *Yiddish in America: Socio-Linguistic Description and Analysis*.
    Bloomington, IN: Indiana University (Indiana University Research Centre in
    Anthropology, Folklore and Linguistics Series No. 36).
GOLD, D. L. 1980, Recent work in the study of Yiddish language planning. *Language
    Problems and Language Planning* 4 (2), 107–21.
GOLDSMITH, E. S. 1976, *Architects of Yiddishism at the Beginning of the Twentieth
    Century: A Study in Jewish Cultural History*. London: Associated University
    Presses.
KLARBERG, M. 1985, Hebrew and Yiddish in Melbourne. In: M. CLYNE (ed.) *Australia,
    Meeting Place of Languages* (pp. 57–62). Canberra: Pacific Linguistics (Series C.
    No. 92).
ROSTEN, L. 1968, *The Joys of Yiddish*. London: Penguin Books.
WEINREICH, M. 1968, Yidishkayt and Yiddish: on the impact of religion on language in
    Ashkenazic Jewry. In: J. A. FISHMAN (ed.) *Readings in the Sociology of Language*
    (pp. 382–413). The Hague: Mouton.
WEINREICH, M. 1980, *History of the Yiddish Language*. Chicago: The University of
    Chicago Press (Translated by S. Noble).